Praise for *Forgetting Fathers*

"*Forgetting Fathers* is a truly remarkable piece of work. The pertinacity of Marshall as a reader, as a critic, as a theorist, impels him on his quest to learn all that he can about his past. The book is riveting."

— Jonathan Freedman, coeditor of *Jewish in America*

"From the Hebrew Orphan Asylum to the history of New York tailors, David Marshall weaves his Jewish family memoir with gripping details. An enlightening contribution to the growing body of research on the lives and institutions of twentieth-century Jewish immigrants."

— Mikhal Dekel, author of *The Universal Jew: Masculinity, Modernity, and the Zionist Moment*

Forgetting Fathers

Forgetting Fathers

Untold Stories from an Orphaned Past

David Marshall

excelsior editions

AN IMPRINT OF STATE UNIVERSITY OF NEW YORK PRESS

Published by State University of New York Press, Albany

Excelsior Editions is an imprint of State University of New York Press

For information, contact State University of New York Press, Albany, NY
www.sunypress.edu

Production, Eileen Nizer
Marketing, Kate R. Seburyamo

Library of Congress Cataloging-in-Publication Data

Marshall, David, 1953 December 20– author.
    Forgetting fathers : untold stories from an orphaned past / David Marshall.
        pages cm
    "Excelsior Editions."
    Includes bibliographical references.
    ISBN 978-1-4384-5892-2 (pbk. : alk. paper)
    ISBN 978-1-4384-5893-9 (e-book)
    1. Marshall, David, 1953—Family.   2. Jews—New York (State)—New York—
Biography.   3. Marshall family.   4. Hebrew Orphan Asylum of New York.
5. Jewish orphanages—New York (State)—New York—Biography.   6. Jews,
Belarusian—New York (State)—New York—Biography.   7. Death certificates—New
York (State)—New York.   8. New York (N.Y.)—Biography.   I. Title.

F128.9.J5M36 2016
974.700492'4—dc23   2015001356

10 9 8 7 6 5 4 3 2 1

For Arthur K. Marshall
and
Daniel Waid Marshall

Contents

Note to the Reader

Although this book incorporates family history, it is not a genealogical work. I have not included a family tree. Nevertheless, a brief summary will help the reader keep track of the main family members who populate the narrative, many of whom were referred to by more than one name during their lifetimes.

Birth dates for relatives born outside the United States are approximate; birth dates for relatives born in the United States match birth certificates, which often contradict other records and personal accounts.

This story focuses on my father's side of the family, especially his father's family, and my grandfather's parents, who were named Harris (or Aaron) and Lena. Harris's father was named David. He married Dorah Garmize (or Debora Germaise), and they seem to have lived in Minsk, Russia. Their children included my great-grandfather Harris (Aaron) (b. 1865?) and his brother Jack (b. 1869?). Aaron, or Harris, seems to have immigrated to New York City between 1885 and 1888.

Lena's parents were Meyer Ruderman (b. 1840?) and Anna (Hannah) Davidow (b. 1846?). They apparently came from Minsk or a nearby village called Gorodok (or Horodok). Meyer immigrated to New York City around 1884. Anna seems to have followed in 1888.

Their children included: Isaac (b.1867?), my great-grandmother Lena (b. 1870?), Abraham (b. 1877?), Fannie (b. 1881?), Bessie (b. 1882?), and Michael (b. 1883?), all of whom were born in Russia. Lena

Ruderman probably immigrated around 1884. Most the Ruderman family seems to have immigrated around 1888. Meyer died in 1935, and Anna died in 1936.

My great-grandparents, Harris and Lena, were married in New York City in 1890. Their children were: Dora (Daisy) (b. 1890); my grandfather David (Dick) (b. 1891); Rubin (Reuben, Ruby) (b. 1893); Mella (Millie, Mildred) (b. 1894); Israel (Isadore, Isi, Irving) (b. 1895); and Harry (Harold) (b. 1901). Harris died in 1901. Lena died in 1960. Millie's daughter, Adele, is my father's first cousin.

My grandfather David, or Dick, married my grandmother Jeanette in 1922. Jeanette was born in 1902 to Louis Levitt (b. 1871?) and Hannah (Anna, Annie) Wolarsky (Waller) (b. 1876?), immigrants from Russia and Poland, who married in New York City in 1894. My grandparents had two children, my father Arthur (b. 1924) and his brother, Stephen (b. 1926). My grandfather died in 1952, and my grandmother died in 1994.

Arthur married Helene (b. 1929), my mother, in 1951. Her parents were Moe (Marcus) Horowitz (1894–1899?) and May (Manya) Alter (1894–1899?), who immigrated to New York City in the early 1920s from Poland. I was born in 1953, my sister Cindy was born in 1956, and my sister Karen was born in 1959. My father died in 2009.

The central figures in this story are my great-grandparents, Harris and Lena, and their eldest son, my grandfather David. I knew almost nothing about Harris and Lena or their families before I wrote this book.

Preface

I was named after my father's father, David Marshall, who died the year before I was born. According to the family story, my grandfather changed the family name to Marshall. We had a Bible inscribed to David Marshall in 1906, on the occasion of his confirmation, from the Hebrew Orphan Asylum of the City of New York. Yet no one knew the original name; my father and grandmother said that they had never asked my grandfather about it. This book has its origins in my search to discover our lost family name.

As a child, I learned about "Ellis Island names"—names that were Americanized or Anglicized by either accident or design. Various relatives had changed their names, or had had their names changed for them. I knew that when my mother set out to become an actress before I was born, she used the name of her maternal grandfather (Alter) because it sounded less Jewish than the name of her father (Horowitz). I remember feeling some satisfaction when, planning to be an actor when I was eleven or twelve years old, a man with some professional experience pronounced "David Marshall" to be a "damn good stage name." I never thought of my own name as a "stage name" (that is, not a "real" name), yet over the years I became increasingly curious about the original name, and especially curious that it was a mystery.

As family history and amateur genealogy started to find a home on the Internet, I made sporadic attempts to search for the family name.

I first opened an *Ancestry.com* account in 2002. It was only after my father's death in April of 2009 that my search became more determined. A casual conversation with my colleague Patricia Cline Cohen, an American historian who knows her way around genealogical search engines as well as archives, led to her taking a generous interest in my search. With her help, I had a breakthrough, and soon I became engaged in a project that combined elements of a hobby, a scholarly research project, and a personal obsession. Discovering the original name was only the beginning.

Over the years, friends and relatives were sometimes puzzled or amused by my pursuit. Many people encouraged and assisted me, and many made invaluable contributions to my research and writing. In a preface to a book about lost origins, missing names, and forgetful and forgotten fathers, I can provide only a partial acknowledgment of my debts. As I noted, Pat Cohen was a tutor and mentor throughout this project, an engaged interlocutor who commented on drafts, advised me about historical research, and even made a few beyond-the-call-of-duty forays into census, municipal, and real estate records. Mark Rose provided encouragement and editorial advice throughout this project, not only reading drafts but also allowing me to engage him in countless conversations about my latest discoveries over weekly Chinese lunches. An ideal reader, he understood my literary and personal investments.

My wife, Candace Waid, and our son, Daniel Waid Marshall, also gave me great encouragement, listening patiently and reading versions of the book as it took shape. Daniel and I both became history majors at around the same time, and I have been inspired by his interest in the meaning of historical memory (and forgetting). Candace, whose own family stories, memories, and even dreams go far back into the nineteenth century, has talked with me and taught me about history, narrative, and autobiography for more than thirty-five years. I benefited from her expertise on topics ranging from labor history to nineteenth-century wedding dresses. My sense of the narrated past was deepened by her grandmother, Harriet Jones, and her father, Donald Waid, master storytellers with deep reservoirs of both inherited and original stories.

My mother, Helene Marshall, and my sisters, Cindy Marshall and Karen Marshall, allowed me to draw upon their memories, knowledge, research, talents, and sympathies to enrich my understanding of our shared history and stories. The stories of the three grandparents that resonated throughout my childhood made me realize what was missing. My father's cousin, Adele Marks, whom I had not seen since I was a child, responded to my out-of-the-blue questions with warmth, generosity, and insight, as well as some important stories and three remarkable family photographs that I had never even imagined. I was fortunate that this project brought us into contact. I am grateful to Jamie Gracer, Judy Shanks, Randy Garr, and Laura Kalman for their interest, support, and professional expertise. Laura Kalman offered detailed comments that improved the manuscript.

Among the other friends and colleagues who had conversations with me, made helpful suggestions, and/or provided encouragement, advice, or assistance, I am especially grateful to Jean-Christophe Agnew, Linda Adler-Kassner, Karen Bowie, Yunte Huang, Rhoda McGraw, Ngũgĩ wa Thiong'o, Ernest Strum, Jennifer Wicke, Erin Cressida Wilson, and Pauline Yu. At the University of California, Santa Barbara, Chancellor Henry Yang generously allowed me to take some weeks of research leave during the summer, and my colleagues and staff in the Division of Humanities and Fine Arts and the College of Letters and Science made it possible for me to take some breaks from administrative responsibilities.

I am grateful to Chip Badley for his editorial work, scrupulous attention to detail, and organizational skills, all of which were of great assistance in preparing the final manuscript. I appreciate the support and assistance I received from the editors and staff of the State University of New York Press, including James Peltz, Amanda Lanne-Camilli, Jessica Kirschner, Jenn Bennett, Eileen Nizer, Kate Seburyamo, and my anonymous copyeditor. The reports from the Press's readers contained insightful comments that helped me to improve the manuscript.

For their assistance with my research, I thank the UC Santa Barbara Library, The Johns Hopkins Medical Institutions, the New York State Archives, and the New York City Municipal Archives; Thomas M.

Savini, Director of the Chancellor Robert R. Livingston Masonic Library of Grand Lodge in New York City; Henry Grossberg, Executive Director of the Stuyvesant High School Alumni Association; Amanda (Miryem-Khaye) Seigel, Librarian, Dorot Jewish Division, The New York Public Library; David P. Rosenberg, Reference Services Librarian, Center for Jewish History; and especially Boni Joi Koelliker, Photo/Reference Archivist, American Jewish Historical Society, who provided reproductions of documents at a crucial moment. Anyone conducting research on the Hebrew Orphan Asylum owes a debt to Hyman Bogen, former "inmate" of the Hebrew Orphan Asylum, President of its Alumni Association, and author of *The Luckiest Orphans: A History of the Hebrew Orphan Asylum of New York*. The materials he saved and collected, including the records of the Solomon Seligman Society, are included in the extensive Hebrew Orphan Asylum archives at the Center for Jewish History in New York City.

I am grateful for the cooperation of Tom Tryniski, whose website, *www.fultonhistory.com*, contains tens of millions of newspaper pages; and Maggie Land Blanck, whose website, *www.maggieblanck.com*, contains wonderful images, as well as *Ancestry.com*. The *Chronicling America* online archive of historical newspapers, sponsored jointly by the National Endowment for the Humanities and the Library of Congress, was a valuable resource. For permission to reproduce images, I gratefully acknowledge the New York Public Library, the Library of Congress, and the Museum of the City of New York. The images on pages 18 and 29 are reproduced by permission of the *New York Times* (on page 18 from the *New York Times*, January 23, 1952, and on page 29 from the *New York Times*, June 4, 1906, © *The New York Times*. All rights reserved. Used by permission and protected by the copyright laws of the United States. The printing, copying, redistribution, or retransmission of this content without express written permission is prohibited). Tony Mastres from Photographic Services at UC Santa Barbara provided timely assistance with scans and photographs.

I am pleased to acknowledge advice, assistance, and/or suggestions from John T. Chiarella, Mary Ann DiNapoli, Christine Finetta, Roger D. Joslyn, Florence Marmor, Arlene Shaner, Daniel Soyer, Maureen Taylor,

Joseph Van Nostrand, and Jerry Waldbaum. Many others allowed me to engage them in conversation about this project—too many to name here—and I thank them for their interest.

When I was just learning how to read, I believed that my father's name was written on the doorknob of the aluminum screen door on the front porch of our house. My father's name was Arthur, but most everyone (besides my mother) called him Art. I recognized the "A" beginning a short word and the "M" beginning a longer word and assumed that the raised metallic letters that circled the doorknob spelled "Art Marshall." I am sure that it made sense to me that the characters of my father's name would be inscribed on our front door. It turns out that the letters spelled "Air Master." At times I've wondered if this screen-door memory was in fact just a screen memory (Freud's name for a memory standing in the place of another more disturbing memory), but I have confirmed that Air Master was and still is a manufacturer of aluminum doors. What I can't remember is whether there was a moment when I realized the mistake in my childish conclusion, or whether one day, opening the door, reading the letters, I remembered what I once believed.

Is it a coincidence that some forty years later I published a book about eighteenth-century aesthetic experience called *The Frame of Art*? Is it a coincidence that my father worked in what was called the "beauty business," selling products destined for beauty salons? It is not a coincidence that I was drawn to my grandfather's and great-grandfather's stories after writing about authors and characters who are obsessed with identity, impersonation, acting, names, conversion, origins, orphans, acts of self-inscription, and autobiographical fictions; but did my interest in those literary obsessions stem from, as well as lead to, my interest in the untold autobiographies of my grandfather and great-grandfather? This book enters into autobiography to reflect on the difficulties of both telling and avoiding one's story. Few books escape family history or life stories altogether.

It is sad to acknowledge that my father, the reader who would have been most interested in my discoveries, will never read this book. Yet sometimes one must dwell on loss if one is not to dwell in loss. This project to undo forgetfulness has helped me to understand the desire of my grandfather and his mother to leave ghosts and memories behind them, even as I have sought to remember and recover what they knew. Eudora Welty wrote: "Remembering is done through the blood, it is a bequeathment, it takes account of what happens before a man is born as if he were taking part. It is a physical absorption through the living body, it is a spiritual heritage. It is also a life's work." This book is dedicated to my father's memory, and to his grandson Daniel, who will remember.

1

Presented to David Marshall

For me, the story begins with a name embossed in gold, Gothic letters on the black cover of a book, inscribed in neat handwriting on the first leaf. The Bible is presented to "David Marshall." It is Wednesday, May 30, 1906, the day he is confirmed. He is, according to the records of the Hebrew Orphan Asylum of the City of New York, fourteen years old. There is an inscription on the first page: "Presented to David Marshall in commemoration of his Confirmation Shabuoth 5666 by the Junior League Hebrew Orphan Asylum." The penmanship is fancy and formal, the capital letters demurely calligraphic; yet the *M* in Marshall loops down with a dramatic flourish to underline the last name. Shabuoth, commemorating the delivery of the tablets with the Ten Commandments to Moses on Mt. Sinai, is in "modern times," according to a contemporary religious instructional manual, "Confirmation Day," the "day of consecration of Israel's youth to the faith of their fathers." For many Reform Jews at the turn of the century, the confirmation ceremony replaced the bar mitzvah.[1]

As he stands there, recognized as a man in the Jewish tradition, receiving the new Bible inscribed with his name, he is fatherless, an orphan. His father died on February 14, 1901, and he has been an "inmate" of the Hebrew Orphan Asylum since March 9, 1903. Some months after his arrival, the new superintendent of the asylum, Rudolf I. Coffee, "abolished the practice of having the children identified by a number and ordered that they be addressed by their first name."[2] His number is 2633. "David Marshall" is not his name.

For me, the story, at least the story about the name, begins with my name. I was born "David Marshall," yet as a child I learned that we came to be called "Marshall," we came to call ourselves and write our name "Marshall," following the Americanization of names so common among late-nineteenth-century Jewish immigrants and their children. I was born in 1953 in New York City, almost two years after my grandfather, David Marshall, died; thus, since the faith of my fathers calls for a child to be named after a parent or grandparent who recently died, I was named David Marshall in memory of my grandfather. According to the family story, it was David Marshall, born more than sixty years

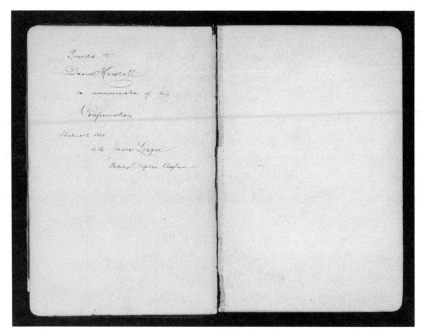

Bible inscribed to David Marshall, Hebrew Orphan Asylum, 1906.

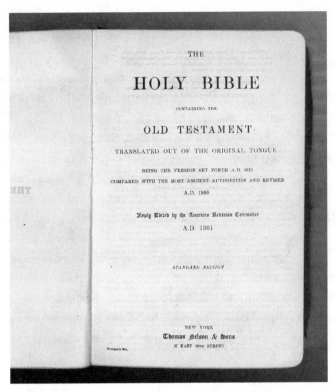

Bible inscribed to David Marshall, Hebrew Orphan Asylum, 1906.

before me in New York City, who changed the family name, not only for himself but also for his mother and siblings—and for those of us who followed. (There is no evidence of a legal name change.)

If this were merely a story about Americanization and assimilation, the replacement of an Eastern European Jewish name with an Anglo-Saxon substitute or abbreviation, there would be no story. What was stranger and more complicated is that no one seemed to know the original name, or the origin of the name. My father and grandmother both said (they insisted) that they did not know the original name. It was not forgotten; it was never known, never spoken. My grandfather's mother, whose first name was Lena, lived until the age of ninety. We called her Grandma Marshall. I was only seven when she died in 1960, and I was too young to ask her about her "real name" or the name of the man she had married seventy years—a lifetime—earlier. I was too young to know that Grandma Marshall had a story. All my father knew about the name was that his grandfather's first name had been Aaron, but he went by the name Harris after he immigrated to New York.

We imagined that the name had been Marshak. In college, I read Russian novels translated by David Margashack and the name resonated. There was speculation about Eastern European names that ended with "-sky." Some relatives believed (rather implausibly, in my opinion) that the last name originally was Harris. I often wondered if my father really knew the name, since he contradicted any theories advanced by our relatives. Either he knew the correct name, I supposed, or he didn't think that anyone could know. I asked him to disclose the secret on his deathbed. There were two weeks in which he knew that he was about to die. Lucid, calm, philosophical, yet sometimes released from inhibitions, he seemed to be mentally reviewing the stories he wanted to know the endings of, the socially unacceptable questions he had always wondered about: whether this person had had an abortion, whether that person had had an affair.

At one point I reminded him that it was the time for *his* deathbed confessions, not those of others. This is your last chance, I pleaded, to tell us what the name had been before it was changed to Marshall. He insisted that he really did not know his father's and grandfather's original name, that he had never known it. He had never asked. My father said that his father did not like to talk about the orphanage, that he seemed bitter about those years. He reported that his mother "always said he was resentful of the fact that he grew up that way."[3] What was it in my father's father's stories (or lack of stories) that proscribed his family's curiosity about his childhood and his name—their name? Was the family name forgotten merely because it was unimportant, a last vestige of an immigrant world left behind by a generation born in New York, discarded in favor of a less ethnic, less foreign, less Jewish name?

If David Marshall's history seemed to stop (or start) at the Hebrew Orphan Asylum, we had stories, or at least the outlines of stories, about the families of my other grandparents. My grandmother Jeanette, my father's mother, who married David Marshall in 1922, was born in New York City to Russian and Polish immigrant parents, Louis and Anna Levitt. She talked about her family and was close to her brothers and sisters. We knew that her father had manufactured children's shoes. (About ten years ago a distant cousin in Israel sent my father a family tree that included my grandmother's mother, listed as Elka Channa Wolarsky, traced back to one Wolf Wolarsky, born in Poland around 1780. It lists my father's parents, Jeanette Levitt and David Marshall, as Janet Levitt and Richard Marshall. Although my grandmother's mother was married under the name Hannah Volarsky, on my grandparents' marriage certificate she is listed as Anna Waller.) My grandmother was raised in Brooklyn. I remember her imitating the Yiddish accents of some of the residents of her North Miami Beach condominium complex, and into her nineties she answered the phone with an upper-class "Hel-*lo* . . ."—the second syllable elongated and almost British—that she must have learned from Hollywood movies. My mother's parents, Moe and May Horowitz, came to New York from Poland in the 1920s. Relatives in New York changed their names from Marcus and Manya to Moe and May. (When I was young, I was embarrassed that my grandfather shared a name with one of the Three Stooges; I didn't even know that Moe Howard's name was actually Moe Horowitz.) We heard the story about how Grandpa Moe's father had come to America to make money to bring over his family from Poland but was cheated out of all his savings by his boss. He returned to Poland "a broken man" and died soon after, leaving my grandfather as the "man of the house" at a young age. We were told that my Grandma May's family had both prominent rabbis and socialist leaders. As I learned, these included Rabbi Yitzchak Meir Rothenberg Alter, the founder of a Hasidic dynasty and the first Gerer Rebbe, born in Poland in 1799 and a descendent of the thirteenth-century Rabbi Meir Ben Baruch of Rothenberg; and Victor Alter, a well-known Bundist activist in Poland and a member of the Central Committee of the Second International, who was executed by Stalin. Growing up, I knew that when my mother had left college to become an actress, she had taken the name Helene Alter as her stage name because Helene Horowitz sounded "too Jewish." When I was in college, and I had to use a pseudonym when submitting some poems for a creative writing prize competition, I used the name "Moses Alter"— re-inscribing Alter in the lineage of a Jewish patriarch whose mother gave him up for adoption to a non-Jewish family.

Just as they had stories, my mother's parents had family photographs from the old country: cabinet-card tableaux of brothers and sisters in formal poses and fine clothes, staged domestic scenes, my grandfather in uniform. Most of their relatives, those who had not emigrated, died in the Holocaust. Growing up, I saw photographs of various great-grandparents, but I never saw a photograph of my father's paternal grandparents, or their relatives from the Old World. I knew of (but do not remember meeting) my grandfather's siblings but did not know of siblings, cousins, or other relatives from my paternal great-grandparents' families. Yet my father's parents and paternal grandparents were not Holocaust survivors who kept their silence about a world that had exiled them, murdered their families, and obliterated their genealogy. Was the family name forgotten, erased, or repressed? Had it disappeared because it was important rather than unimportant?

American Jews were wary of anti-Semitism and Jewish quotas; they were insistent that they were American, especially those born in New York in large immigrant communities around the turn of the century. At the fiftieth anniversary of the first building of the Hebrew Orphan Asylum (HOA) on April 10, 1910, twelve hundred orphans marched onto the stage of the New York Hippodrome before five thousand spectators (including New York City Mayor William J. Gaynor) and sang "America" and "The Star-Spangled Banner." David had been discharged from the orphanage by this time, but his brothers Rubin and Isadore were still inmates so they must have been on this stage. The boys wore military-style suits; the cadet corps of the Hebrew Orphan Asylum performed a patriotic number called "Rally 'Round the Flag" and fired real rifles with blanks.[4] Color postcards of the orphanage from this decade display two American flags flying prominently from the turrets of the building.

Postcard, Hebrew Orphan Asylum.

Postcard, Hebrew Orphan Asylum.

Upon entering the main hall of the Hebrew Orphan Asylum in the first years of the twentieth century, one would have encountered a twelve-foot-high bronze sculpture representing a wishful allegory of America and the Old World: "the ruins of three dynasties—Assyria, Egypt, and ancient Rome—and upon this base a red marble column of fasces stands, emblematic of the United States." According to a description published in the *New York Times*, "The serpent of intolerance winds its way through these ruins and tries to coil itself around the column of the Union, but is being destroyed by the American eagle."

Sculpted by Moses Ezekiel, a Jewish, Confederate army veteran whose bust of Thomas Jefferson is in the United States Capitol, the sculpture was designed as a memorial to Jesse Seligman, a prominent banker and former president of the Hebrew Orphan Asylum. Beside the column that held Seligman's bust, "an orphan girl stands holding a scroll upon which is inscribed, 'His Character Knew No Race or Creed.' "[5] Although the sculpture stands in what was called the Memorial Hall, the orphan, like the United States, stands on the ruins of the past, as if freed from historical memory.

The Hebrew Orphan Asylum of the City of New York, founded in 1860, was a nationally respected institution that rescued thousands of orphaned children from loss and poverty, educating and training them for productive lives. It was located between 136th and 138th streets on Amsterdam Avenue, across the street from where the campus of the City University of New York was built between 1903 and 1907. The imposing Second Empire Renaissance–style building was designed by William H. Hume, a prominent architect of commercial and institutional buildings. A former inmate who had arrived as a child in 1929 recalled: "Its Victorian Gothic crenellated architecture—crowned with a tall clock tower—made newly arriving children think of fairytale castles."[6]

About 75 percent of the children, like my grandfather and his two brothers, had a living parent who could not afford to care for them. There is a photograph of the Hebrew Orphan Asylum published in *King's Views of New York* in 1903, the year my grandfather and his brothers arrived at the orphanage, with the caption: "Maintains large

Memorial Hall, Hebrew Orphan Asylum, *Eighty-Third Report of the Hebrew Orphan Asylum of the City of New York*, 1906. Courtesy of the Collection of the American Jewish Historical Society.

asylum, very finely equipped, where 1,000 orphans and indigent boys and girls are sheltered and educated. Hebrews rarely neglect their poor and unprotected."[7] The orphanage had many wealthy and influential trustees and patrons, many from the German-Jewish aristocracy of New York, such as department store magnates Isador Strauss and Louis Stern, and the stockbroker Emmanuel Lehman. An April 29, 1912, article in the *New York Times* described a meeting of the HOA trustees at which the political leader and lawyer Edward Lauterbach and the banker Jacob Schiff broke down in "sobs" as they paid tribute to their fellow trustees

Isador Stern and Benjamin Guggenheim, who two weeks earlier had perished on the *Titanic*. There were thousands of loyal alumni.[8]

In the months after David and his younger brothers Rubin and Isadore arrived in March of 1903, Superintendent Coffee began his appointment by introducing a period of liberalization and "de-institutionalization." In 1904, addressing a system of discipline reminiscent of English boarding schools, Coffee announced "the absolute abolition of corporal punishment." (He was neither the first nor the last superintendent to make such a pronouncement.)[9] In addition to changing the practice of addressing children by their numbers rather than their names, Coffee allowed the children to speak during meals, and he changed the boys' clothing to make their uniforms less institutional. Writing in 1905, in the *Report of the Eighty-Second Annual Meeting of the Hebrew Orphan Asylum of the City of New York,* Coffee proudly stated: "I have frequently attended public schools and other assemblies where our children are gathered. At present there is nothing in their attire to give the slightest hint of an institutional home."

Noting that there were 1,034 inmates (614 boys and 420 girls), Coffee wrote, "despite the large number of children, it has ever been our aim to pay individual attention to the needs of every child in our Home. If our workers cannot bestow parental love on our wards, they at least are able to apply scientific methods to the study of each of our children, so as to develop the very highest traits of character there found. It is no small matter to know the individual needs of each of our wards—and we want every child to have individual traits—but we cherish the fond hope that our efforts are successful."[10] In the annual report of 1906, when the population of the orphanage included 1,020 children, Coffee's successor, Superintendent Solomon Lowenstein, wrote, "The abolition of uniform clothing, the substitution of chairs for benches in the dining room, to mention only two recent changes, are evidences of our care for the child's individuality."[11]

In the photograph of the Hebrew Orphan Asylum published in the 1903 edition of *King's Views of New York*, the expansive building stands alone on its two city blocks behind a short fence, set back from

One Hundred and Thirty-sixth Street   Amsterdam Avenue   One Hundred and Thirty-eighth Street
HEBREW BENEVOLENT AND ORPHAN ASYLUM, Amsterdam Ave., 136th to 138th Sts.
Founded 1823. Maintains large asylum, very finely equipped, where 1,000 orphans and indigent boys and girls
are sheltered and educated. Hebrews rarely neglect their poor and unprotected. Louis Stern, President.

Hebrew Orphan Asylum, *King's Views of New York*, 1903.

a wide empty street and a wide empty sidewalk, as two small boys sit by themselves, posed, on the curb. It is difficult to see them, so small are they in the photograph, sitting by themselves, far from what most likely was their old neighborhood, the Lower East Side, at that moment said to be the most densely populated place on the planet. Who are they? The boys can't be more than five or six years old. They have no caps; one has his hands crossed awkwardly on his knees. I imagine that they are inmates, brought outside to represent 998 unseen children, or to provide a measure of the magnificent scale of the building behind them, which already towers above the bare branches of the trees. They seem alone, but perhaps less alone than they might have felt among a thousand children behind the walls of the orphanage.

Accounts of the Hebrew Orphan Asylum in the early twentieth century suggest a spartan regimen. Since David and his brothers arrived in 1903, they would have experienced the old regime. However, even the reforms introduced by Coffee and Lowenstein were relative, and not necessarily effective, despite "scientific methods" and good intentions. In an unpublished memoir, *All Still: Life Among A Thousand Siblings,* Maurice Bernstein, who entered the Hebrew Orphan Asylum at the age of six or seven in 1911, the year after Isadore and Ruby were discharged, recalled that upon arrival: "I was given a number. This was sewn into my suits, my mackinaw, and other garments, serving as a laundry mark for the seamstresses who sewed the clothes. It also indicated where I stood in the frequent 'lineups,' where I sat in the synagogue, in the dining-room and where my bed was located." Bernstein described the children's experience attending local public schools: "there was no way of escaping the consciousness of difference from other children. A teacher would say, 'All boys and girls from the Orphan Asylum, stand up.' The other children would gaze at us. . . . The stereotype classification of 'orphan' made us squirm. We tried to conceal the fact that we came from the Home."[12]

In *The Luckiest Orphans: A History of the Hebrew Orphan Asylum of New York,* Hyman Bogen describes the admission and induction process in the first years (and indeed decades) of the century as "utterly traumatic" for the children.[13] Children had their heads shaved and were placed in an isolation ward called the "Reception House" for weeks. According to Maurice Bernstein: "More than a hundred boys slept in each dormitory, with an aisle down the length of the room and, in those days, no partitions. They slept in beds without mattresses, on taut springs covered by a blanket, on which there were two sheets topped by two army style blankets." (Apparently mattresses were impractical because of bed-wetting.) Bernstein recalls: "The dining-room seated all the children at one time—as many as almost 1200 in 1911 . . . with a center aisle dividing girls and boys. We marched into the dining-room in two lines as we also did when we went to the bathing rooms, to the synagogue, to the playrooms for lineups, so that order could be maintained."[14] A boarding-school and militaristic system in which older boys acted as "monitors" for the younger ones encouraged violence and sadism. During Superintendent Coffee's regime, there was an internal investigation of sexual abuse.[15]

All of this I learned later. Only later, in thinking about my grandfather's silence about his name, did it occur to me that the Hebrew Orphan Asylum was what my grandfather might have wanted to forget. Only later did it occur to me that he might have wanted to forget the death of his father. Only later did it occur to me that he might have wanted to forget the life of his father. At first, it was the story of the name that intrigued me: the story of the name of the father, the original name; and the story of how my grandfather came to be called, came to call himself and write his name, "David Marshall." Then there was the story of why the name of the father was forgotten. The story of the orphanage, the story of my grandfather's father—his life and his death—were at first secondary to the story of the name. Of course, there would be no story if I did not have the Bible that was presented to my grandfather at the moment he was confirmed. The inscription in the Bible seemed both a mystery and a dead end since it—implausibly—named a fourteen-year-old boy with a name that was not his own and could not be traced. Yet it is the inscription, which placed my grandfather in the Hebrew Orphan Asylum of the City of New York, that led to the missing name.

The fact that I have the Bible, 112 years later, is significant. Neither my father nor his father was religious or observant. My grandfather appears to have saved no other memorabilia from his childhood. Relatively little from the rest of his life survives. When I was a child, my father gave me a wallet that had belonged to his father on which was monogrammed the initials "DHM," for David Henry Marshall. (There is also an ingeniously carved walking stick, fashioned from the branch of a tree.) No other childhood possession of my grandfather remains, at least in our immediate family, besides "The Holy Bible Containing the Old Testament Translated Out of the Original Tongue Being the Version Set Forth AD 1611 Compared with the Most Ancient Authorities and Revised AD 1885 Newly Edited by the American Revision Committee AD 1901." He saved this Bible, carrying it from the New York Hebrew Orphan Asylum to Brooklyn (410 Hopkinson Avenue to 474 Saratoga Avenue to 443 Hopkinson Avenue to 408 Saratoga Avenue to 1276 Union Street), with other stops in between, including the U.S. Army.

Recalling the Bible with his name embossed in gold letters that he was given in a comparable Hebrew Orphan Asylum ceremony, Maurice Bernstein writes that he saved his for over fifty years.[16] I don't know how my grandfather's Bible ended up in our house or when I took it. (In an interview with my sister Cindy in 1991, my father recalled vaguely: "I remember I have a Bible, that he was bar mitzvahed from there, the Hebrew Home.")[17] I might have felt entitled to it because it bore my name. Although the cover is now coming off and the pages are starting to crumble, the Bible was not well read. The copyright page, by coincidence, inscribes the date of my grandfather's father's death: A.D. 1901. The Bible's inscription marks the moment, five years and five months after the death of his father, that he named himself. This was something to be remembered.

I assume that my grandfather named himself. The *only* story about the family name that was passed down was that my grandfather had changed it. Although the Junior League of the Hebrew Orphan Asylum was formed (according to the *New York Times*) "particularly to assist in caring for the children after they leave that institution,"[18] it seems unlikely that its mostly young, female, unmarried members would have taken it upon themselves, in presenting the boy with the new Bible marking his confirmation, to present him with a new name—to baptize him, as it were, with an American identity for use in the outside world upon "graduation," just as Americanized relatives changed the names of my maternal grandparents from Marcus and Manya to Moe and May upon their arrival in New York from Poland some fifteen years later. It is difficult to imagine how a fourteen-year-old boy, who may or may not have known that he would be discharged four months after this ceremony, could convince the women of the Junior League to write, "Presented to David Marshall in Commemoration of his Confirmation Shabuoth 5666," to conspire in a ceremony in which he replaced his father's name, rejected the name of his grandfather, as they presented him with a book in the ceremony that inscribed him in the faith of his fathers in a commemoration of the delivery of the tablets at Mt. Sinai. Even in the Hebrew Orphan Asylum, even for Reform Jews in

1906, it seems unlikely that this rite of passage would have been a rite of assimilation. There appears to be a smudge on the inscription around the word "Marshall," possibly a sign of erasure and rewriting. Yet if the name was altered, the re-inscription must have been contemporaneous with the original inscription and confirmation ceremony. Both handwriting and ink are uniform and consistent, and the solemn, Gothic letters embossed in gold on the cover boldly pronounce, "David Marshall."

2

---◆◈◆---

Finding Names

I did not plan to write a book or even to take up family history, but I began to search for the family name. Over the years, I had acted on my curiosity in fits and starts. Once, when my sisters and I were visiting our parents' home in New Jersey on some holiday, I convinced my father to drive us to the New York City Municipal Archives on Chambers Street to look through microfilms of birth certificates. We didn't know where to begin. I remember a time from my childhood when my father tried to show me that one could look up a word in the dictionary to learn how to spell it. I could not believe that one could look up a word that one could not spell. We didn't know how to look for a name that we did not know. Everything turned on a single, unknown, unspoken word. Only later did I learn that we did not even have the correct year of birth for my grandfather.

It took me several years, trying sporadically, to locate "David Marshall" in the records of the Hebrew Orphan Asylum of the City of New York. According to our abbreviated family history, after my grandfather's father died, his widowed mother could not afford to take care of her six children, one of whom was a baby; so the three older boys were sent to the orphanage. I knew that my grandfather's father's first name was supposed to have been Harris, or Aaron. His mother's first name was Lena. His siblings were named Daisy, Reuben (or Ruby), Irving, Millie, and Harry. The January 23, 1952, *New York Times* obituary notice for David H. Marshall identifies him as "beloved husband of Jeanette, devoted father of Arthur and Stephen, darling son of Lena, brother of Mildred Levine, Daisy Braverman, Harry, Irving, and Ruby."[1] Harry was the youngest child, so Ruby and Irving must have been sent to the orphanage with David.

In 2002, I contacted the disclosure coordinator of the Jewish Child Care Association in search of records of the Hebrew Orphan Asylum. Although she warned me that New York State law forbade disclosures, she told me that she saw nothing relevant in her files, and referred me to the American Jewish Historical Society, where I unsuccessfully leafed through some Hebrew Orphan Asylum ledgers in search of my

> MARSHALL—David H., beloved husband of Jeanette, devoted father of Arthur and Stephen, darling son of Lena, brother of Mildred Levine, Daisy Braveman, Harry, Irving and Ruby. Services today 10 A. M., "The Riverside," Brooklyn, Ocean Parkway at Prospect Park.
> MARSHALL—David H. Gothic Lodge, No. 934, F. and A. M., regretfully announces the passing of Brother David H. Marshall, father of Brothers Arthur K. and Stephen E. Marshall. Brethren are requested to attend Masonic Services Wednesday morning. Jan. 23. 1952. at 10 o'clock at Riverside Memorial Chapel, 1 Ocean Parkway, Brooklyn, N. Y.
> JOSEPH SLONIM, Master.
> WM. GREENZWEIG, Secretary.
> MARSHALL—David H. Officers and members of the Hebrew Mutual Benefit Society announce with regret the loss of their esteemed member. Funeral services at 10 A. M., on Jan. 23. 1952, at "The Riverside," Brooklyn, Ocean Parkway at Prospect Park.
> B. W. CANTER, President.
> KARL A. KOHN, Secretary.

grandfather and his brothers. The Hebrew Orphan Asylum archives are housed in the Center for Jewish History on 16th Street in New York City.[2] In the summer of 1971, I lived in an apartment in a worn brownstone (originally built in 1852) just across the street from where the Center for Jewish History would open twenty-nine years later. Walking down the stone stairs each day, I could not imagine that almost forty years later I would find myself in a library across the street reading a heavy ledger in which the names of my grandfather and great-grandmother were inscribed.

My first visit to those archives was unsuccessful. I wasn't sure what I was looking for, and some of the volumes I wanted to consult were off-site being microfilmed. Eventually I would be able to see those pages on my computer. Over the years, more and more documents were microfilmed, scanned, and made available in online, searchable data bases. I occasionally would search for David Marshall and his family. I knew (or thought I knew) my grandfather's date of birth, I knew he had been at the orphanage in 1906, and I knew the names of his parents. David, Harris, and Lena were common names. I encountered many false starts and dead ends. Knowing that spellings, names, and dates in these records were often unreliable, I sometimes tried to rationalize inconvenient inconsistencies. At first I searched records from the Brooklyn Hebrew Orphan Asylum, since I knew only of the family's Brooklyn roots. In 2008, I discovered some online records and tried to declare the mystery solved after I located a David Wallach, born in 1892 to parents named Harry and Lena, who had been admitted to the Brooklyn Hebrew Orphan Asylum in 1901.

In response to my e-mail declaring the case closed, my father correctly pointed out that the details didn't really match the facts as we knew them, and he asked: "Why would a name be changed from Wallach to Marshall??" He wrote: "David, If you are trying to put a round peg into a square hole you must have some way to make one smaller or larger to fit. It is an exercise to make things fit. The Lena and Harry fit but the rest seems to be fudged." Looking back at these e-mails, written nine months before my father's death, I am surprised by the wishful (indeed willful) thinking in my rationalizations, and by a response on my father's part that tried to transcend our somewhat argumentative e-mail exchange. He continued: "Just believe that you are the 3rd generation Marshall and Daniel is the 4th, and a rose will smell as sweet regardless of the name. I'm glad that my grandparents on both sides came to the USA and that you are my son. So no matter the original name we come from great stock. My father was a great guy and picked up his 5'3" to become a successful individual in trying times. He left us at too early a time and he would have loved you as I do."

This sort of comment was not exactly uncharacteristic of my father, but it was not typical either. My father didn't really understand my investment in this question, but it made him think about fathers and sons, sons and grandsons, and the death of fathers. Nine months before my father's death, I did not understand what my investment in this question would become.

I eventually discovered my grandfather in the Hebrew Orphan Asylum of the City of New York. I first searched the Hebrew Orphan Asylum registers for boys named Marshall, since, according to the Bible, this was his name when he had his confirmation there. Nothing matched. There was no David Marshall in the Hebrew Orphan Asylum. Eventually, because I was able to cross-reference the first names of the three brothers and the first names of the parents in an online database, and because I knew their approximate ages and the time frame in which the boys were at the orphanage, I finally was able to match records and locate my grandfather and his brothers. I subsequently identified them in the Hebrew Orphan Asylum applications for admission, the register of admissions and discharges, some other HOA registers, and then eventually in census records and New York City archives and records.

The boy who would become David Marshall is inscribed in the voluminous files of Hebrew Orphan Asylum applications for admission as David Roshafsky, along with his brothers Rubin Roshafsky and Isadore Roshafsky. In many of the Orphan Asylum ledgers the spelling looks like "Roshofsky." The date of admission is March 9, 1903. In the margin, the letters "C of C" indicate that "certificates of commitment"

Application for Admission, Hebrew Orphan Asylum, 1903. Courtesy of the Collection of American Jewish Historical Society.

were obtained. According to Application for Admission No. 3132, filed on March 3, 1903, David Roshafsky is eleven; the date of birth noted on the application is January 5, 1892. Rubin or Reuben, known in the family as Ruby, is ten, born on January 14, 1893; Isi or Isidore, later known as Irving, is seven, born on December 7, 1895. (None of these dates are quite correct, according to the dates I later would find on their birth certificates.) At home are two sisters, ages twelve and nine, and a two-year-old brother. (Daisy, Millie, and Harry are unnamed on the application form.) Lena Roshafsky, their mother, is thirty-three years old. Born in Russia, she has lived in "the city" for nineteen years; her address is 130 Suffolk Street. Next to "Occupation" is written, "Washing, etc." Next to "Special Circumstances of the Case," we read: "Husband dead 2 yrs."[3]

Index of Children, Hebrew Orphan Asylum. Courtesy of the Collection of American Jewish Historical Society.

page		page	
2	Hyman Ranthum	45	Gertrude Rabiner
2	Louis Rifkin	45	Rebecca Rabinowitz
2	Joseph Roeder	45	Benjamin Rosenthal
2	Moses Roeder	45	Sarah Rabinowitz
2	Isaac Rosenberg	45	Emanuel Reich
2	Jacob Rosenblum	45	Rose Reich
43	Samuel Randel	45	Birdie Reich
43	Max Rosenblum	45	Harry Rosenthal
42	Max Rosenblum	45	Fannie Rappaport
43	Mary Rosenthal	45	Isidor Rubin
43	Maurice Rimmer	46	Bessie Reiff
43	Fannie Rosenbaum	46	Nathan Reiff
43	Martha Rotsky	46	Abraham Rothman
43	Herman Rosenmuff	46	David Ruskin
43	Mary Rosenberg	46	Ida Rosenblum
44	Philip Richard	46	Hyman Rosenblum
44	Abe Richard	46	Michael Rosenblum
44	Pincus Richard	46	Isidor Rosenzweig
44	Abraham Rothman	46	Charles Rosenzweig
44	David Rothman	46	Ida Rubin
44	Frank Roth	46	Abraham Rosenmuff
44	Esther Ringel	46	Leo Rosenberg
44	Moritz Ringel	46	Richard Rottman
44	Herman Rosenberg	46	Lizzie Rosenberg
44	Nathan Rappaport	46	Mary Rosenberg
44	Ethel Racoosin	46	Fred Rosenzweig
44	Reuben Racoosin	47	George Rosenzweig
44	Jennie Rosenberg	47	Sophie Rothlein
44	Hyman Rothfeld	47	Samuel Rothlein
44	Julius Rabiner	47	Isidor Rothlein
44	Leo Rabiner	47	Hyman Rosenblum
45	Julius Reuter	47	William Rothlein
45	Harry Rappaport	47	Della Rabiner
45	Reuben Roshofsky	47	David Rauch
45	Isidor Roshofsky	47	Harry Roth
45	Rose Rosen	47	David Roth
45	Julia Rosen	47	Simon Rothlein
		47	Esther Rosenberg

Index of Children, Hebrew Orphan Asylum. Courtesy of the Collection of American Jewish Historical Society.

I found in the archives of the American Jewish Historical Society undated, bound ledger books that include an "Index of Children" in the orphanage. One register of names lists David Roshofsky (Number 2633), Rubin Roshofsky (Number 2634), and Isidore Roshofsky (Number 2635). Another list includes only Reuben Roshofsky and Isador Roshofsky.[4]

The 1905 New York census lists David Roshafsky (age fourteen), Isador Roshafsky (age ten), and Ruben Roshafsky (age twelve) among

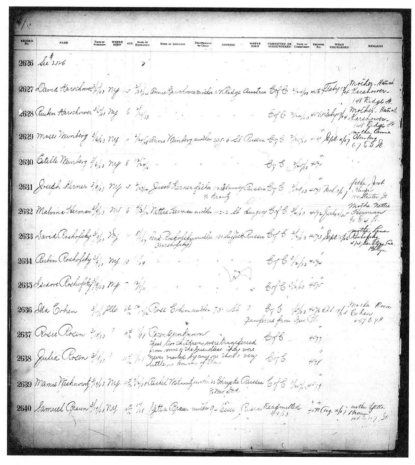

Admissions and Discharges, Hebrew Orphan Asylum, 1884–1907. Courtesy of the Collection of American Jewish Historical Society.

the inmates of the Hebrew Orphan Asylum. The 1910 U.S. census records Isador Roshofsky (age fourteen) and Ruben Roshofsky (age seventeen) as residents there. According to a ledger book showing admissions and discharges, David Roshafsky, the oldest son, was discharged to his "mother Lena Roshafsky" living at 474 Saratoga Avenue in Brooklyn, on September 5, 1906.[5]

Rubin Roshafsky and Isidor Roshafsky leave with "Mrs. Roshofsky" four years after David on August 10, 1910. A smaller booklet of discharge records documents Mrs. Roshofsky's declaration to "The Board of Trustees of the Hebrew Orphan Asylum of the City of New York" that she is withdrawing her sons Reuben and Isidor.[6] There is a gap in the pages for September 1906, so no comparable record exists for David.

Another register recording admissions and discharges that includes Reuben and Isidore indicates that Reuben stayed in the orphan asylum for almost two years after he (according to the asylum records) turned sixteen years old and was moved to what was called the "free list," which

Discharge Records, Hebrew Orphan Asylum, 1909–1911. Courtesy of the Collection of American Jewish Historical Society.

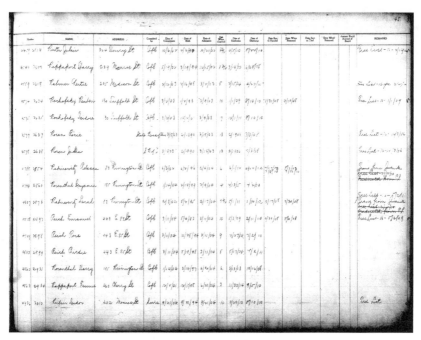

Admissions and Discharges, Hebrew Orphan Asylum, 1892–1910. Courtesy of the Collection of American Jewish Historical Society.

indicated that he received no city or state subsidies and was supported entirely by the orphan asylum.[7]

I also found in the archives a "Register of Visitors to Inmates" between 1903 and 1905, a large and heavy ledger wrapped carefully in intricately folded paper and tied with string. Although most of the inmates in the Hebrew Orphan Asylum had a living parent, children were allowed only four visits a year from family members. The 1906 *Report of the Eighty-Second Annual Meeting of the Hebrew Orphan Asylum of the City of New York* states: "Relatives and friends of the inmates may visit the Asylum on the first Sundays in January, April, July and October, from 2 to 4 o'clock, P.M."[8] The 1903 annual report lists the same hours. In the ledger, neat handwriting shows Mrs. Roshafsky visiting her sons at these regular intervals, each time bringing a different relative with her: "Grandma," "Grandpa," "Aunt," "Uncle," "Sister." With the exception of Daisy, the boys' oldest sister and the oldest child in the family, these relatives are all from the Ruderman family, Lena's family, first listed as residing at 82 Essex Street in New York City, and then later residing at 410 Hopkinson Avenue in Brooklyn. It seems that Lena was living with her parents and siblings during this time, and when the boys are

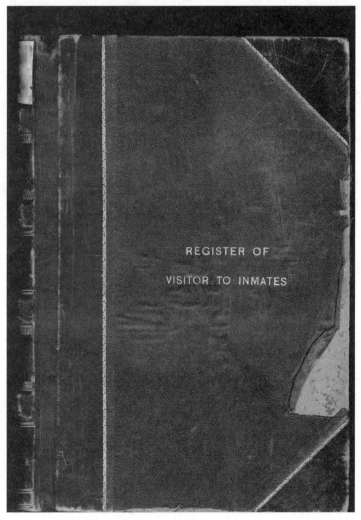

Register of Visits to Inmates, Hebrew Orphan Asylum. Courtesy of the Collection of American Jewish Historical Society.

233

DATE	NAME OF INMATE	NAME OF VISITOR	ADDRESS OF VISITOR	Relationship to Inmate	Date of Visit

Register of Visits to Inmates, Hebrew Orphan Asylum. Courtesy of the Collection of American Jewish Historical Society.

discharged from the orphan asylum, Lena's address is the same as the Rudermans', 474 Saratoga Avenue in Brooklyn.[9]

In fact, neither Roshafsky nor Roshofsky is the "real" family name. David's mother is inscribed on the March 2, 1903, application for admission as "Lena Roshafsky (Warshowsky)." The family name, it turned out,

was in fact *Warshawsky*—or Warschawsky, Warshowsky, Warshafsky, Warshofsky, Warschawski, Warshawski, Wishafzki, and Wasschafsky, along
with a seemingly infinite number of other variations. As far as I can tell,
the Hebrew Orphan Asylum is the only place that anyone in the family is
known as Roshofsky or Roshafsky. Looking through the Hebrew Orphan
Asylum application records for this period, I find no other instance of
a variant spelling or alternate version of a name added in parentheses.

$1,000 IN CASH PRIZES FOR HEBREW ORPHANS

Annual Distribution to Bright Pupils at Asylum.

FINE KINDERGARTEN WORK

Prizes Ranged from $100 Down to $5, and Some Got Medals and Watches.

Franklin Brush Meyer Prizes—Simon Michael-
son and Jacob Satz, $10 each; Harry Einst
and Mamie Schnitzer, $5 each.
Kate Kleinent Memorial Prizes—David Warshawsky, Esther Goodman, Jacob Kostofsky,
Martha Brandt, and Hyman Pfiefenmacher,
$10 each.
Betty Frankenheimer Prizes—Jacob Hepner
and Sarah Parleser, $10 each.
Hettie Levy Prize—Tillie Stiefler, $10.

"$1,000 in Cash Prizes for Hebrew Orphans." Courtesy of *The New York Times*,
June, 4, 1906. © *The New York Times*. All rights reserved. Used by permission
and protected by the copyright laws of the United States. The printing, copying, redistribution, or retransmission of this content without express written
permission is prohibited.

It is as if the registrar knew that "Roshafsky" was wrong the moment the name was recorded, surrounded by a vertiginous variety of mother tongues, accents, non-standardized spellings, transliterations, and Ellis Island mishaps. Whether an afterthought, a correction, a translation, or a note of clarification, the name "Warshowsky" does not appear in any other Hebrew Orphan Asylum record that I have found. Yet the *New York Times* reported on June 4, 1906, just a week after "David Marshall" received his Bible, that "David Warshawsky" was one of the winners of the Kate Kleinert Memorial Prize in the annual awards ceremony organized by the Hebrew Orphan Asylum.[10]

There were no other children with the name Warshawsky who were inmates at the time, besides David's brothers. It would not be surprising if the family name, spoken with a Russian or Yiddish accent, had been heard or transcribed as either Roshafsky, Roshofsky, Warshofsky, or Warshowksy, but why would two names or two pronunciations have been noted, with the actual name, Warshowsky, noted parenthetically and then apparently eclipsed bureaucratically, if not forgotten, for the next seven years? The family seems to have been Roshafsky on the official books of the Hebrew Orphan Asylum and Warshowsky (or Warshawsky) in other contexts, including, the *New York Times* report suggests, in their everyday life in the orphanage. According to the *Times,* the prize that was awarded in June of 1906 went to David Warshawsky, not David Marshall.

The double inscription of "Roshafsky (Warshowsky)" stands as a reminder, a strange acknowledgment, of the labile character of names in this story, the transformation of names through transcription and re-inscription. It provides a trace of what is lost and found in translation and transliteration. I have not yet mentioned that sometime during his youth, David started calling himself, or was called, Dick, a nickname that stayed with him throughout his adult life and afterward. My grandmother and father referred to the grandfather who died before I was born as my Grandpa Dick. According to the family story, he did so to distinguish himself from other boys in the neighborhood named David. I do not know whether he was known as either Dick Roshafsky or Dick Warshowsky in the Hebrew Orphan Asylum.

Application for Admission, Hebrew Orphan Asylum, 1903. Courtesy of the Collection of American Jewish Historical Society.

Without that parenthetical notation of "(Warshowsky)," the name Roshafsky would have been both a revelation and a closed door for me in my search for autobiographical origins. Although I would have had evidence of the original name before it became Marshall, it would have been false or at least misleading evidence. Roshafsky alone would have been a dead end, since it would not have led to the various public documents that allow one to reconstruct life stories and family histories: birth certificates, marriage certificates, death certificates, census records, military records, immigration and naturalization records, city directories, death notices and obituaries, newspaper stories, and reports of the New York State legislature—as well as a wide variety of obscure, late-nineteenth- and early-twentieth-century books and journals that, because of their publication date, size, and shape, were among the more than 20 million books selected almost randomly for digitization by a consortium of research libraries in the massive Google Books project. Without "(Warshowsky)" I would not have become an occasional visitor to and correspondent of the bureaucracies of the New York City Municipal Archives on Chambers Street, the United States District Court for the Southern District of New York on Varick Street, and the Queens County Clerk's Office (where I could never seem to send the right combination of forms, self-addressed, stamped envelopes, and money orders)—as well as a sometimes obsessive visitor to the virtual world of *Ancestry. com*, *Familysearch.com*, *Jewishgen.org*, *Italiangen.org*, and other addictive search engines of family history. That parenthetical aside, like a whisper to the audience, provided the opening in what might have worked as a screen memory, a misleading cover story, for the story of the name that hid behind the name Marshall. As if an explanatory translation, "(Warshowsky)" was the key to other texts and other names.

3

⟨⟨⟩⟩

Inscribing Names

I now know that the boy receiving the Bible inscribed to "David Marshall" at the beginning of June 1906, misfiled in the Hebrew Orphan Asylum as "David Roshafsky, Number 2633," was inscribed on his State of New York Certificate of Birth as David Warshafsky, second child and oldest son of "Harrie Warshafsky," tailor, age twenty-six, and "Lena Warshafsky" (previously "Ruderman"), age twenty-three, both born in Russia. My grandfather listed October 5, 1892, as his birthday, but—perhaps unknown to him—his birth certificate records his date of birth as October 4, 1891.[1] The midwife, Yetta Bokser, who lived at 83 Essex Street, where his mother's family, the Rudermans, lived and where the Warshawskys had lived before David's birth, seems to have registered the birth certificate on October 16.

Harris Warshafsky, age twenty-four, and Lena Ruderman, age twenty, were married in New York City on January 27, 1890. The State of New York Certificate of Marriage, which the groom signs "Haris Warshofsky," records Harris's father as "David Worshafsky" and his mother as "Dorah Garmize." David, the first son, was named after his grandfather. Harris and Lena's first child, David's older sister Daisy, was born Dora Warshafsky on November 15, 1890, and she was named after her grandmother. The names of Dora and David indicate that

33

Harris's parents had died before the children were born, since it would be expected in the Jewish tradition to name one's first son and daughter after one's father and mother only if they had died. On the marriage certificate, Lena's parents are listed as "Meyer Ruderman" and "Minna Davidow." Lena's mother later appears in various records as "Hanah," "Anna," "Annie," and "Any." There is one document in which she appears as "Annie Davidson," either an Americanization or a misreading. "Minna" was no doubt a misreading of "Anna"; even at the time, people seemed to have had trouble reading each other's handwriting. Lena's parents, Meyer and Anna Ruderman, lived until 1935 and 1936, respectively, and the Warshawsky family often lived with them and Lena's siblings. As I reconstruct the family, Meyer and Anna Ruderman's children were (in birth order) Isaac, Lena, Abraham, Fannie, Bessie, and Michael—all born in Russia, all immigrants who came to New York.

Birth Certificate, David Warshafsky, New York City Department of Records.

Birth certificates for all of the Warshawsky children document variations in names, sometimes due to the discrepancy between Hebrew and American names, and variations in spelling and transcription, due perhaps to the varying orthographic skills of both midwives and parents, as well as non-standardized transliterations of Russian, Hebrew, and Yiddish names. When Rubin (later Ruby) is born, on February 12, 1893 (his birth date is later listed as February 14, 1893, February 14, 1894, and January 14, 1895), the father is recorded as "Haris Warshawsky." (His mother's name before marriage is listed as "Lena Faderman.") Millie's birth certificate names her as "Mella Warshawski," and lists her parents as "Harris Warshawski" and "Lena Warshawski" (previously "Lena Ruderman"); her birthday is recorded as August 16, 1894, although later records show different birth years. Isadore's birth certificate names him as "Israel Warsawsky" (he would later become Isi and Irving) and records his parents as "Harris Warsawsky" and "Lena Warsawsky" (previously "Lena Rooderman"). His birth date, December 22, 1895, is given in later years as December 15, 1895, and December 15, 1896. Harry Warshawsky is born on August 17, 1901, to "Lena Rudderman Warshawsky." According to the birth certificate, he has "no father."

I found the Warshawsky family in the 1900 U.S. census, living at 151 Norfolk Street in New York City. Listed are: Harris (age thirty-five), Lena (age twenty-eight), Daisy (age nine), David (age eight), Ruby (age seven), Millie (age five), and Isador (age four). Harry is not yet born, and not yet conceived. This record was difficult to find with the genealogical search engines because the scribes at *Ancestry.com* transcribed the last name as "Fasha???" Only a search for the right combination of first names and birth dates located the family at this address. Sheet No. 29 of the 71 pages recorded for district 223 is difficult to read. The page is smudged, blotted, and faded, as if someone had spilled water on it and the ink began to bleed. Furthermore, Joseph Bissert, the census enumerator who visited 151 Norfolk Street on June 11, 1900, had a habit of drawing a bold line marked with an X over the name of the head of the household. This makes the names even more difficult to read. The last name is overwritten, and almost illegible.

7—224.

TWELFTH CENSUS OF THE UNITED STATES.

257 A 29

SCHEDULE No. 1.—POPULATION.

State *New York*
County *New York*

Township or other division of county *Borough of Manhattan* Name of Institution, X
Name of incorporated city, town, or village, within the above-named division *New York* Ward of city, X
Enumerated by me on the 11th day of June, 1900, *Joseph Bisset*, Enumerator.

Supervisor's District No. *2* Sheet No.
Enumeration District No. *223* 29

US Census, 1900. Courtesy of *Ancestry.com*.

Yet looking carefully, one can see that Joseph Bissert had rendered the family name as Fashafsky. Is this another version of Rashafsky or Roshafsky, another effort to transcribe Lena's Russian or Yiddish pronunciation of Warshafsky? Census enumerators were required to get a "verbal utterance to every question" (as the *New York Times* explained on June 2, 1900), much to the annoyance of respondents asked to state whether they were male or female and to say their address while standing at the door of their apartment. Five years later, a New York State census enumerator in Brooklyn with better hearing but worse spelling would record "Lina Wishafzki" and her children "Daysie Wishafzki, Milie Wishafzki, and Herry Wishafzki."

According to Bissert, Harris and Lena Fashafsky are from Finland, as are the Cohen, Katz, Goldstein, Rosenberg, Silverblatt, and Schwartz families, and indeed most of their other neighbors on Norfolk Street. The February Manifesto of 1899 issued by Emperor Nicholas II declared Russia's control over Finland in a period of Russification. In the 246 numbered "instructions to enumerators" issued for the 1900 census, Number 40 stated: "Write Finland rather than Russia for persons born in Finland." Joseph Bissert seems to have misunderstood this directive and written Finland for an entire block of Jewish immigrants born in Russia. He did not have an easy job. The New York newspapers that week had stories describing the massive deployment of thousands of census enumerators who had only fifteen days to account for "every person living on June 1, 1900" in their district in New York City.

Articles described the many "troubles" and "stumbling blocks in the way of an easy count" experienced by the census-takers as they knocked on doors, encountering languages they could not even identify, pleading for cooperation from people who, despite the threat of arrest, refused to answer their questions. Women were said to "resent inquiries about their ages." Men didn't know their ages or the year in which they were born—including a man in Brooklyn who stubbornly insisted that he was born in a year after his mother's death. Enumerators inundated their supervisors with demands for interpreters and police protection, as well as answers to such questions as how to list the race of an Indian man in Brooklyn when the "Montauk tribe down on Long Island is so intermingled with the negro race." They called in sick or quit, claiming family emergencies.[2]

Joseph Bissert himself does not seem to appear in the 1900 census as a respondent (presumably he was never at home when the census enumerator in his neighborhood visited his residence during the first two weeks of June), but according to 1910 census, he was (or by then had become) a policeman. I picture Joseph Bissert, then twenty-three years old, climbing dark tenement staircases, children crowding around him as he tried to balance his large ledger and his papers. The Warshawsky family seems to have come up in the world in the ten years since their first apartment on Essex Street, but I imagine that Joseph Bissert's experience on Norfolk Street was similar to the experience that Jacob Riis described on Ludlow Street in 1890: "Up two flights of dark stairs, three, four, with new smells of cabbage, of onions, of frying fish, on every landing, whirring sewing machines behind closed doors betraying what goes on within . . ."[3]

Climbing those stairs, Joseph Bissert could not have imagined me sitting at my computer, trying to decipher his blotted pages and thick black penmanship, imagining him walking up and down Norfolk Street on June 11, 1900, talking to tailors, shirtmakers, necktie makers, pressers, dressmakers, peddlers, carpenters, painters, and housewives. Unlike the printed city directories, with their impersonal type, the images of the census pages on *Ancestry.com* promise more than names and information. I study his handwriting, rich and rushed, the textured pages that echo the voices and accents that can be heard on the staircase, as I trace his

US Census, 1900. Courtesy of *Ancestry.com*.

trajectory through the Warshawskys' neighborhood. According to Joseph Bissert's entry under "Occupation, Trade, or Profession," Harris was a "contractor," which indicates that he was not only a tailor but that he employed other people in the garment industry. He was a thirty-five-year-old naturalized citizen, married for ten years, who could read, write, and speak English. Joseph Bissert did not imagine, as he inscribed in his book of life who was living on June 1, 1900, that seven months after he filled out his form, Harris Warshawsky would be dead.

Carl Weinberg was the 1905 New York State census enumerator who found the "Wishafzki" and Ruderman families living at 418 Hopkinson Avenue in Brooklyn. According to the Hebrew Orphan Asylum visitors register, they moved from 410 Hopkinson Avenue to 418 Hopkinson Avenue sometime between April and July of 1905. Carl Weinberg, who either spelled phonetically or sought an accurate transliteration of what he heard, listed Lina Wishafzki, age thirty-two, as the head of the household, with "Home work" as her occupation. This suggests that she took in sewing or did some sort of piecework for a contractor in the garment industry. In addition to her children, Daysie Wishafzki, age thirteen, Milie Wishafzki, age ten, and Herry Wishafzki, age four, we see: Mayer Ruderman, age fifty-six, tailor, and head of his household; Any Ruderman, age fifty-four, who also did "home work," and their children Bessie, age twenty-three; Abraham, age twenty-six;

Wishalzki Lina	head	w	f	32	Russia	19	Ci	home work
Daysie	daughter	w	f	13	U States		Ci	at school
Milie	daughter	w	f	10	U States		Ci	at school
Herry	son	w	m	4	U States		Ci	home
Ruderman Mayer	head	w	m	56	Russia	23	Al	Tailor
Anie	wife	w	f	54	Russia	17	Al	home work
Bessie	daughter	w	f	23	Russia	17	Al	home
Abraham	son	w	m	26	Russia	17	Al	Tailor
Fanie	daughter	w	f	24	Russia	17	Al	Halk wear
Michel	son	w	m	22	Russia	Al	Cl	Book keeper
Rosie	daughter	w	f	10	U States		Ci	at school

New York State Census, 1905. Courtesy of *Ancestry.com.*

New York State Census, 1905. Courtesy of *Ancestry.com*.

Fanie, age twenty-four, Michel, age twenty-two; and grandchildren Rosie, age ten, and Lilie, age eight. Lena's brother, Michael, was naturalized in the same year. As I noted, the 1905 census finds David, Isidor, and Rubin Roshafsky among the list of inmates of the Hebrew Orphan Asylum.

Five years later, four years after "David Roshofsky" is discharged from the Hebrew Orphan Asylum in 1906, the 1910 U.S. census enumerator finds David H. Warshawsky residing at 441 Hopkinson Avenue in Brooklyn. The "H" stands for, or will stand for, Henry. Despite the testimony of the Bible, David Roshofsky (Warshowsky) is not yet David Marshall in the eyes of the U.S. government. The census records him as a seventeen-year-old "office boy in a jewelry factory." He lives with his mother, Mrs. Lena Warshawsky, who has a candy store, and his sisters Daisy (age eighteen) and Millie (age fourteen), and his brother Harold (age eight). Daisy is a bookkeeper in a clothing factory. According to the census, "Isidor Roshafsky" and "Ruben Roshafsky" are still inmates in the Hebrew Orphan Asylum in Manhattan. The Ruderman family lives near the Warshawksy family at 474 Saratoga Avenue in Brooklyn, and this is the address that Lena lists when she finally discharges Isi and Ruby on August 10, 1910.[4]

Two years later, in 1912, a listing in the July 3 *Brooklyn Standard Union* announced: "Daisy Warshawsky, 441 Hopkinson Street, age 20, engaged to Herman Braverman, age 21, New Jersey." Three years after that, on December 20, 1915, the day that would become my birthday thirty-eight years later, the *Brooklyn Daily Eagle* announced a marriage license issued to Reuben Marshall of 408 Saratoga Avenue in Brooklyn and Minnie Goldberg of 1053 Broadway. Sometime between August 31, 1912, when Daisy Warshawsky, identified on her marriage certificate as the daughter of "Harris Warshawsky" and "Lina Ruderman," and

US Census, 1910. Courtesy of *Ancestry.com.*

December 25, 1915, when Reuben Marshall, son of "Harold" and "Lena Rudderman," is married, the family seems to have officially changed its name from Warshawsky to Marshall. Strangely, although the Rudermans appear in the 1915 New York State census, living at 470 Saratoga Avenue, neither the Warshawsky family nor the Marshall family is to be found.[5] There is an intriguing reference to "Dick Marshall" in an April 20, 1913, article in the *Brooklyn Daily Eagle* about a dance held by the Krimson Klub, a social and athletic club that frequently organized events and outings in 1912 and 1913. The dance was said to be "attended by some well-known people of the East New York and Brownsville sections." "Dick Marshall" appears in a long list of almost entirely Jewish names. This is the first public reference that links my grandfather to the name Marshall.[6] He would have been twenty-two or twenty-three years old. Later in the decade there would be several Brooklyn newspaper articles associating Dick Marshall (aka David H. Marshall and D. H. Marshall) to the Huron Club, another active social club.

We don't find "David Marshall" inscribed in an official record until June 5, 1917, when he registers for the draft following the April 6 entry of the United States into World War I: He is now David H. Marshall, age twenty-five, born October 5, 1892, living at 408 Saratoga Avenue in Brooklyn. His brothers, Ruben Marshall and Isadore Marshall, also register on this day. We don't know when my grandfather started using the name, whether he started using it publicly or professionally before the rest of his family, or whether he waited for a collective decision that included Ruby, Irving, Millie, and Lena to change the family name. With so much mystery about the family name, I don't know why my grandfather would have told his family that he had changed the name if in fact his brothers or mother had preceded him in changing from Warshawskys to Marshalls. As I have noted, there is no record of a legal petition to change their name.

In an age before photo identification cards, Social Security numbers, drivers' licenses, and photocopies, there were few ways to document one's identity. Reuben lists his occupation as "chauffeur" on his 1915 marriage certificate. Although New York City did not require drivers to be licensed until 1917 (New York State instituted drivers' licenses in 1924), New York began to require chauffeurs to be licensed on January 1, 1915.[7] This effectively would constitute a legal name change, as would registering with the U.S. government in the massive national mobilization of 1917. In Philip Roth's novel *The Human Stain*, the light-skinned African American protagonist effectively changes his race to white when he fills out Navy enlistment forms at the start of World War II. Perhaps this was a comparable moment. If David Warshawsky had not already officially inscribed himself as David Marshall, this would have been the moment of legal transformation.

In fact, all that was required to register with the Selective Service on June 5, 1917, was to show up at one's local election precinct, report one's name, address, and occupation to one of the eight thousand men who had volunteered to be registrars in New York City, and sign the

Form 1

1 **Name in full** David H Marshall   Age 25
   (Given name)   (Family name)

2 **Home address** 408 Saratoga Ave Bkly
  (No.) (Street) (City) (State)

3 **Date of birth** Oct 5   1892
  (Month)   (Day)   (Year)

4 Are you (1) a natural-born citizen, (2) a naturalized citizen, (3) an alien, (4) or have you declared your
intention (specify which)?   Native Born

5 **Where were you born?** N Y   N Y   US
  (Town)   (State)   (Nation)

6 If not a citizen, of what country are you a citizen or subject? _____

7 **What is your present trade, occupation, or office?** Accountant 28

8 **By whom employed?** William L Werner Inc
Where employed? 5 W 37th St N Y

9 Have you a father, mother, wife, child under 12, or a sister or brother under 12, solely dependent on you for
support (specify which)? Mother to Support

10 **Married or single (which)?** Single   **Race (specify which)?** White

11 **What military service have you had? Rank** None   **; branch** None
years None **; Nation or State** None

12 **Do you claim exemption from draft (specify grounds)?** Support of home & Mother

I affirm that I have verified above answers and that they are true.

David H Marshall
(Signature or mark)

If person is of African descent, tear off this corner.

31-9-8

1 **Tall, medium, or short (specify which)?** 5 ft 3"   **Slender, medium, or stout (which)?** Slender

2 **Color of eyes?** Brown   **Color of hair?** Dk Brown   **Bald?** No

3 Has person lost arm, leg, hand, foot, or both eyes, or is he otherwise disabled (specify)? None

I certify that my answers are true, that the person registered has read his own answers, that I have witnessed his signature, and that all of his answers of which I have knowledge are true, except as follows:

_____

H Lovitch
(Signature of registrar)

Precinct 165

City or County Kings

State N Y

June 5 17
(Date of registration)

World War I Registration Card, 1917.

card that the registrar filled out. In the weeks following May 18, when Congress passed the Selective Service Act, newspapers published several articles a day about the upcoming June 5 registration, in which all men between the ages of twenty-one and thirty-one would be required to register.[8] A reproduction of the registration form was published in the newspapers so everyone would be prepared, along with a guide written by the federal government advising registrants how to fill out the form: "Write your birthday (month, day, and year,) on a piece of paper before going to the registrar, and give the paper to him the first thing. Example: Aug. 5, 1894." Acknowledging that "many people do not carry in mind the year they were born," the guide advises: "This may be obtained by the registrar by subtracting the age in years on this year's birthday from 1917."[9] It was not expected that anyone would possess a birth certificate. No documents were needed; no proof of name or identity. Men left the precinct with a certificate that was proof that they had registered; they were advised to keep it on their persons. All that was required was a signature: *David H. Marshall, Reuben Marshall, Isadore Marshall.*

The first line on the registration card, which is mostly structured as a series of questions, numbered from 1 to 12, is: "Name in full," with a space for "Given name" and "Family name." Unlike numbers 4 through 12, which include question marks ("Where were you born?" or "Married or single (which)?"), No. 1 is not posed as a question, but one can imagine that it posed a question to the three brothers who had entered the Hebrew Orphan Asylum as "Roshafsky (Warshowsky)." We know from the registration cards that in 1917 David and Isadore live together at 408 Saratoga Avenue when they register at Precinct 31. Ruby (who signs his name "Reuben") registers at Precinct 86—he lives at 1596 Eastern Parkway—but we know from the cards that Ruby and Isadore work together as automobile mechanics at the American Motor Service Co. at 2119 Bergen Street in Brooklyn. I imagine that in the weeks between May 18 and June 5, they might have talked about this moment as the culmination of their plan, their pact, following the lead of the oldest brother, the oldest son. All they had to do was tell the registrar their names, to sign their signatures.

Eleven years and six days after he received the Bible inscribed to David Marshall at the Hebrew Orphan Asylum, David and his brothers are now all legally inscribed as *Marshall*. When Millie changes her name in marrying Isadore (later Irving) Levine at 408 Saratoga Avenue on March 30, 1919, her name has already been changed: she signs her name Mildred Marshall on the marriage certificate. Nine months later, on January 2, 1920, a census enumerator named Minerva Moskowitz (they probably called her Minnie) finds the "Marshal" family at 408 Saratoga Avenue: "Lena (age 50), David (age 27, accountant), Irving (age 23, auto mechanic), and Harold (age 18, clerk in the Army)." Fourteen years after David Marshall received the Bible at the Hebrew Orphan Asylum, his mother is now named Marshall.

U.S. Census, 1920. Courtesy of *Ancestry.com*.

When my grandfather marries my grandmother on November 12, 1922, he is "David Henry Marshall."[10] The only mention of the Warshawsky family name in any document that I have found after Daisy's 1912 marriage certificate is a 1922 alumni souvenir program that I discovered in a box in the Hebrew Orphan Asylum archives in which an "Honor Roll" of "Graduates of the Hebrew Orphan Asylum

THE HEBREW ORPHAN ASYLUM

HONOR ROLL

GRADUATES OF THE HEBREW ORPHAN ASYLUM WHO SERVED THEIR COUNTRY
DURING THE WORLD WAR

Markowitz, David
Marshal, Isidore
Maxwell, A. M.

Wachter, Jacob W.
Warshafsky, Reuben
Weber, Ben

Hebrew Orphan Asylum Centennial Souvenir Program, 1922. Courtesy of the Collection of American Jewish Historical Society.

who Served their Country during the World War" includes the name "Warshafsky, Reuben." Reuben's younger brother, Irving, appears as "Marshal, Isidore."[11] Perhaps Ruby decided to list himself as Reuben Warshafsky because he reasoned that his fellow alumni, the friends of the Roshafsky or Warshafsky brothers, would not know who Reuben Marshall was. David, although also a veteran who served his country during World War I, does not appear at all on this list. Perhaps he had no interest in being associated with this alumni event. Perhaps he did not know how to name himself in the program.

4

---•≈•---

A Posthumous Child

So I picture him, standing there on May 30, 1906, at the moment of his confirmation, receiving the Bible. I picture him: David Roshafsky, standing in for David Warshafsky, or David Warshawsky, grandson of David Worshafsky, naming himself and becoming David Marshall in an autobiographical act of self-inscription that would prescribe the naming, shortly after his death in 1952, of a grandson he never would know—named, just as he was, for his late grandfather David. It is his brother Harry, born after his father's death, who could have said, like David Copperfield, "I was a posthumous child," but David Marshall stands here as if he were a posthumous child. An orphan, an inmate under an assumed name, the oldest son: Did David or Dick feel free to reinvent himself, a self-made man like Horatio Alger's orphan, Ragged Dick, or a hero like the male protagonist of Alger's *The Mad Heiress*, Henry Marshall, both of whom he could have encountered (along with the orphan David Copperfield) in the Hebrew Orphan Asylum library?[1]

How did he arrive at the name *Marshall*? There may have been relatives from Russia named Marshak. Records from Minsk and surrounding villages show families named Marshak as well as Varshavski and Ruderman.[2] The prominent attorney and philanthropist Louis Marshall was a well-known patron of the Hebrew Orphan Asylum in 1905, but

49

businessman Seelig Warshawsky also was a donor. (I have found no evidence of any family relation.) The Hebrew Orphan Asylum library contained books by the children's author Emma Marshall, as well as *The History of the United States Naval Academy* by Edward Chauncey Marshall. "Warshawsky" appears in so many forms, not just from one document to the next but even within the same document, recorded by the same hand: Warshawsky, Warshafsky, Warshofsky, Warschawsky, Warshavsky, Worshafsky, Warschafske, Wishafzki, Roshofsky, Roshafsky, Fashafsky. One can see how easily names are transformed by misreading, mishearing, transliteration, transcription, bad penmanship. On Ruby's birth certificate, Lena's maiden name is listed as Federman rather than Ruderman, a simple misreading of an *R* for an *F* and an *e* for a *u*.

As my eyes glance at the name on his birth certificate, at the peaks of the flourish of the *W*, I can see how David arrived at *Marshall*. The *W* becomes an *M*, inverted, a mirror image; the *arsha* of W̲arshawsky remains. I found a listing in a city directory for a tailor named "D. Marchovsky." There is a "Marschauski" in the 1915 New York State census. One of the genealogical websites incorrectly lists Isadore's birth certificate information under the name "Marsawsky," presumably a recent act of misreading. In city directories, among the variants of Warshawsky, one finds both Warshaw and Warshall. In the handwriting of the time, the slanted, cursive *W* resembles an *M*. How easily, either accidentally or intentionally, through the misreading of handwriting, in the evolutionary Anglicization of spelling, the second *w* in Warshawsky becomes a double *ll*: Warshaw becomes Warshall. One can picture the child writing his name, practicing his penmanship, his signature, with the flourishes of the capital letter: once the *W* and the *M* are transformed, the name Marshall is almost there.

Indeed, if the inscription of the confirmation Bible has been altered, as the smudge on the page might suggest, if Warshawsky has been changed to Marshall on this very page, all that has been changed is the beginning and end of the last name: the *arsha* that forms the center of both Warshawsky and Marshall seems undisturbed. If there is a smudge, a sign of erasure and rewriting, it appears in the flourish of

Birth Certificate, David Warshafsky, New York City Department of Records.

the *M* and the flourish of the double *ll* that frame the name. This possible smudge came to light only a few years ago when I photographed the page, like an X-ray of a Da Vinci painting that revealed a false start. I think it has become more visible over the past decade, like invisible ink that came to the surface after one hundred years of concealment. Yet if there were an erasure and rewriting, it seems unlikely that, years later, sometime between 1906 and 1915, David would have decided to change his name, presumably in concert with the rest of his family, and *then* gone back and changed the inscription in the Bible in perfect and identical penmanship. This was not a legal document that would authorize other legal documents, like a birth certificate. The Bible would have been a historical curiosity ("I received this Bible when we were still named Warshawsky," he might have told his sons) rather than evidence of a conspiracy. Who would even have seen the Bible? Furthermore, the gold letters on the cover of the Bible that pronounce *David Marshall* must have been contemporaneous with the original gift.

Maurice Bernstein, the boy who arrived in the Hebrew Orphan Asylum in 1911, a year after Ruby and Isi were discharged, recalling his confirmation and bar mitzvah gifts more than half a century later, wrote that each "boy was given a Bible with his name engraved in golden letters."[3] Would David Marshall, alias David Warshawsky, have gone to the trouble and expense, years later, of scraping off the golden letters and then adding newly embossed gold, Gothic letters on the cover of the Bible in a gesture meant to seal a retroactive imposture, to hide the name from his future wife and sons? What made him keep this Bible, apparently the only keepsake of his years in the Hebrew Orphan Asylum?

It seems more likely that, at the moment of his confirmation, recognized as a man, poised to go out into the world, he was determined

Bible inscribed to David Marshall, Hebrew Orphan Asylum, 1906.

to leave the name of his father and grandfather behind. Perhaps the Junior League of the Hebrew Orphan Asylum had not gotten the message; perhaps no one had remembered to tell the secretary, Miss Alma Rosenberg, or that woman with the nice handwriting who was chosen to inscribe the Bibles, that he no longer wanted to be known as David Warshawsky or David Roshafsky. Or perhaps one of the Junior League ladies noticed the mistake just in time and corrected it. Perhaps his name change was not sanctioned by the school authorities. Just a week after the confirmation ceremony, as the *New York Times* reported on June 4, 1906, David Warshawsky won the Kate Kleinert Memorial Prize in the annual Hebrew Orphan Asylum awards ceremony. (At least it was not awarded to David Roshafsky.) Or was he disappointed, after being called up to the bema of the synagogue to receive his Bible, to read the inscription? A special Bible like this could not be discarded or replaced. The young women of the Junior League were not much older than he was: Did he plead or charm, showing them that the name could be easily fixed to become his chosen name, *Marshall*? Or did he originally have another name in mind? Did he stare at the letters of *Warshawsky* and wonder what could be made of the name until suddenly *Marshall* took shape and the solution was in sight? Countless names were altered at Ellis Island under comparably accidental or arbitrary circumstances. Whether the Bible was inscribed to David Marshall from the outset, or "corrected" after the original inscription was made, I imagine that when he left the Hebrew Orphan Asylum on September 5, 1905—just one month before his fifteenth birthday according to his birth certificate—he carried with him the Bible inscribed to David Marshall. Naming him, perhaps proleptically, as David Marshall, the Bible stands as a birth certificate. It becomes a passport to a future. In transforming Warshawsky into Marshall, it erases—either figuratively or literally, or both—the name of the father.

Yet if the name of the father is transformed, translated, effaced, its trace returns in the children's names. The name of the father returns in the *H*. Harry, the son born some six months after the death of his father, memorializes the name of Harris, just as Dora bore her late grandmother's name and David bore his late grandfather's name. The *H* circulates further. The Warshawsky birth certificates include no middle names or initials, yet in the 1910 census, David becomes "David H.," and Daisy, his oldest sister and the first-born Warshawsky child, becomes "Daisy H." Daisy's first son, born in 1913, twelve years after her father's death, is named Harold, despite the presence of her youngest brother, who presumably discharged the family of any obligation to name another child after Harris. On his World War I draft registration card, David becomes "David H. Marshall." On his marriage certificate and his World War II registration card, David is "David Henry Marshall." Is "Henry" a variation of "Harry" or a rejection of "Harry" that still maintains the *H*? His brother, on his World War II registration card, becomes "Ruben Harold Marshall," echoing the name of the father, along with his orphaned brother Harold, whose 1901 birth certificate, which records "no father" on the line reserved for "Father's Name," names him as "Harry."

The trace of the father is also found in the letter *A,* which echoes Harris's "real" name (or Hebrew name), Aaron. The Social Security Death Index lists Harry, from birth named after his father, as Harry A. Marshall. Harry's son-in-law lists him on a family tree as "Harry Aaron Marshall," suggesting that he was named, or later named himself, after his father doubly. American Jews often fulfill the traditional family obligation to name a child after a deceased parent by maintaining the

Bible inscribed to David Marshall, Hebrew Orphan Asylum, 1906.

first letter of the name or by assigning a separate Hebrew name. Ruby's first son, born in 1917, is named Arnold. David's first son, my father, born in 1924, is named Arthur. My father's Hebrew name was Aaron. I assume that this was true of Arnold as well. Millie's daughter, born in 1925, is named Adele. Thus the name of the father is memorialized. His alphabetic trace is dutifully disseminated, if transformed, throughout the family. Yet if Harris Warshawsky is remembered, why does he seem to disappear? The mystery of the name turned out to be the easiest mystery to solve. The deeper mystery is why *Warshawsky* was erased, beyond the re-inscription of *Harris* and *Aaron* in successive generations. This mystery is, I imagine, related to the mystery of the death of the father. This is also a story about how stories unexpectedly open up onto other stories.

5

———⋆⋆⋆———

Traces of the Father

On Thursday, February 28, 1901, the *Newtown Register*, a small biweekly paper published in Newtown, Long Island, printed a notice titled "Queens Vital Statistics" that included a list of deaths. Near ads for "Edison Phonographs and Recordings" and "Broadway Styles in Hats and Men's Furnishings—Now Ready at Half of Broadway Prices," is this death notice: "Astoria—Harris Warshawsky, 36 years."[1] This is the only public acknowledgment of Harris Warshawsky's death. I have not found Harris Warshawsky in any published death notices or obituaries in New York City or Brooklyn, or in any other newspaper article or listing.

There are traces of his life in New York City municipal records and archives, directories, and even in published state reports. The names Warshawsky and Warshafsky were not uncommon, and with so many variants and variant spellings, and a few appearances of another Harris Warschawsky in the garment industry, I have had to cross-reference each record with an address or some biographical detail to confirm its relevance. Harris Warshawsky was a tailor; like the large majority of his neighbors on the Lower East Side, he was part of the rapidly expanding "needle trade" in the 1890s. City directories list his residence and work addresses between 1890 and 1900, and I have found documents

Queens Vital Statistics.

For the week ending February 23, there were recorded in the Health Department of Queens Borough 46 births, 19 marriages, 62 deaths. Of the deaths 22 were in the First Ward, 18 in the Second, 13 in the Third, 9 in the Fourth and none in the Fifth. One of the deaths was from accident or violence, 16 were under 5 years of age. The following were the deaths recorded:

Astoria—Harris Warshawsky, 36 years; Samuel S Betts, 56 years; Sophie Schneider Koch, 42 years; Mamie Sullivan, 2 months.

"Queens Vital Statistics," *The Newtown Register*, February 28, 1901.

that locate him in every year between 1890, the year of his marriage, and 1901, the year of his death. Ship registries are suggestive but inconclusive. I have located a marriage certificate from 1890, naturalization papers from 1892, a death certificate from 1901, and birth certificates for each of the six Warshawsky children. We have the 1900 U.S. census, but the 1890 census was destroyed by a fire.

These records suggest that Harris (or Aaron) Warshawsky was born in 1865 in Russia in Minsk. The 1900 census record for the family indicates that he immigrated around 1887. Perhaps Aaron Warshawsky's early life paralleled that of David Levinsky, the protagonist of Abraham Cahan's partly autobiographical novel, *The Rise of David Levinsky*, who is born in 1865 and immigrates to New York in 1885 along with tens of thousands of Russian Jews fleeing the anti-Semitic pogroms and political violence that spread through Russia in the early 1880s. David Levinsky is a young Talmudic scholar who arrives in New York with four cents in his pocket and becomes a rich cloak manufacturer in the 1890s, a period in which immigrant Russian Jews come to dominate the garment industry. Aaron Warshawsky might have been the typical *cheder* boy described by Cahan and other authors of the time, gradually removing layers of orthodoxy and observance, changing his name from Aaron to Harris, ashamed to be seen as a "greenhorn," seduced by Americanization. Compelled to make a living, like so many thousands of his fellow Russian Jewish immigrants, he reinvents himself as a tailor and eventually a businessman in an industry that had an insatiable appetite for both exploited workers and would-be entrepreneurs.

The card registering Harris Warshawky's petition for naturalization leaves blank the boxes noting "Port of Arrival in the United States" and "Date of Arrival." Many of the documents from this era have inaccuracies and inconsistencies, and sometimes approximate dating; people did not always keep track or remember correctly years and dates, even of birthdays. A ship called the SS *Republic* arrived in New York from Liverpool on March 17, 1884, with a twenty-year-old "laborer" named Aron Wasschafsky. He is said to be from Poland, but there was often political and geographical confusion between Russia and Poland. On August 18, 1885, a ship called the SS *Moravia* arrived from Hamburg with a twenty-year-old Russian named Aron Warschawski on board; he traveled steerage (*Zwishendeck*) along with Wolf Warschawski, also age twenty. Aron Warschawski is identified as a "dealer" (or merchant) under "Occupation or Calling." Perhaps he was an aspiring capitalist, arriving with savings to invest.[2]

Could Aaron (Harris) and Wolf be brothers or cousins? I haven't found a trace of this Wolf Warschawski in subsequent records.[3] I have discovered that Harris had a younger brother in New York named Jack Warshafsky, who married Annie Blecher in New York City on October 5, 1893, at the age of twenty-four. On the marriage certificate, his parents are listed as David Warshafsky and Debora Germoise from Minsk, which matches the record of Harris's parents on his 1890 marriage certificate: David Worshafsky and Dorah Garmize. The address given is 110 Norfolk Street, the address of Harris and Lena between 1891 and 1894. There is no record of Jack Warshafsky after this. I have a theory that he moved to Newark, New Jersey, where he was known as Isaac Warshoff.[4] Both Wolf Warschawski and Jack Warshafsky could have changed their names.

Changes in names and even variations in spellings make relatives difficult to track. In 1890, the same year in which Harris and Lena were married, the *New York Herald* ran a story titled, "Why Many People Change Their Names," which describes a Russian immigrant in the "clothing and hat business" named Louis Warshowsky. According to Louis Warshowsky's petition to change his name from Warshowsky to Warshor (filed with the New York City Clerk's Office and cited in full in the article): "your petitioner desires but one name and that pronounceable by the average persons with whom he deals, and that the name of 'Warshor,' by which he has been called and is now generally known, is acceptable to him and his family. . . . That it will materially assist him in his business, as the new name is one easily remembered and better adapted to business purposes than to be called, as he sometimes has, as the man with the unpronounceable name."[5] This statement may represent what David Warshawksy came to feel, even as a child. Despite his unpronounceable (and unspellable) name, Aaron Warshawsky changed only his first name. I don't know if any of the people listed in New York City directories in the 1890s as Warshawsky, Warshafsky, Warshow, Warshaw, Warshor, Warshof, Warner, etc., were related to him.

I don't know what Harris Warshawsky was called by his family, friends, employers, employees, or how he introduced himself. On most official documents, he is "Harris Warshawsky" (with variants in spelling), but on David's birth certificate he is named "Harrie," like his posthumous son Harry. Harris and Harry were very common names on the Lower East Side. Perhaps his wife and brother called him Aaron, pronounced in the Russian or Yiddish way, or perhaps they used a diminutive. Since no one spoke of him or named him in my family, there is no family tradition to follow. I will call him Harris Warshawsky or Harris, the way he is named by official documents. I hesitate to call him Harry or Aaron, the way that biographers call their famous subjects by their first names in their early chapters, caught between a false intimacy and the false teleology caused by the retrospective illusion that Sartre named in describing how a book called *The Childhood of Famous Men* ruined his childhood. If I call him Harris Warshawsky, knowing that this may have been only his public or bureaucratic or American persona, this is also to acknowledge the difficulty of knowing the story that the name stands for.

There is a family story (recounted by my father's cousin Adele) that Harris Warshawsky and Lena Ruderman had an arranged marriage; this would not have been unusual. The Ruderman family seems to have come from a town called Gorodok (or Horodok) near Minsk, and it was typical for immigrants to maintain their Old Country communities through both informal associations and formal organizations.[6] Lena appears to have been born in about 1870, immigrating to New York City in 1884,

Certificate of Marriage, Harris Warshafsky and Lena Ruderman, New York City Department of Records.

CERTIFICATE OF MARRIAGE.

1. *Full Name of* GROOM, _Harris Warshafsky_

2. *Place of Residence,* _83 Essex_

3. *Age next Birthday,* _25_ years, Color,*

4. *Occupation,* _Tailor_

5. *Place of Birth,* _Russia_

6. *Father's Name,* _David Warshafsky_

7. *Mother's Maiden Name,* _Dorah Gerning_

8. *No. of Groom's Marriage,*

9. *Full Name of* BRIDE _Lena Ruderman_

   Maiden Name, if a Widow,

10. *Place of Residence,* _83 Essex_

11. *Age next Birthday,* _21_ years, Color,*

12. *Place of Birth,* _Russia_

13. *Father's Name,* _Meyer Ruderman_

14. *Mother's Maiden Name,* _Minna Davidow_

15. *No. of Bride's Marriage,*

*If of other races, specify what. At Nos. 8 and 15 state whether 1st, 2d, 3d, &c., Marriage of each. The signatures below of Bride and Groom should be written out in full for the "given" and family names.

New York, _January 27_ 18_80_

We, the Groom and Bride named in the above Certificate, hereby Certify that the information given is correct, to the best of our knowledge and belief.

Harris Warshofsky (Groom.)

Lena Ruderman (Bride.)

Signed in the presence of _Harris Steach_

and _Abram Udelow_

Marriage Ceremony performed by _Rabbi H. Lass_

Residence, _2 & 4 Suffolk_

Certificate of Marriage, Harris Warshafsky and Lena Ruderman, New York City Department of Records.

probably with her father, Meyer Ruderman, although my father's cousin Adele believes that she may have come alone in advance of her family. She likely had other relatives in New York. Her mother, her brothers Isaac, Abraham, and Michael, and her sisters Fannie and Bessie, seem to have arrived later, in 1888.[7] This "chain migration," as historians call it, typically consisted of "husbands and fathers leaving first, securing a job and a place to live, and then sending funds home to bring over the rest of the family."[8] Lena's arrival at the age of fourteen, with or without her father, preceding her mother and five siblings (including her older brother), suggests independence, responsibility, and courage. Surely she went to work when she arrived in New York, presumably in the garment industry, along with her father, who worked as a tailor for decades. Her income would have been important to her family, especially as she and her father saved money to bring over the rest of the family. We do not know what her life was like in the five or six years between her arrival in New York and her marriage at the age of twenty. Perhaps Harris and Lena met while working in the same shop. Perhaps Harris Warshawsky worked with Lena's father or with her brothers, who also were tailors.

In 1890, Meyer and Hannah Ruderman would have had six children living with them at 83 Essex Street: Isaac (age twenty-four), Lena (age twenty), Abraham (age thirteen), Fannie (age nine), Bessie (age eight), and Michael (age seven). Both Harris and Lena list 83 Essex Street as their address on the marriage certificate. Perhaps Harris was a boarder already living with the Rudermans. The Rudermans lived at 83 Essex Street and then later at 82 Essex Street for many of the years between 1889 and 1905. Harris and Lena lived with the Ruderman family at 83 Essex Street not only when they were married in January of 1890, but also when their first child, Daisy, was born in November of 1890, and, according to Trow's Directory, for at least part of 1891. If they were all living in the same tenement apartment at 83 Essex Street, there would have been (at least) ten or eleven people living there after Daisy's birth in 1890, not counting any other relatives or boarders. It is possible that they lived in neighboring apartments in the same tenement, but this would not have been typical. In 1890, in his chapter "Jewtown" in *How the Other Half Lives*, Jacob Riis writes: "In Essex Street two small rooms in a six-story tenement were made to hold a 'family' of father and mother, twelve children and six boarders."[9]

By 1892, Harris and Lena had moved to 110 Norfolk Street, where they would live until 1897. Three of their children were born there. Harris Warshawsky lists his residence as 110 Norfolk Street when he is naturalized in 1892. I found the October 25, 1892, proclamation of the District Court of the United States for the Southern District of New York that grants him American citizenship. There is no record of Lena's naturalization. The 1920 U.S. census indicates that Mrs. Lena Marshal was naturalized in 1891. After 1855, a wife was legally naturalized at the moment that her husband became a citizen. Harris's naturalization papers would have made both husband and wife citizens simultaneously.[10]

While he signs "Haris Warshofsky" on the line next to "Groom" on his 1890 marriage certificate in a careful but somewhat shaky hand,

Postcard, Essex Street, New York City.

the signature of the man who renounces and abjures all allegiance to the Czar of Russia in his naturalization papers is considerably fancier and more sophisticated than the signature of the man who was married two years earlier. However, the flourishes of the capital "H" differ even within the document. The most calligraphically ornate signature is that of the witness, Hyman Lewis, of 173 Delancey Street, who swears that "Harris Warschawsky" has "behaved as a man of good moral character, attached to the principles of the Constitution of the United States, and well disposed to the good order and happiness of the same." According to the 1900 census, Hyman Lewis was a teacher. The handwriting of the census enumerator is difficult to decipher, but I think that he lists Lewis's occupation as "teacher of languages." Although there was a Hyman Lewis who was a tailor and contractor in the 1890s, the Hyman Lewis who was a teacher living at 173 Delancey Street can be followed in the New York State and U.S. census records over the next thirty years. In 1930, his occupation is listed as a teacher of English.[11] He was thirty-three years old in 1900, having come to New York from Poland twenty-five years earlier when he was eight.

When I figured out that Hyman Lewis was a language teacher, I imagined that after helping Harris Warshawsky to learn English, Hyman Lewis helped him with the ceremony (and perhaps with the signature) that inscribed him as an American. In Abraham Cahan's 1917 novel, *The Rise of David Levinsky*, the protagonist's English teacher becomes his mentor, friend, and eventually his partner. In Cahan's stories, teaching English is a common sideline for educated immigrants, and in the 1890s it might have been a lucrative business. In 1890 Jacob Riis describes "whole settlements on this East Side where English is practically an unknown tongue, though the people be both willing and anxious to learn." He describes crowds "babbling, and shouting in foreign tongues, a veritable Babel of confusion" in which an "English word falls upon the ear almost with a sense of shock, as something unexpected and strange."[12] I subsequently discovered that Hyman Lewis was a witness for dozens of naturalization petitions in this period—for example, in 1891 for Joe Richmond, a trimmings maker living at 263 Division Street; Max

Petition for Naturalization, Harris Warschwasky, District Court, United States District Court for the Southern District of New York.

Resnick, a tailor living at 232 Goerck Street; and Abram Oslag, a tailor living at 32 Willett Street; and in 1892 for Isaac Peters, a tailor living at 143 Essex Street; and in 1894 for Nathan Ehrich, a cloak maker living at 87 Attorney Street. On most of the petition cards, Hyman Lewis is identified as a teacher. Before moving to 173 Delancey Street, he lived at 192 Broome Street, a few doors down from where Harris Warshawsky would have his coat-manufacturing firm at 198 Broome Street.

I imagine that Hyman Lewis included in the price of his English lessons a promise that he would not only prepare his students for citizenship but also accompany them to the naturalization ceremony and help them fill out the forms. This connection suggests that Harris Warshawsky, who seems to have arrived in New York between 1885 and 1887, was still learning English around 1892, when he became a naturalized citizen. This was a year after his second child, David, was born. In looking through these records, I discovered that two years later Harris Warshawsky himself served as a witness for the naturalization of Abraham Sametzsky, a tailor living at 17 Attorney Street, in October of 1894. Perhaps Abraham Sametzsky worked for Harris Warshawsky. I have found no other record for him.

Since 110 Norfolk Street is the address that Jack Warshafsky gives when he marries Annie Blecher in 1893, it is possible that Jack and Annie lived there with Harris and Lena and their children after their marriage, or at least that Jack Warshafsky lived with the Warhsawsky family before he married. The 1893 Trow's Directory reports Meyer Ruderman living at 110 Norfolk Street as well, suggesting that the Rudermans and Warshawskys moved together from 83 Essex Street; the Rudermans are at 82 Essex Street by 1898, but we do not know if they lived with the Warshawskys during the entire intervening period. An article in the November 26, 1898, *New York American* (about court fees that poor people were required to pay) depicts a man named Benjamin Wolff, "a poor cabinet-maker who lives with a numerous family at No. 110 Norfolk Street."[13] The Warshawsky family remains at 110 Norfolk Street until 1897 or 1898; they move next to 176 Rivington Street and stay for two or three years. The Rudermans are absent from the 1900

U.S. census. They do not appear among the 124 people that the census enumerator Arthur Tackler found at 82 Essex Street in 1900. In 1900, the Warshawsky family is living at 151 Norfolk Street. Many of the pages for Norfolk Street, including 151, are partially illegible because of some sort of water stain. Perhaps the Rudermans are there. In any case, we know that the Warshawksy family did not stay there for very long.

Wandering the streets of the Lower East Side on a summer Sunday, I found 151 Norfolk Street, a large six-story apartment building with a parallel entrance and address at 153 Norfolk. I stopped a resident opening the door and asked if I could see the lobby. There was an exposed brick wall and an old airshaft that looked at least a century old. Asked about the history of the building, the man recounted the story he had heard of a frightening, dark basement with strange wooden partitions.

"The Ghetto, New York, N.Y.," c. 1909. Courtesy of the Library of Congress, Prints and Photographs Division.

151 Norfolk Street, New York City.

They say, he repeated in an ominous tone, that this is where they had the sweatshops. By 1900, the Tenement Act prohibited shops in apartments, but the law was difficult to enforce. An 1892 article called "The Jews in New York" in *Century Magazine* cited Riis's account that in an overcrowded tenement he had "found that several people slept in a subcellar four feet by six, on a pile of clothing that was being made."[14] We know that throughout most of the 1890s Harris Warshawsky produced coats in a shop that was inspected and approved by the New York State factory inspectors.

It is difficult to know what standard of living or social class these addresses reflected at the turn of the century in the notoriously overcrowded Lower East Side, what was then "the most crowded neighborhood on the planet," with "more than 700 people per acre."[15] According to the 1900 census, the Warshawskys' immediate neighbors at 151 Norfolk included a peddler, a furrier, a presser, a shirtmaker, a pocketbook maker, a dressmaker, a corset maker, an umbrella maker, a cap maker, an embroiderer, and many tailors, as well as a carpenter, a tinsmith, a news agent, a laundryman, a boat operator, a hair dresser, a liquor dealer, a bartender, and a musician. There were many young children. Although the heads of households all seem to be gainfully employed, these occupations do not indicate that this was a residence for the nouveaux riches. This list of occupations is entirely typical of what one finds in the census records for the entire neighborhood. The same *New York American* article that depicts a poor cabinetmaker at 110 Norfolk Street depicts a poor servant girl named Fannie Follick, "whose earnings help to keep the hungry mouths filled at her home, No. 153 Norfolk street."[16]

I wonder where the Warshawsky children went to school. On Suffolk Street approaching Rivington Street, I found an imposing neo-Gothic building that (I later learned) originally was a grammar school. It opened in 1898, which is about when the family moved to 176 Rivington Street, just around the corner; 130 Suffolk Street, where the children lived with their mother after their father's death, would have been even closer. The school is now the home of the Clemente Soto Vélez Cultural and Educational Center, which sponsors Puerto Rican and Latino arts programs on the Lower East Side. Although obscured by scaffolding when I saw it, it still presided over the neighborhood with majestic architecture that was designed by C. B. J. Snyder, a prolific architect who was the New York City Board of Education superintendent of school buildings between 1891 and 1923. (He also designed Erasmus Hall High School in Brooklyn, which my father attended.) An article in the *New York Times* on December 13, 1898, announced the completion of four new schools, the largest of which was "Public School No. 160, at Suffolk and Rivington Streets," a "five-story structure, containing 39 classrooms, each capable of seating 45 pupils, or 2,755 in all, besides the kindergarten rooms." The opening of the buildings was delayed by "the lack of school furniture supplied by the State Prison Commission." On April 8, 1897, the *Times* had reported that a "new grammar school

Jacob Riis, "Public School, Suffolk and Rivington Streets," c. 1897. Courtesy of the Museum of the City of New York.

building" would be "erected on Rivington Street between Forsyth and Eldridge Streets" to "replace the old Chrystie Street schoolhouse, erected in 1856, which has been rendered so dark from adjoining high buildings that gas and electric light must be used constantly."[17]

The last decade of the nineteenth century, David Warshawsky's first decade, was a time of transformation in the New York City schools. The School Reform Law of 1874 had required a minimum of fourteen weeks of schooling for children between the ages of eight and fourteen. The School Reform Law of 1894 instituted compulsory education between October and June. The *Annual Report of the Board of Education of the City of New York for the Year Ending December 31, 1886* reported: "Insufficient school accommodations have furnished cause for very general complaint on the part of the citizens of New York during the past ten years. The unprecedented growth of the city, together with unexpected movements of population, rendered it almost impossible to keep pace with the demands in given localities or to anticipate the needs of certain sections of the city that speedily outgrew the accommodations that were provided."[18]

Despite the new schools, it was difficult to keep up: the *New York Times* ran an article on September 12, 1900, with the headline, "Some Schools Overcrowded. Superintendent Jasper Thinks Half-Day Classes Will Be Necessary for 8,000 Pupils." School No. 4 on Rivington Street reported "fourteen part-day classes." An article published one year later, on September 10, 1901, titled "Too Few Schools for New York's Children. Thousands Turned Away at Their Opening for Lack of Room," also described "Half-day classes at School No. 4, Rivington and Ridge Streets," and reported that police had to be called in to deal with "almost riotous efforts on the part of parents to get their children into the buildings without delay." Among the impacted schools on the Lower East Side was "School No, 140, at 116 Norfolk Street," a primary school with a capacity of eleven hundred. The article (which that day also reported special assemblies to pray for the recovery of President McKinley, who had just been shot) noted the "work public schools are doing in making homogeneous the foreign peoples in this Nation" by assimilating "Italians, Russian and Polish Jews, Irish and Germans, Greeks and Armenians" and even Chinese.[19]

David would have been eight years old in October of 1899 (assuming that the family used his actual birthdate of 1891). David and Daisy (and perhaps Ruby) would have been among those thousands of children trying to go to school. With half-days of schools and many children not required to attend—not to mention truants—the streets would have been filled with children. Many were put to work in shops and homes, and in the spaces in between. Photographs from this decade and the next show children on the streets carrying stacks of unfinished garments, shining shoes, and selling newspapers, as well as working in tenement apartments and shops. Did David (who later was always entrepreneurial) ever work in his father's shop, or help with piecework at home? The Warshawsky children, all born in New York, may have been the first in their family to attend school, and surely their parents, like the *New York Times*, would have seen education as critical to the family's success and assimilation.

I have three photographs, sent to me late in my search by Harris and Lena's sole surviving grandchild, my father's cousin Adele, Millie's daughter: a portrait of Harris and Lena Warshawsky, a portrait of Lena, and a portrait of Daisy and David when they were young children. These photographs must have been saved by Lena and passed down to Millie. I assume that my grandfather, who lived with his mother from the age of fourteen to the age of thirty-one, did not own copies. Indeed, when I began this search, I had no idea that such photographs existed. The formal portrait of Harris and Lena Warshawsky, in the genre of the cabinet card, in many ways looks like a traditional wedding portrait: in the formal pose typical of wedding portraits of the time, Harris is seated and Lena is standing on his right; her hand barely touches his wrist, her folded fingers resting on his arm not intimately but as if it were a table. Both Harris and Lena are impeccably dressed: he has a fine suit, fashionably unbuttoned above the waist to reveal a watch chain. His dark hair is neatly parted in the middle, and he has a moustache with the ends waxed and tilted up. He has no beard; he bears no trace of the Russian Jewish immigrant, unless it is a portly, European bourgeois sense of gravity, or a drive to assimilate described so often in the literature of the period. Although his pose is formal, he does not seem stiff or awkward. It is no doubt several years since he underwent the transformation described by Abraham Cahan in "The Imported Bridegroom": "Instead of his uncouth cap and the draggling coat which had hidden his top boots from view, he was now arrayed in the costliest 'Prince Albert,' the finest summer derby, and the most elegant button shoes the store contained." These clothes, and "a starched shirt-front, a turned-down collar, and a gaudy puff-tie," are described as "the garb of Gentile civilization."[20]

Lena seems somewhat more exotic, her dark hair pulled back, also parted in the middle. Like her husband, her head is uncovered, and of course she has no wig. She has a formal, dark dress, no doubt her best dress, or the best dress in the family, with the fashionable puffed "mutton leg" sleeves that were popular in the 1890s, an intricate lace

Harris and Lena. Courtesy of Adele Marks.

front above a corseted bodice, with a chain or tassel pinned to it like a watch chain. Lace falls over her shoulders from behind her head where it ties back her hair. There is a belt with a ribbon and a lace handkerchief. One hand rests on her hip behind her back. Her sleeves have gauzy, sheer cuffs. Harris is seated on a plush chair next to a potted plant. His frame is solid; he must be considerably taller than his wife since, seated,

Lena. Courtesy of Adele Marks.

his head rises above her shoulders. Both seem serious, businesslike; they seem less awkward than the typical cabinet-card portrait of a couple in the 1890s, as if they are comfortable posing. There is an accompanying portrait of Lena shot from the torso up: looking off to her right, she displays an earring in her left ear; her hair is pulled back tightly and the lace frames her face. This portrait seems vaguely romantic, even artistic; the dress is a work of art, and it frames her delicate face.

As I dwell on these pictures, I try to picture their lives, to bring them into focus, to imagine their situation and prospects in life at the time. The portraits reflect social stature, and perhaps even more so, social aspirations. They fit squarely into the portrait genre of the time; no one would make a formal portrait wearing anything but his or her best clothes (or someone else's best clothes). It was possible to rent clothes for a wedding, but a family of tailors, immersed in a sea of tailors, would have been able to produce a fine set of clothes. It is more likely that the acquisition of fine new clothing would be the occasion for a formal portrait than it would be that clothing would be acquired for the occasion of a portrait. These portraits mark some occasion, some moment of arrival.

In Harris's careful tailor's hands, there is a rectangular piece of paper, held lightly between each thumb and forefinger. The edge barely touched by the thick thumb and forefinger of his left hand may be slightly frayed, as if it were a ceremonial document. Assuming that this was a wedding portrait, I assumed that this piece of paper, held horizontally, was the *ketubah* or marriage contract, or at least their New York City marriage certificate. (The Hebrew word *ketubah* means, literally, "the document.") If this were a wedding portrait, it would date the photograph around January 27, 1890. However, an expert in photographs and family history assured me that this was not a wedding photograph. Although it was not uncommon for a bride to wear her best dress, even if it were not a white bridal gown, for her wedding and subsequently her wedding portrait, she insisted that Lena's dress, with its sleeves puffed out at the shoulders, was not characteristic of a dress, especially a wedding dress, worn at the beginning of the decade. She did not think that it was common for a couple in a wedding portrait to pose with a marriage certificate. Surveying such photographs in web-based library and museum archives, I have seen only one other photograph in which a couple holds some sort of document. The expert asked if this could be a deed to a property or some other document that represented a personal landmark in business.

If this is not a wedding photograph, what moment of accomplishment or prosperity does it commemorate? What document is Harris holding so carefully in his hands? The document might be the proclamation of the District Court of the United States for the Southern District of New York that granted Harris Warshawsky (and by extension his wife) U.S. citizenship on October 25, 1892.[21] This would have been a moment to commemorate for a young, ambitious couple. However, since Ruby was born on February 12, 1893, Lena would have been at least five months pregnant at the end of October of 1892, assuming that he was not born prematurely. Looking at her midsection below the tight-waisted bodice, it does not seem obvious that she was pregnant when this photograph was made, but nor does it seem impossible that she was pregnant.[22] Perhaps they would have waited until after the baby was born to have posed with the document that made them American.

These portraits bear the imprimatur of the New York photographic studio Newman & Co., which was located at 183 Essex Street, down the block from the Ruderman residence. Founded in 1886 by Samuel Newman and Edward Leaming, the studio had an elaborate notice in an 1888 volume titled *Illustrated New York: The Metropolis of To-Day* that boasted that the photographers "are familiar with the requirements of the best classes of the public" and that "the character of the work done here compares favorably with the finest on Broadway and Union Square at one half the prices."[23]

Next to the Newman imprimatur on the card, an insignia cites a diploma and a medal from the Photographers Association of America dated 1894 and 1896, respectively. If the prints were made in 1896 or later, they might have been reprints. It was common for studios to retain negatives, including the stock of their predecessors, and offer duplicates or reprints of photographs.[24] It is possible that Harris and Lena Warshawsky purchased a new copy of this portrait, perhaps at the moment they moved from 110 Norfolk Street to 176 Rivington Street between 1896 and 1897; perhaps this was the moment they moved into a nicer, larger apartment. Perhaps they had a parlor for the first time; they do not appear to live with the Rudermans in the middle of the 1890s.

If the photograph were taken in the middle of the decade, it could mark a moment of professional accomplishment and success. Shortly before the Warshawsky family moved from 110 Norfolk Street to 176

Rivington Street, Harris appears to have started his own factory. *The Report of the Factory Inspector of the State of New York* first records him with a coat-manufacturing firm at 198 Broome Street in 1895. Up to this point, he was listed in the city directory as a tailor working at 84 Suffolk Street. In 1895, H. Warschowsky's factory had over twenty employees, the largest number recorded for him in the reports that the factory inspector issued annually. Might the document in the photograph be a lease or some sort of certificate of incorporation? Might it be a deed, perhaps to one of the parcels in Brooklyn that were the subject of so much speculation in the New York real estate market toward the end of the decade? Or is it possible that Harris and Lena, too poor to have a wedding portrait made in January of 1890, chose to restage a wedding portrait in 1896, posing with their marriage certificate to name the occasion?

The photograph tells a story that has a text at its center: a document, a certificate, a memorial, a deed. The piece of paper, although illegible, tells a story that the photograph incorporates, as if it were self-evident. The word "deed" comes from the Old English *dæd*: "a doing, act, action, transaction, event." What does this document do, what does it transact? Does it enact as well as mark an event? I picture them carrying this piece of paper, held so carefully in the photograph, as if the ink were not yet dry, through the crowds of Essex Street—assuming that it is not a photographer's prop. I cannot read beneath its blank surface.

The photograph of Daisy and David, which bears the insignia of another Essex Street photographer's studio located at 183 Essex Street, also reflects class aspirations. Daisy, the oldest, could be about four years old; her face and head look older than her body. David wears a gown rather than pants, and he could be closer to two years old than to three. Both children are in elegant white dresses with lace curtains behind them. David is seated on a small chair, holding some kind of ball; Daisy stands next to him, leaning one hand on the arm of the chair, holding a knit pocketbook. David bears an uncanny resemblance to my father at the same age. Daisy, who has a somewhat solemn and even furtive look, resembles Lena, intense and older than her years. Neither child seems

David and Daisy. Courtesy of Adele Marks.

pleased by the occasion, or comfortable in their poses or clothes. This is also a formal portrait that fits into a contemporary cabinet-card genre. It declares prosperity and social stature; this was not the sort of portrait that a struggling immigrant tailor would have had made. These American-born children were not expected to work in a sweatshop. Yet with its lace curtains and ornate child's rocking chair, the portrait seems more Victorian than American. This seems to be a stage set with costumes, a nouveau-riche fantasy of the prosperous American, or perhaps an echo of an old-world Europe left behind in Minsk. It is difficult to picture these children in the streets of the Lower East Side in the last decade of the nineteenth century. The photograph imagines another world.

Did the children leave costumes and props behind in the photographer's studio when they stepped back into the noises and smells of Essex Street, or was this the nouveau-riche milieu that their parents designed for them? In March of 1898, Michael Ruderman (the uncle who must have been more like an older brother to David) appears to have acted in a production of *The Mikado* performed by "Hebrew boys," the oldest of whom was sixteen years old, at the Hebrew Institute on Jefferson Street and East Broadway. According to the April 2, 1898, issue of the *School Journal*, this "most unique entertainment" was presented by members of the Altruist chapter of the Patriotic League and the Alliance Literary Society. Reporting that "some of the boys had surprisingly clear and powerful voices," the critic singled out "Michael Ruderman as Ko-Ko," among a few others. (In Gilbert and Sullivan's comic opera, Ko-Ko was a "cheap tailor" who accidentally finds himself in a more elevated position.) Picturing David Warshawsky in the audience, I imagine a world of educational improvement, cultural enrichment, and aspirational assimilation in the lively cultural milieu of the Lower East Side, which, like Gilbert and Sullivan's Victorian fantasy of Japan, was also a strange world of multicultural mixing, translation, and performance. Unlike Michael Ruderman, who was born in Russia, David was a New Yorker, an American.

Although Meyer Ruderman lived to be ninety-five years old, when he arrived from Russia he was already about forty-four, not at all a young man in the 1880s. His wife, who died at age ninety, was about forty-two when she arrived; all her children were born in Russia. I picture them, in the first decade of my grandfather's life (the first decade of their life in New York, the last decade of the nineteenth century) as typical Lower East Side immigrants, working in tenement or factory shops, living with a dozen relatives, speaking mostly Yiddish. Harris was about twenty when he arrived in New York, and Lena was about fourteen. On David's birth certificate, Harris is said to be twenty-six and Lena twenty-three. Their "greenhorn" days were long behind them, but we don't know how good their English was or how often they spoke it, or whether the Warshawskys and Rudermans spoke Yiddish at home. Harris probably spoke English with an accent; Adele does not remember Lena speaking with an accent in her later years. We don't know how comfortable or privileged David Warshawsky's life was in the ten years before his father died, or what he would have looked like if photographed on the street rather than in the photographer's studio.

In *The Spirit of the Ghetto*, published in 1902, Hutchins Hapgood sees in the "shrewd-faced boy with the melancholy eyes that one sees everywhere in the streets of New York's Ghetto" a "mixture of almost unprecedented hope and excitement on the one hand, and of doubt, confusion, and self-distrust on the other hand." Drawn more to the streets than to the "chaider," shaped by "heterogeneous and worldly" public schools, he is portrayed as "a rising businessman" who "yet a child, acquires a self-sufficiency, an independence, and sometimes an arrogance which not unnaturally, at least in form, is extended even toward his parents." The boy is portrayed as "aware, and rather ashamed, of the limitations of his parents," who remain nonetheless "his conscience, the visible representatives of a moral and religious tradition by which the boy may regulate his inner life." Perhaps influenced by my father's stories of how he played stickball in the streets of Brooklyn in the 1920s and 30s, I picture David Warshawsky in the years before he was sent to the Hebrew Orphan Asylum not as Henry Roth's timid David in his novel *Call It Sleep*, pampered by his mother and terrorized by his father, but rather as one of a group of scrappy New York–born friends who teach him how to cross from one tenement roof to another. Perhaps he was both. Hapwood sees "the Ghetto boy's growing Americanism" as "easily triumphant at once over the old traditions and the new socialism."[25] This was the path of David Warshawsky, the oldest son of an immigrant tailor turned contractor, who would become a Republican businessman but not enter the garment industry, except for a period as an accountant.[26]

These images come in and out of focus. It is difficult for me to reconcile the face of Lena in these photographs with my only childhood memory of Grandma Marshall. Opening a door more than fifty years ago, I found myself unexpectedly standing face to face with a seemingly ancient woman, my great-grandmother ("What's so great about her?" asked my younger sister Cindy) in the small dining room of our home in New Jersey. What did she see in my face, in me, a boy who bore the name of her firstborn son, a boy just two or three years younger than the son described in his obituary as her "darling David" when his father died over fifty years earlier and their world changed? I do not recall my father talking about his grandmother; nor does my mother, who does not remember seeing her very often. He spoke sometimes about his mother's parents, with whom his family shared a house when he was growing up. It seems that Lena, Grandma Marshall, came to our house only once, the time that I remember from my childhood. My father does not seem to have had much contact with his father's family after his marriage and his father's death. My grandfather does not appear to have had much contact with his siblings (with the exception of Millie) after his marriage.

Alfred S. Campbell, "In Hester Street, N.Y. Candy," c. 1896. Courtesy of the Library of Congress, Prints and Photographs Division.

" 'How the Other Half Lives' in a Crowded Hebrew District, Lower East Side, N.Y. City," c. 1907. Courtesy of the Library of Congress, Prints and Photographs Division.

My father passed on no stories about his father's childhood in the last decade of the nineteenth century. After my grandfather left the Hebrew Orphan Asylum, he seems to have lived with his mother and extended family until he got married at the age of thirty-one; but even if he rejoined his family, the Hebrew Orphan Asylum must have been a dividing line: a River Lethe that all the orphans drank from in a country of oblivion that made them forget their past lives. (Many of the orphans would have barely remembered a past life, only coming to consciousness, as it were, in the orphan asylum.) Did my grandfather tell my father and his brother Stephen stories about his childhood? When he was four years old, he lived in an airless tenement apartment during the deadly 1896 ten-day heat wave that killed close to fifteen hundred people in New York City; when he was eight years old, he lived in an unheated tenement apartment during the Great Blizzard of 1899, when the temperature fell to –6 degrees Fahrenheit. Did he tell them about the crowded and unsanitary living and working conditions on the Lower East Side in the first decade of his life, before he was sent to the Hebrew Orphan Asylum? This decade was bracketed by the publication of Jacob Riis's exposé of tenement life, *How the Other Half Lives: Studies Among the Tenements of New York*, published in 1890, the year before he was born, and the New York State Tenement House Act of 1901, the year that he turned ten.

When my grandfather brought his sons with him to his office when they were eight or ten years old, did he tell them about how he visited his father's shop or coat factory at the same age, recalling the men hunched over sewing machines in either crowded sweatshops or an airy new factory? Although he lived in Brooklyn, my grandfather worked in Midtown Manhattan. Did he ever visit Essex Street, Norfolk Street, Rivington Street, Suffolk Street, Broome Street? How my grandfather remembered his Lower East Side childhood, how he remembered his father, we do not know. My father passed on no stories about Harris Warshawsky, the grandfather he had never known, or about the world that his grandfather had left behind. We learned that his maternal grandfather, Louis Levitt, had been a shoemaker who became a manufacturer of children's shoes. I don't think that my father knew that his paternal grandfather had been a tailor—not to mention his paternal grandmother's father and brothers.

When my father was four and a half years old, his parents might have taken him to see the new Harold Lloyd film, *Speedy,* which opened with great fanfare on April 7, 1928, in part because it featured an extended comic scene with Babe Ruth. My father liked baseball, and he often told us stories about playing stickball in the streets of Brooklyn, using manhole covers and cars as bases. A brief, handwritten reminiscence that he wrote titled "Growing Up in Bklyn," begins (in the tradition of Defoe and Dickens) with the lines: "I was born across the street from Ebbets Field although I doubt that I realized the importance of the home of the Brooklyn Dodgers for another 6 or 7 years."[27] (He never forgave the Dodgers for leaving Brooklyn.) After breaking box office records at the Rivoli Theater in Manhattan, *Speedy* played in multiple theaters in Brooklyn from May through August. In the film, Harold Lloyd, who plays a taxi driver, discovers Babe Ruth handing out baseballs to a group of excited orphan boys at an orphanage, and then drives him across town at breakneck speed to Yankee Stadium, narrowly avoiding collisions at every moment. Ruth got good reviews for his performance.

Had my grandfather been in the movie theater audience, he would have been surprised to see Babe Ruth surrounded by a group of real orphans in front of the Hebrew Orphan Asylum. The stone pillars at the gate before the portico entryway to the building are clearly visible and repeatedly pictured in the scene, which lasts for a minute and eight seconds. Surely my grandfather would have watched with a shock of recognition as the uniformed boys with close-cropped hair clamor for

"Babe Ruth Signs Balls For Crowd of Kids," 1927. Courtesy of Corbis Images.

the baseballs that the Babe throws into the air against the backdrop of the building. Perhaps he recalled that (as Bogen reported) in 1904 Superintendent Coffee "became a hero to the boys when he had the HOA buy their first, real, factory-made baseballs" rather than "improvise their own from scrap materials."

If my grandfather had brought my father to see the movie, he might have concluded that his son was too young to understand that his father had lived in that building and been one of those boys. If my grandmother had been there, she might have felt my grandfather flinch as the uncanny scene flashed before him in the dark theater while the audience laughed. Did my grandfather's brothers Ruby and Irving call him that summer to ask if he had seen the film? Noting how New York City was featured in the film, the reviewer for the *New York Times* wrote: "The introduction of the city itself is done in a fashion that will make every New Yorker proud of the Empire City. And for that matter, wherever Mr. Lloyd takes you in this film he rather makes you regret that you haven't been there for some time." Had my grandfather been in the audience, he would not have regretted that he hadn't been to the Hebrew Orphan Asylum for a long time. I imagine that he kept his thoughts to himself as he walked home.[28]

6

------◆◇◆------

Traces of the Tailor

Becoming a Contractor

At the turn of the twentieth century, two hundred thousand Jews worked in the needle trade in New York, including Harris Warshawsky, Meyer Ruderman, and Lena's brothers, Isaac and Abraham. (Lena and her mother and sisters may have worked alongside them, or done piecework at home while taking care of their children.) There are numerous records that identify Harris Warshawsky as a tailor, and he is listed in the 1900 census as a "contractor." This term (sometimes used interchangeably with "sweater" in the context of the "sweating system" or "sweatshops") covers a wide range of arrangements in the garment industry, from bringing a worker or two into one's tenement apartment in the service of a clothing manufacturer to running a shop or a factory. The contractor was responsible for supplying and organizing the labor that assembled ready-made clothes for the manufacturer. The manufacturer paid the contractor for each item of completed clothing, and he had to hire the workers needed to turn the cut fabric into (for example) coats.

During the 1890s, there were major transitions in the garment industry. What David Levinsky described as an "army of tailors" arrived in New York; Russian Jews replaced German Jews in manufacturing, and cheap immigrant labor, especially following the Panic of 1893 and a subsequent Depression, filled shops and factories. Although only 11 percent of Jewish immigrants were tailors when they arrived in New York, by 1890 60 percent worked in the garment industry.[1] Many shops were tenement apartments where the contractor lived with his family and worked with two or three other workers. In the "outside shop" and the "task system," according to a brief history that prefaced a 1916 report by the U.S. Department of Commerce, "the Russian Jewish contractor" presided over "a 'team' of three: one did the machine sewing or operating, another the basting, and another the finishing. . . . The contractor, who was usually more skilled, did the trimming and fitting and the off pressing." The report recounts how the "Tenement House Act of 1892 in New York, which prohibited contractors from manufacturing in their homes," led contractors to rent "shops and lofts built for manufacturing purposes," where they "installed many machines, and entered into the making of clothes on a large scale."[2]

My grandfather's younger sister Millie told her daughter Adele that her father had collapsed in his factory and died. (Adele repeated this story to me 110 years after Harris Warshawsky's death.) Harris Warshawsky turns up at least six times in the *Report of the Factory Inspector of the State of New York,* which was published annually by the state assembly beginning in 1886. In 1894, 1896, 1897, 1898, 1900, and 1901, the factory inspectors included in their lists of inspected "firms" Harris Warshofsky or Harris Warschawsky or Harris Warschowsky. There was at least one other Harris Warshawsky who worked as a tailor around this time, but we can correlate the addresses of the firms associated with our Harris Warshawsky, which manufactured coats, to the business and home addresses given in city directories, which correspond to family documents.

The 1891 Trow's Directory locates Harris Warschawsky, a tailor, whose residence is at 83 Essex Street, working at 16 Monroe Street, the location of a manufacturer of shirts by the name of Samuel Warshofsky, and Harris Warshawsky's work address in 1892 as well. According to the 1893 *Report of the Factory Inspector,* in 1892 this shop employed nine men and nine women; minors worked sixty-six hours per week, and there were eleven hours of work on Sunday.[3] Harris must have been one of those workers. He might have been a partner, but it seems likely that he got his start working for a relative before starting his own shop. The 1889 directory locates "Samuel Warshowsky, pedlar" at 84 Suffolk Street. It would not have been unusual for an immigrant to begin as a peddler, become a tailor, and then start a shop in his tenement apartment. In 1894 and 1895, Trow's Directory locates Harris Warshafsky, a tailor, working at 84 Suffolk Street and living at 110 Norfolk Street (the home address listed on three of his children's birth certificates and Harris's naturalization papers).

"Jewish Life—Jewish Peddler." Courtesy of the Library of Congress, Prints and Photographs Division.

The 1894 *Report of the Factory Inspector* tells us that in 1893 Harris Warshofsky ran a shop at 84 Suffolk Street that employed an average of nine men and two women; both women were under the age of twenty-one. Minors worked an average of sixty hours a week, and there was a ten-hour workday on Sunday. The inspector ordered the shop to "provide separate water closet for use of women" and to "obtain workshop permit." There is also a note that references "section 13." Section 13 of the New York Factory Inspection Law states: "No room or apartment in any tenement or dwelling-house, shall be used, except by the immediate members of the family living therein, for the manufacture" of clothes; and, "No person, firm or corporation shall hire or employ any person to work in any room or apartment, in any rear building or building in the rear of a tenement nor dwelling house at making in whole or in part any of the articles mentioned in this section, without first obtaining a written permit."[4] The fact that 84 Suffolk Street appears to have been Samuel Warshofsky's residence in 1889 and the reference to the permit and Section 13 seem to confirm that this shop was in a tenement building and not in a factory building.

Discussing the 1890s, the Lower East Side Tenement Museum in New York City reports: "Research shows that in one year shops were in existence in tenements along Delancey, Sheriff, Division, Hester, Essex, Ridge, Cherry, Ludlow, Monroe, Mulberry, Mott, Baxter, Pitt, Rivington, Suffolk, Norfolk, Canal, Henry, Cannon, Stanton, East Houston, Attorney, Allen, Eldridge, Bayard, Chrystie, Orchard (No. 180, in addition to 97), Willett, Jefferson, Columbia, Clinton and Madison streets."[5] The Warshawsky family lived on Essex Street, Suffolk Street, Norfolk Street, and Rivington Street, and Harris worked on Monroe Street, Suffolk Street, and Broome Street in this decade. Although the city directories that list Meyer Ruderman as a tailor give a work address for him only once (in 1900), Harris Warshawsky has a separate work address from the time he first appears in Trow's in 1891.

According to the 1916 Department of Commerce report, "From about 1895 we find the establishment and extension of the large inside shop, with its better light, ventilation, and sanitary conditions, and the introduction of factory methods."[6] In 1896, Trow's locates Harris Warshafsky, a tailor, working at 198 Broome Street and living at 110 Norfolk Street. His shop at 198 Broome Street seems to have been in operation for five or six years. In 1895, according to the factory inspector, the "firm" employed seventeen men, including one under the age of eighteen, and four women, including one under the age of twenty-one. Minors worked fifty-nine hours per week; there were nine hours of work on Sunday and none on Saturday. In 1896, there were ten men and one woman employed; in 1897, thirteen men and five women, with sixty-four hours of labor reported; in 1900, twelve men and two women, with sixty hours of labor reported. In a sixty-four-hour workweek, with only nine hours on Sunday, the average workday would be eleven hours. Only hours per week for minors were reported; presumably this was a minimum number for everyone else, since many workers were paid by the piece and worked longer hours. (There were busy and fallow seasons in the garment industry, so these statistics must have varied throughout the year in which the inspectors made their visits.) The only infraction noted at 198 Broome Street was a failure to "post law and labor schedule." In 1900, Harris's coat-manufacturing shop was in compliance with all regulations and had no changes ordered.[7] The only city directory listing for Meyer Ruderman that gives a work address (the 1900 Trow's Directory) lists: "Meyer Ruderman, 298 Broome, h. 82 Essex." Surely this is a typographical error; Meyer Ruderman must have worked in his son-in-law's factory at 198 Broome Street. It seems likely that he worked there for the last half of the 1890s. Perhaps Lena's brothers Isaac and Abe worked there as well.

The New York Factory Inspection Law of 1886, which was revised and amended throughout the 1890s, aimed to end the worst health, safety, and working conditions of the sweatshops, in part by prohibiting tenement-based shops that employed non-family members. It required contractors to relocate their shops to factory buildings. The *Eighth Annual Report of the Factory Inspector*, published in 1894, reported approvingly the construction of fifty-nine "modern, well-appointed factory buildings erected upon sites formerly occupied by tenements swarming with people who lived, worked, ate, slept and—all too many—died therein." It reported that eighty-five tenement buildings had been "remodeled and made over into shop buildings, their use for domestic purposes having been stopped entirely."[8] According to a list of "New factory buildings erected during 1893 on sites formerly occupied by tenement sweat shops and cleared of occupants by order of the Factory Inspectors" included in the eighth annual report, in 1893 a building was erected at Suffolk and Broome Streets, containing five shop floors, five shops, and 165 workers. This is about where 198 Broome Street would be, just down the block from 84 Suffolk Street, where Harris worked 1893 to 1895.

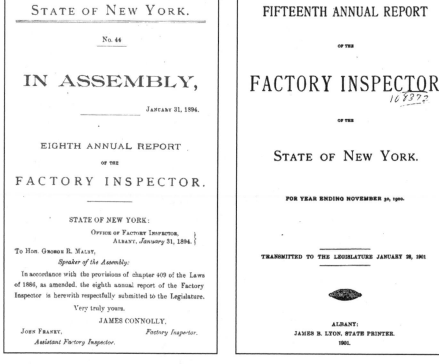

Left: *Eighth Annual Report of the Factory Inspector of the State of New York*, New York State Factory Inspector, 1894. Right: *Fifteenth Annual Report of the Factory Inspector of the State of New York*, 1901.

Eighth Annual Report of the Factory Inspector of the State of New York, New York State Factory Inspector, 1894.

No.	Name	Remarks
4870	Wasser, Louis †	Post law and labor schedule; reduce the hours of labor for minors; provide separate water closets for the use of women; limewash walls; erect fire-escape.
4871	Wagler, Nicholas —	Post law and labor schedule; erect fire-escape.
4872	Ward, Abraham & Sons —	Post law and labor schedule; discharge illiterate child; place handrail on stairway; keep register of outside employés in order; report incident.
4873	Ward, Marcus & Co.—	Post labor schedule. The children's certificate; provide separate water-closets for women;
4874	Wardener, R. Wolfers in order; report incident.	
4875	Warner, Wm. C.—	Post law and labor schedule.
4876	Warner, Wm. C.—	Post law and labor schedule;
4877	Warner & King—	Post law and labor schedule; file child's certificate; place handrail on stairways;
4878	Warnlanskiz, F. Loralis.†	Post law; screen stairs; obtain workshop permit.
4879	Warshauer, Jacob.—	Post law; obtain water-closet; erect fire-escape.
4880	Warshauer & Greenberg.†	Post law and labor schedule.
4881	Warschauer, Joseph.†—	Discharge all persons not members of family
4882	Warslopsky, Joseph.†	Post law; discharge all persons not members of family
4883	Warslopsky, Louis.†—	Screen stairways; keep register of outside employés and send copy of same to factory inspector.
4885	Washolsky, Harris.†	Post law and labor schedule; provide separate water-closet for use of women; obtain workshop permit.
4886	Wit, Israel †—	Discharge all persons not members of family.

† Firms marked thus (†) come under the provisions of section 13.

No.	Name	Address	Product
4875	Warner, L. W. & Co	60 Murray street †	Patent medicines
4876	Warner, Wm. C.	85 Centre street	Brushes
4877	Warner & King*	404 Sixth avenue	Bedding
4878	Warehausky, Louis*	205 Allen street, rear	Coats
4879	Warehauer, F. & Bro.†	69 Chrystie street	Cape
4880	Warehauer, Isaac*	17 Rutgers place	Coats
4881	Warehauer, Jacob	7 Rutgers place	Coats
4882	Warshauer & Greenberg†	75 and 77 Stanton street	Coats
4883	Warshawsky, Joseph†	169 Elizabeth street	Men's clothing
4884	Warshawsky, Louis*	205 Allen street, rear	Coats
4885	Warshofsky, Harris†	84 Suffolk street	Coats
4886	Warshofsky, Jacob†	19 Pitt street	Trousers
4887	Warslopsky, Israel†	47 Pike street	Coats
4888	Warwick Steam Laundry*	872 Eighth avenue	Laundry work
4889	Washington Cigar Factory*	255 and 257 Greenwich st.	Cigars
4890	Wasserman, Isaac†	8 Pitt street	Dresses and cloaks
4800	Wasserman, Louis	8 Pitt street	Coats

† Firms marked thus (†) come under the provisions of section 13.

In 1893, 198 Broome Street was the location of Harris Brenner, whose twenty-four employees manufactured coats; John Muskovitz, whose thirty-eight employees manufactured coats; Samuel Cohn, whose eighteen employees manufactured cloaks; and Bernhard Wurtzel, whose five employees manufactured cloaks.[9] Although there were "thousands of tiny shops, most of them belonging to contractors" in the New York City garment industry,[10] judging by the number of firms and the number of employees, 198 Broome Street, shared by four or five shops, would appear to be the sort of factory building described in the 1893 report, and perhaps even the actual building described. This is where Harris Warshawsky produced coats for the last half of the 1890s. The number of employees in his firm seems about average, or sometimes below average, judging from the annual reports.

In an article titled, "The Sweating System," published in 1896 by the U.S. Department of Labor, Henry White, the general secretary of the United Garment Workers of America, wrote that the new factory buildings "improved the condition of 17,147 persons who manufacture clothing in New York City," but he noted that the improvement "relates only to their sanitary welfare, and has nothing to do with the serious question of their ill-paid labor."[11] A *New York Times* article in 1895, the year that Harris Warshawsky moved his coat shop from 84 Suffolk Street to 198 Broome Street, reported the testimony before a state assembly committee investigating the "sweating-shop system," of a Mrs. Tessie Devio, whose job was to put "the last touches on little trousers for small boys, turning up the hems at the bottom of the legs, and sewing on the buttons. For this work she gets from 7 to 10 cents a dozen pairs." Although she described working all day and night at home in her two-room apartment, earning between $2.00 and $2.50 a week, "Mrs. Devio said that she worked for a man doing business at 198 Broome Street. She did not know his name."[12]

If Harris Warshawsky was a contractor employing workers in a shop, firm, or factory, this does not necessarily mean that he was wealthy or successful. A lengthy article in the *New York Times* on July 3, 1904, describes the contractor as "the middle man" between the manufacturers and the workers, noting that in "some instances one coat is handled by forty different persons before it is completed."[13] In his 1890 exposé, *How the Other Half Lives: Studies Among the Tenements of New York*, Jacob Riis wrote: "The sweater is simply the middleman, the sub-contractor, a workman like his fellows, perhaps with the single distinction from the rest that he knows a little English; perhaps not even that, but with the accidental possession of two or three sewing machines, or of credit enough to hire them, as his capital, who drums up work among the clothing-houses. Of workmen he can always get enough. Every ship-load from German ports brings them to his door in droves, clamoring for work."[14]

According to a 1901 report prepared by John R. Commons for the U.S. Industrial Commission on Immigration, the "Jewish contractor" was "not a mere middleman; he was necessarily a tailor and an organizer of labor." Noting that the contractor lives among his workers in an isolated immigrant community, he continues: "The man best fitted to be a contractor is the man who is well acquainted with his neighbors, who is able to speak the language of several classes of immigrants, who can easily persuade his neighbors or their wives and children to work for him. . . ."[15] According to the 1916 Commerce Department report, "The large number of friendless immigrants whose only acquaintance might be their fellow countryman who was a tailor, gave such an energetic tailor the opportunity to become a contractor."[16] However, as the Lower East Side Tenement Museum explains, "The line that contractors straddled between being helpful employers and ruthless exploiter to their fellow countrymen was indeed thin, and varied from shop to shop."[17] Commentators at the time emphasized the contractor's place among the workers he hired.

In a 1913 article in *McClure's Magazine* called "The Jewish Invasion of America," Burton J. Hendrick offers a brief history of the garment industry: "The contractor was himself an immigrant. He had reached this country poor and wretched, and had spent his few years of apprenticeship in the tailoring trades. He was usually the exceptional workman—the typical ambitious Jew, who early saw in the malodorous sweatshop the road to fortune. At the beginning this feverish ambition was practically his only stock in trade. He had a room or two in a tenement—perhaps his own home, perhaps a rented apartment."

"The path from worker to contractor, or even to small manufac-turer, was not a particularly difficult one to take," writes historian Daniel Soyer: "The contractor only had to buy or rent a couple of sewing machines, find a space to put them, and supply a pressing table and a

Lewis Hine, "Group of sweatshop workers in shop of M. Silverman. 30 Suffolk St., N.Y. Feb. 21, 1908," 1908. Courtesy of the Library of Congress, Prints and Photographs Division.

Lewis Hine, "Sweatshop of Mr. Goldstein 30 Suffolk St. Witness Mrs. L. Hosford," 1908. Courtesy of the Library of Congress, Prints and Photographs Division.

stove on which to heat the irons." According to Irving Howe, "During prosperous times thousands of contractors made good returns on their tiny capital investments, often no more than $50 to $100—the cost of a few used sewing machines."[18]

Commons describes how, just as in the "sweating system," in which "the foreman becomes a contractor, with his own small shop and foot-power machine," the contractor could become a "small merchant manufacturer." Citing the "racial characteristics of the Jew," he notes that "the Jew likes to be 'his own boss.' "[19] In a monograph published in 1905, *The Clothing Industry in New York*, Jesse Eliphalet Pope noted that "the average contractor possessed little more capital than the men who worked under him," often buying his machinery "on the instalment plan," typically needing to borrow money from a pawn shop between the end of the week, when he had to pay his workers, and the next Monday, when he was paid by the manufacturer. Pope also suggests that "the tendency of the Jew to become an employer is strong, and that his entrance to this sphere is in the clothing industry through the contract system."[20] In his 1896 article, Henry White writes that the "petty contractor" (who works out of tenement apartments rather than in "large, healthy shops") "has made possible the sweating evil" because since "little capital and not much general knowledge of the trade are required to become a contractor, almost any ordinary workman can enter the field and compete with the others on even ground. This soon results in such keen competition between the contractors for the opportunity to obtain work that prices are reduced to a ruinous figure."[21]

Indeed, if the contractor was the middleman, he often seemed caught in the middle, and not necessarily much better off than his workers. Pope notes that in 1901 the United Garment Workers of America acknowledged that the contractors, who are "forced to compete mercilessly against each other, are driven to extraordinary straits in order to do the work at a minimum cost." In the same year, the U.S. Industrial Commission stated: "There is always a cut-throat competition among contractors." Pope also notes that in 1895 the former secretary of the United Garment Workers said: "The contractor is certainly losing money.

That is what makes the contractor kick so hard and that is what makes us call the contractor a fool."[22] As Soyer notes, although it was possible "to make good money as a contractor," it also was easy to fail: "The average firm in the men's clothing trade in the first couple of decades of the twentieth century lasted seven years. One-third of all contractors went out of business each year." Contractors typically had a small profit margin and sometimes made little more than their workers. If the shop had "unlimited hours of work," stated Commons, the "contractor himself works unlimited hours." Hendricks writes that the contractor "was himself one of the hardest workers in the 'team.'"[23]

Harris Warshawsky could have been a successful entrepreneur, or a struggling tailor with onerous responsibilities and anxieties, or both. I imagine him in these years, which included an economic depression, as a struggling tailor who became a successful "worker-entrepreneur." Working for—or perhaps with—Samuel Warshofsky, an uncle or cousin, he would have worked his way up from being a tailor in someone else's shop, to organizing a tenement shop, to renting factory space to set up his own firm. When we first see Harris and Lena in public documents, in their 1890 marriage certificate, they are living with Lena's parents at 83 Essex Street. Perhaps he was a boarder there before he married Lena, but perhaps he began working alongside Meyer Ruderman and his sons in a "landsman" shop.

We can picture, then, an upward trajectory for Harris Warshawsky, rising from tailor to contractor or "small merchant manufacturer," the "ambitious Jew" figured in the *McClure's* article who "saw in the malodorous sweatshop the road to fortune" and who, according to the U.S. Industrial Commission on Immigration, liked "to be his own boss." Although Pope considers the "small master" to be dangerous because "he is forced to assume risks for which he is unfitted, and his business standards do not deter him from resorting to methods to which the large manufacturer would not stoop," he sees the contractor becoming "through trade union agitation, state regulation, and the general advance in the clothing industry," a "person of larger responsibility, of more intellect and higher business standards." Indeed, in his view, "the contractor becomes a man of larger affairs" who "partakes more and more of the nature of the entrepreneur," becoming "an enlightened and responsible employer of labor."[24] We don't know if this is what Harris Warshawsky was on his way to becoming in 1901, but we might conclude that, as a contractor, he had a combination of entrepreneurial ambition, organizational ability, and interpersonal skills. His "most important assets," as Soyer characterizes the contractor, would have been his "social network and his knowledge of the language and conditions in the community."

I think of the qualities that made my grandfather and father successful as manufacturers' representatives in the cosmetic and beauty supplies business, as well as the strains and uncertainties that they experienced as middlemen and salesmen running their own business. According to my parents, my grandfather had a strong personality and was admired and well liked by his business associates. He may have developed survival skills in the orphanage, but (reading backwards) I imagine that he inherited or learned certain personality traits from his father, who must have displayed both survival and social skills. A charismatic, self-made man whose career had ups and downs, perhaps my grandfather recalled his father in his ambition and entrepreneurial drive. My father built the business he took over at the time of my grandfather's death, at that time a small family business barely able to support the new families of my father and uncle and their widowed mother. In my own case, I thought I was following the family line of my mother's maternal great-grandparents, which included both prominent rabbinical scholars and socialist Bund organizers. When I was around thirteen or fourteen, at some industry trade show with my parents in New York, I laughed when a business associate of my father asked me if I planned to follow in my father's footsteps. I've thought about how my professional path in academic administration drew upon an inheritance from both of my grandfathers as well as my father, but I never imagined that my own social, organizational, and entrepreneurial skills might also be an inheritance from a tailor-turned-contractor in the 1890s.

At the time of his death, Harris Warshawsky seems to have been associated with the Order of B'rith Abraham (OBA), one of the most popular Jewish fraternal orders of the hundreds of fraternal orders, lodges, *landsmanshaftn*, and mutual benefit societies that populated the Lower East Side. (*B'rith Abraham* means *Covenant of Abraham*.) In 1901, the Order of B'rith Abraham, which had 253 lodges nationally, listed eighty lodges in New York City and eight in Brooklyn; OBA lodges met twice a month down the block from every home and work address but one that we have for Harris Warshawsky. Like Masonic lodges, these Jewish orders promoted assimilation and Americanization, often with hybrid rituals that combined American and Hebrew traditions. According to Daniel Soyer, "young men joined B'rith Abraham with the hope of advancing their business or professional careers, and in so doing furthered the order's image as American, 'progressive,' and success-ful." In Anzia Yezierska's 1925 novel, *The Bread Givers*, set earlier in the

"Street Scene—Lower East Side 1898 from Intersection of Hester and Suffolk Sts," 1898. Courtesy of the Museum of the City of New York.

century, Sara Smolinsky's suitor, Max Goldstein, boasts that he belongs to a dozen lodges: "Money making is the biggest game in America. At the lodge meetings I combine my business and my pleasure. It's meeting people." (Sara's father, Reb Smolinsky, "belonged to so many societies and lodges" but most of them are charities.) Perhaps Harris Warshawsky belonged to several societies. There were dozens associated with Minsk, including OBA lodges; they would have been part of his social network and probably his business network as well.[25]

We don't know if the Warshawsky family's moves from 83 Essex Street to 110 Norfolk Street to 176 Rivington Street to 151 Norfolk Street between 1890 and 1900 represented steps up or steps down. All of these apartments were in the same small neighborhood, and the socio-economic class of the neighbors in each of these buildings was the same. Harris's coat-manufacturing firm at 198 Broome Street had an average of twenty-one employees in 1895 yet only fourteen in 1900. Not only was the world of the contractor highly competitive, speculative, and unstable, labor unrest, union organizing, and strikes increased exponentially in the garment industry throughout the 1890s, a decade that began with the founding of the United Brotherhood of Tailors and the United Garment Workers of America and ended with the founding of the International Ladies' Garment Workers' Union. The United Hebrew Trades (a large labor federation affiliating some forty unions) at first made no distinction between contractors and workmen. However, according to historian Moses Rischin, "In 1890, the United Hebrew Trades defined contractors as employers, barring them from the unions."[26] This meant that throughout the 1890s, a time of great labor unrest, the contractor became the target of his brother tailors. Whether he was a boss or one of the hardest-working members of the team, a helpful employer or a ruthless exploiter, it would have been difficult for a contractor to have a successful and stable business in the 1890s.

---◆◈◆---

Traces of the Tailor

On Strike

On Labor Day, September 3, 1894, between ten thousand and
fourteen thousand tailors went on strike in New York City and
Brooklyn. According to the September 4, 1894, *New York Herald*, "About
twelve thousand tailors struck yesterday to force the manufacturers and
contractors for whom they work to abolish the task or sweating system and establish a ten hour work day, with regular weekly pay. It is
expected that by the end of the week thirty thousand men, women and
children who work in the tenements and sweat shops of the east side
will be idle." The strikers emphasized their poverty and declining wages.
Meyer Schoenfeld, a member of the Operators' Union Local 21 and
the Brotherhood of United Tailors executive board who had emerged
from obscurity as a coat maker to become a leader of the strike, told
a crowd: "It is as easy for us to starve idle as to starve working. Let us
then remain idle until the bosses pay us enough to keep us from starvation."[1] (Schoenfeld, according to a later article in the *New York Herald*,
was "a product of the sweat shop" who "began work pulling 'basting'
threads when he was ten years old.")[2] Financial instability and panics,
and the Depression of 1893, created a desperate situation for much of
the country. Economists estimate that the national unemployment level

was between 12 and 18 percent. The only other time that the unemployment rate exceeded 10 percent for five or six consecutive years was during the Great Depression of the 1930s.[3]

In the garment industry, cutthroat competition among contractors was exacerbated by a seemingly endless supply of immigrant labor. According to Henry White's report in the 1896 "Bulletin of the Department of Labor," as the "industrial prostration of 1893 and 1894 set in," tailors were "reduced to a condition bordering on pauperism. Special relief works were started in the large clothing cities to prevent actual starvation."[4] These were the years in which Harris and Lena Warshawsky started a family. Their fourth child, Millie, was born at 110 Norfolk Street on August 16, 1894, less than three weeks before the tailors went on strike. Daisy was almost four, David was almost three, and Rubin was about eighteen months old.

TWELVE THOUSAND STRIKE.

Tailors Stop Work, and by the End of the Week It Is Expected 30,000 Will Be Idle.

About twelve thousand tailors struck yesterday to force the manufacturers and contractors for whom they work to abolish the task or sweating system and establish a ten hour work day, with regular weekly pay. It is expected that by the end of the week thirty thousand men, women and children who work in the tenements and sweat shops of the east side will be idle.

"Twelve Thousand Strike," *New York Herald*, September 4, 1894.

If the strike was about the difference between a living wage and starvation, it was also about the working hours demanded by the task system. Newspaper articles described how an operator who had received about $3 for finishing seven coats in three days now saw the task "increased to ten, twelve and, in some cases, even fifteen coats, while the pay has remained the same." The operators had to work twice as long to make the same $6 a week. Abraham Harrison, another United Brotherhood of Tailors executive board member, told a crowd of three thousand meeting at New Irving Hall on Broome Street: "We are not Socialists nor Anarchists. We who were born here and who came here from tyrannical and monarchial countries want to do well as decent Americans in the liberty-loving United States. We are not on strike for money . . . but to be treated as Americans. At present we labor under conditions which do not prevail in the mines of Siberia." Disarming public fears about imported Russian revolutionaries by emphasizing the tailors' aspirations to be Americans, yet implying that the czar of Russia may have treated them better than American capitalism did, Harrison insisted that the strike for a ten-hour workday was about families more than wages: "We leave our homes every day when our families are yet sound asleep, and we return at an hour when they have long since retired. We see them awake but once a week, when religious influence compels the observance of one day as a time of rest. We are strangers to our own children, and our offspring often call others papa because they see them daily." Meyer Schoenfeld presented a similar picture: "For fifteen years, we have been working from 4 o'clock in the morning until 10 at night. We never have a chance to see our families, and I challenge any physician to deny that there are more than ten per cent of the unfortunate 'sweaters' who are not cripples."[5] It is likely that Daisy, David, Ruby, and now Millie were among those children who rarely saw their father.

In a mass meeting held two days after the strike began in the Apollo Hall on Clinton Street, near Broome Street, Meyer Schoenfeld (according to the *New York Herald*) was "the favorite speaker" in a series of speeches than ran from noon to night.[6] The *Herald* printed a small sketch portrait of the young Schoenfeld. Wearing a high collar and

AIMED AT THE SWEAT SYSTEM

SEVERAL THOUSAND GARMENT WORKERS ON STRIKE.

THE EAST SIDE STREETS CROWDED WITH EX-CITED MEN—DISCUSSING THEIR GRIEV-ANCES—TROUBLE ALSO AMONG THE CARPENTERS.

"Is a Giant Strike. Between 12,000 and 14,000 Coatmakers Now Arrayed Against the Sweating System," *New York Tribune*, September 5, 1894.

a wide tie, he is handsome, almost swarthy, with thick eyebrows and a moustache. Schoenfeld was later described by the *Herald* as "under middle height, but stocky and muscular," and "a man of force, and of a steadiness, both mental and physical, seldom found among his people. He is both a talker and a business man—a rare combination. He can sway his audience to tears and laughter, and five minutes later can drive a shrewd bargain with an employer."[7]

In Apollo Hall, Schoenfeld evoked the Bible with almost messianic rhetoric, declaring: "Our forefathers were in slavery in Egypt, and threw off the yoke of their oppressors. We are in far worse slavery than they were. We must follow their example. 'Ah, but we have no Moses,' you say. Oh, yes, we have a Moses. Our trade union is our Moses, and will lead us out of slavery and out of the wilderness into a land of prosperity." The article reports that the "enthusiastic Hebrews" interrupted Schoenfeld: "'You are our Moses,' they cried, 'and will lead us out of slavery.'"[8] According to White, "This strike was akin to a revolution in its suddenness and sweep. It began in New York, Brooklyn, and Newark in September, 1894, and was continued in Boston and Baltimore."[9] The Warshawsky and Ruderman families were literally surrounded by this revolutionary scene in the first weeks of September.

MEYER SCHOENFELD.

"Meyer Schoenfeld," "Is a Giant Strike. Between 12,000 and 14,000 Coatmakers Now Arrayed Against the Sweating System," *New York Herald*, September 5, 1894.

ENTHUSIASM AT THE MEETINGS.

There was a big meeting in Apollo Hall, in Clinton street, near Broome, yesterday afternoon. It began at one o'clock and lasted till nightfall. An endless succession of speakers appeared on the platform and harangued the ever shifting crowd in German and Hebrew.

Meyer Schoenfeld, leader of the strike, was the favorite speaker. He was received with cheers.

"It is as easy," he shouted, 'for us to starve idle as to starve working. Let us then remain idle until the bosses pay us enough to keep us from starvation.

"Our forefathers were in slavery in Egypt, and threw off the yoke of their oppressors. We are in far worse slavery than they were. We must follow their example.

"'Ah, but we have no Moses,' you say. Oh, yes, we have a Moses. Our trade union is our Moses, and will lead us out of slavery and out of the wilderness into a land of prosperity."

Shout upon shout went up from the enthusiastic Hebrews at these words. They cheered till they fairly stopped the speaker.

"You are our Moses," they cried, "and will lead us out of slavery!"

Schoenfeld has come into prominence in the last two or three weeks. Before that he was known only as a coatmaker, and an executive member of his union.

"Aimed At The Sweat System. Several Thousands Garment Workers On Strike," *New York Tribune*, September 4, 1894.

In the "thickly populated tenement-house districts on the East Side," as the *New York Tribune* reported, a "big labor parade" attracted "thousands of onlookers" and at New Irving Hall on Broome Street, there was "a crowd of fully 2,000 people, who stood here and there in groups, each group discussing excitedly the chance of winning the strike."[10] New Irving Hall was just a three-minute walk from 110 Norfolk Street. It would have taken about two minutes to walk from 84 Suffolk Street, the location of the shop where Harris manufactured coats from 1893 to 1895. (In 1893, he employed an average of thirteen people, perhaps including Lena's father and brothers.) Suffolk Street seems to have been the epicenter of the strike. The strikers, from Local Unions 2, 13, 17, and 20 of the United Garment Workers, had their headquarters at 145 Suffolk Street. The headquarters of the Brotherhood of United Tailors was at 71 Suffolk Street; and the American Federation of Labor had its headquarters at 89 Suffolk Street. Another local met at 59 Suffolk Street.[11] The *Tribune* accompanied its articles with illustrations depicting crowds of men in suits and bowler hats, many with beards, standing on Suffolk Street, arguing or speaking animatedly with each other.

The Clothing Contractors' Mutual Protective Association met on the third floor of 200 East Broadway, just around the corner from Essex Street. On September 5, under the title, "THRONGS IN THE STREETS," the *Tribune* reported: "Broome-st., Attorney-st., Suffolk-st., Orchard-st., and thoroughfares continuous to these were made impass-able in many places yesterday by crowds, who were moving to and fro all day, talking and gesticulating."[12] According to another article, "The sweat shops, which are scattered all over the east side, usually in lofts over stores and in tenement houses, are wholly deserted. The tailors are in the streets. They stand on corners in groups and crowd the buildings where the headquarters are located. They are an orderly lot. They are not of a turbulent, drunken or violent race. But they are excitable and chatter loudly."[13]

We do not know what role Harris Warshawsky or his family played in these discussions, debates, and negotiations, but we know that they lived in the middle of the turmoil. They were deeply interested parties;

STRIKERS IN SUFFOLK STREET.

"Strikers in Suffolk Street," "Is a Giant Strike. Between 12,000 and 14,000 Coatmakers Now Arrayed Against the Sweating System," *New York Tribune*, October 12, 1894.

they had everything at stake, and not only because they would have shared the working hours and working conditions denounced by the strikers. The strike was directed largely at the contractors. According to the *Tribune*, "More than 3000 of the United Brotherhood of Tailors assembled in and around New Irving Hall on Broome-st. early yesterday afternoon and delivered some fiery speeches to one another, in which the contractor as well as the merchant was denounced in vigorous terms."[14] On September 5, the *Herald-Tribune* reported "rioters" and a "mob" in Brooklyn, where a confrontation with the police took place as a man shouted, "Kill the contractors!" The strikers on the Lower East Side were generally more peaceful, although there were confrontations with the police. (A "too strict enforcement of the law by Policeman 'Issy' Rosenberg" was blamed for a clash between strikers and police on "Broome Street, between Norfolk and Ludlow," described in a headline as a "RIOT IN BROOME STREET," that resulted in the arrest of fifteen tailors.) Even after the strike was settled, a contractor named Isaac Cohn, living at 132 Broome Street, was "assaulted by a crowd of strikers, who hurled rotten eggs and vegetables at him and chased him" into a shop. He had to be rescued by police after a "mob of about 2,000 gathered and demanded that Cohn be brought out, as they wanted to kill him."[15] A month later, on October 12, the *New York Tribune* would report a police riot, with the headline, "The Police Gone Mad. Furious Clubbing Assault. They Attack a Crowd of Striking Cloakmakers." One of the victims among a crowd assembled at Rutgers Square to march to a rally at Union Square was one Israel German of 186 Suffolk Street.[16]

During the September tailors' strike, the contractors insisted that they were just middlemen at the mercy of the manufacturers, who paid them less and less for each completed garment. Meyer Schoenfeld declared in one of his speeches: "If the contractors would make common cause with us against the big merchants of Broadway and Mercer-st. we would succeed."[17] The contractor, unlike a distant boss, typically worked alongside the other workers, sharing many of the same working conditions that the tailors denounced. Furthermore, some of the garment workers that Harris Warshawsky employed were probably his relatives,

THE POLICE GONE MAD.

FURIOUS CLUBBING ASSAULT.

THEY ATTACK A QUIET CROWD OF STRIK-
ING CLOAKMAKERS.

LED BY CAPTAIN GRANT THEY RUSH ON THE
WORKING-PEOPLE ASSEMBLED FOR A PARADE
IN RUTGERS SQUARE—BLOWS SHOWERED
ON MEN AND WOMEN ALIKE—JOSEPH
BARONDESS PLEADS FOR HIS
FOLLOWERS IN VAIN.

"The Police Gone Mad," *New York Tribune*, October 12, 1894.

such as the Rudermans. The unions acknowledged that the practices of the manufacturers left contractors with a very small profit margin. On September 6, the *New York Tribune* reported that many of the contractors "said they were prepared to make common cause with the strikers and do all that they could to bring about an increase in the wages of the men."[18]

This was a theme in the subsequent strikes that occurred with regularity for the rest of the decade, despite the enmity against contractors who had broken agreements. During a strike in the summer of 1896, the *New York Times* noted: "Of course the contractors themselves make only a small margin in consequence of the keen competition that exists among themselves." A subsequent *Times* article bore the headline, "Contractors May Join Tailors," and predicted "an alliance of tailors with contractors against the manufacturers." At a meeting of the contractors, "one-half of their number, it was said, were in favor of fraternizing with the tailors, while the remainder positively refused to entertain any such proposal." The *Tribune* ran a headline, "Contractors May Side with Tailors." Almost a year later, on May 20, 1897, the *Tribune* ran an article with the headline, "Sympathy for the Tailors" (this referred to the manufacturers' sympathy) that detailed the contractors' plight. It quoted the secretary of the executive committee of the Contractors' Association, who declared that "the contractors were worse off than the men, because the latter had some wages at least to take home at the end of the week, whereas the contractors often went home in debt. Those of the contractors who had some capital, he said, had lost it all in the last two or three years."[19] In October of 1897, on behalf of the United Brotherhood of Tailors, Meyer Schoenfeld issued a public statement addressed to "ALL CLOTHING MANUFACTURERS OF NEW YORK." Citing both the successes and failures of "periodical strikes" over the "past four years," and the inevitability that the competition of the contract system would "drive the operative into performing an inhuman task for less than a living wage and amid the poorest and unhealthy conditions," he declared that "in the year 1899, the clothing workers of this city will refuse to work for any contractor or middle man."[20] Whether or not this claim would prove to be feasible, contractors could read the writing on the wall, and they no doubt agreed that their situation was untenable.

In the first strike of 1894, the contractors quickly capitulated. On September 6, the *Tribune* reported that "leading contractors" went to the executive board of the Brotherhood of United Tailors at 71 Suffolk Street, just a few doors down from Harris Warshawsky's no doubt idle shop, and "implored the Executive Board to bring the strike to an end. . . . The contractors said that they were prepared to make common cause with the strikers and to do all that they could to bring about an increase in the wages of the men, but that this was not possible so long as the Broadway merchants continued to treat the contractors in the matter of price as shabbily as they do at present." Another article on the same day, under the headline, "STRIKERS VICTORIOUS," announced: "CONTRACTORS MAKE TERMS . . . DEATH BLOW TO SWEAT SHOPS." The article reported that "sixteen contractors," representing "considerably more than half of the employing interest of the trade," and "the largest in the city," met the demands of the striking workers with complete acquiescence." It also noted that "many of the smaller contractors still hold out against the strikers," but that the cutters had refused to work for any contractor who did not agree and that the contractors "have organized a union of their own" and "entered into an alliance with the cutters and tailors to freeze out the small contractors who refuse to abide by the union rules."[21]

Of course, the announcement of the union leaders that the settlement "means the total abolition of the sweating system in the tailoring trade in this city" proved premature, as were similar announcements following the strikes that were repeated over the next few years. The *Tribune* acknowledged on September 7 that "if the manufacturers do not yield to the demands of the contractors for an increase in their payments this apparent submission of the men who directly employ the strikers will not avail much." It was further noted that the Contractors' Association had "300 members out of a total of about 700 whose hands are on strike." In the next days, the contractors' refusal of the union demand that each contractor provide an individual bond of $500, a sort of security deposit guaranteeing that he would honor the agreement, caused a renewal of the strike. On September 11, the *Tribune* described the jubilation at the United Brotherhood of Tailors headquarters at 71 Suffolk Street: "All day long the contractors kept going to the place to sign individual bonds for the faithful performance of their contracts with their employees." A list of thirty-seven contractors published in the paper does not include Harris Warshawsky, but the article emphasizes two contractors, who had 110 and 150 employees respectively; these shops were some five times larger than Harris Warshawsky's coat firm.[22]

The final agreement called on contractors to provide bonds of $100 if they had two machines or less, $200 if they ran three machines or more, and $500 if they ran over five machines. An article on September 16, again announcing the end of the strike, reported that the Contractors' Association had disbanded; the president is "alleged" to have said, "It's no use, boys; our association is 'busted.' Every contractor should settle with the Brotherhood as best he can." According to the *Herald*, after this declaration of surrender, "there was an instant stampede" to the Brotherhood of Tailors executive board as "[e]ach contractor came with his bondsman to sign the agreement and give individual bonds. So great was the rush that several policemen were sent from the Delancey street station to preserve order."[23] Presumably Harris Warshawsky was one of those contractors, signing his careful signature before the tailors.

Among the vignettes published in articles in the *New York Herald* on August 18, 1895, entitled, "The Ghetto of New York: The Daily Life of the Russian and Polish Inhabitants of the Jewish Quarter," there is a description of contractors humbly appearing before the executive board of the tailors' union.[24] (Earlier in the month, another strike had been called because the contractors were not living up to their previous agreements and would not sign new agreements; in the end, the contractors again agreed to the union demands.)[25] An illustration with the caption, "Contractors Trying to Make Terms," shows a man standing, depicted with his back turned mostly to the beholder, addressing a group of about twelve men who are seated in a semi-circle. The contractor's face is not visible, so I can imagine that this is Harris Warshawsky. In the center of the listening men (and the illustration) is a seated figure, a stern man with a mustache who seems to be presiding. I imagine this to be Meyer Schoenfeld. An engraving printed in the *Herald* later that year, which shows Schoenfeld with a fuller moustache than he had the year before, and emphasizes his fine suit, resembles the figure of authority in this illustration. According to the *Herald*, "The workmen worship him and the contractors fear him, but even the contractors never had a suspicion to cast on his honesty or integrity."[26]

The presiding figure sits on a raised platform, like a judge surrounded by a jury. A man seated next to him whispers confidentially in his ear, covering his mouth with his hand. The men are mostly attentive, although one or two seem pensive, lost in thought. The standing man has his hand extended, as if making a point as he pleads his case. The reporter notes that he has been admitted to witness "a contractor being examined by the Board" and remarks, "Nothing quite like this scene can be witnessed anywhere else." He continues: "Lining the walls are

CONTRACTOR TRYING TO MAKE TERMS.

"Contractor Trying to Make Terms," "The Ghetto of New York: The Daily Life of the Russian and Polish Inhabitants of the Jewish Quarter," *New York Herald*, August 18, 1895.

men, young and old, listening intently to the proceedings, but never interrupting then. The contractor has his say: he is responded to by this or that member of the Board. The language used is either Yiddish or German. There is a plentitude of gesticulations, a vehement play of the hands and some rude eloquence. But the appeal on both sides is made to reason, or at least, to sentiment—to the emotions, not to the passions." The contractor, as commentators and historians have described him, is a man of some charisma, "who is well acquainted with his neighbors, who is able to speak the language of several classes of immigrants, who can easily persuade his neighbors or their wives and children to work for him."[27] Here he stands as his own advocate, using his powers of persuasion to plead his own cause.

MEYER SCHOENFELD.
Who Will Probably Lead the Striking Tailors.

"Meyer Schoenfeld. Who Will Probably Lead the Striking Tailors," "Big Strike Begins To-Day," *New York Herald*, December 15, 1895.

According to the reporter, who is presumably translating from the Yiddish: "The contractor explains how willing he is to do the right thing: he insists that he is a kind master, that he has always looked after the welfare and well being of his men, has treated them well and never taken advantage of their necessities. But after all, he, too, must live." The reporter continues: "He is questioned as to his willingness to live up to the contract imposed by the Board, and if his answers are satisfactory he will be allowed to sign a bond pledging him to the fulfillment of his promises. There is no organization among the contractors. Each represents only himself, and is treated as an individual and not as a representative of his class."[28] This is not the traditional image that one has of a sweatshop boss. The reporter seems to feel that the tables have been turned. Perhaps this is not a scene of personal advocacy or rhetorical bravura but rather a scene of ritual humiliation with a foregone conclusion. A few months later, following a lockout of tailors by contractors, a contractor named Herman Bolaski complained that the contractor had become "only a figurehead, who was useful to pay the men their wages."[29]

Harris Warshawsky must have acquitted himself well enough in such pleadings, or at least agreed to all the necessary terms. In 1895, he moved his coat-manufacturing shop from 84 Suffolk Street to the factory building at 198 Broome Street and employed twenty-one people, according to the *Tenth Annual Report of the Factory Inspector*, the largest shop he had for which we have a record. His shop at 84 Suffolk Street, according to the *Eighth Annual Report of the Factory Inspector*, employed eleven people. Presumably this means he was no longer a petty contractor working out of tenement conditions but rather a manager with a modern shop that had "better light, ventilation, and sanitary conditions" and "factory methods."[30] The outcome of the 1894 strike would have had some benefits for contractors since it would have eliminated some of the cutthroat competition, including the smallest, most unscrupulous contractors, who drove down prices. The playing field would be leveled, at least for a while. Perhaps it also improved the working conditions for the contractor; the ten-hour day might allow him to get home to see his wife and children. The photograph of Harris and Lena from the Newman studio was printed sometime after 1896. Harris Warshawsky seems to have prospered during these years.

Writing in the *Commercial Advertiser* on August 25, 1900, about ten weeks after Harris Warshawsky was listed in the 1900 census as a contractor living at 151 Norfolk Street, Abraham Cahan speculated about the "disappearance of the annual tailor strike," which "used to break out, like a sort of summer complaint" every July or August: "It came every year, regular as the heat, unavoidable as malaria in swampy districts. . . . The big annual tailor strike, *the* strike of the East Side, where hundreds of sweatshops were deserted, the streets of the ghetto were swarming with gesticulating, chattering, groaning men and women, and the newspapers were full of pictures of long-bearded patriarchs, has been gone now three years." Cahan quotes a "labor philosopher" named George Pine who suggests that "the contract system in the tailoring industries makes old-time strikes futile" because

Postcard, Lower East Side.

the clothing firms were "their real employers" and the "contractors or sweaters"—whom he calls "cockroach capitalists"—were "a poor irresponsible lot, who were willing to sign any contract and yield to any demand of the union simply because their contracts were not worth the paper they were written on." One of Cahan's sources describes the "seeming disappearance of the annual tailor strike" as "only the calm which precedes the storm," after which the struggle between labor and capital will lead to "the abolition of the 'un-American' sweating system." According to George Pine, "by and by the middleman must go altogether. Why can't we work in large, well-ventilated factories instead of in tenement house pestholes? Do away with the sweating system and all the filth of the East Side, physical and moral, will disappear, like the perennial strike."[31]

With or without a large tailors' strike, the second half of the decade was filled with labor unrest and uncertainty: regular strikes throughout the garment industry, lockouts and repudiations of agreements by contractors who claimed they couldn't make a profit and couldn't run their own shops, and pressures from both unions and state regulators. The *Fifteenth Annual Report of the Factory Inspector*, published in 1901, reporting on the year ending November 30, 1900, marks the last time that we see Harris Warshawsky in these state records.[32] Whereas his coat-manufacturing firm had an average of twenty-one employees in 1895, it had fourteen employees in 1900. This is about when the Warshawsky family moved from 176 Rivington Street to 151 Norfolk Street. We do not know if Harris Warshawsky's shop was faltering, if he was a powerless middleman, part of a dying breed of cockroach capitalists, or whether at the time of his death he was (or was on his way to becoming) a successful manufacturer whose clothing firm was thriving in the changing landscape of the garment industry. The 1901 *Report of the Factory Inspector* was officially transmitted to the legislature on January 28, 1901, a day after the eleventh wedding anniversary of Harris and Lena. Less than three weeks later, on February 14, 1901, Harris would be dead. As the second year of the twentieth century began, David Warshawsky was nine years old. Lena Warshawsky was about two months pregnant.

———◆———

Special Circumstances of the Case

The thousands of pages of the applications for admission to the Hebrew Orphan Asylum from the years around the turn of the century offer few biographical details about the applicants, and these are mostly about the parents, not the children. The details recorded on the application forms are not very different from the details recorded by the census enumerator: the applicants' names, place of birth, age, occupation, residence, the length of time they had lived in the city, the number and ages of brothers and sisters of the children. The application form asks: "Was any money left to the applicant or the Children from Lodges or Societies?" and "Has the Child (or Children) been sick before?" There is a line for "References," but this section is for the most part left blank, and the blank space is often used to note additional details about the national origins of the deceased or missing parents. The section marked "Special Circumstances of the Case" is the one place where the registrar (or whoever filled out these intake forms) telegraphically notes the outline of the story that led to the application for admission.

Sometimes these "special circumstances" read like notes for a novel. For example, in the application for Harold Stock, an eight-and-a-half-year-old boy brought in by a "friend," George C. Mansel, we read:

"Father & mother divorced—mother received custody of the child, whom she deserted and left him in the hands of Mrs. Mansel—mother an actress—a disreputable woman." One has the sense that the registrar is more likely to note such details of plot if the story is still fresh. We read of Mary, Hannah, and Rebecca Jacobowitz, close in age to David, Ruby, and Isi: "Mother died in Bellevue Hospital 3 weeks ago. She was insane & committed suicide."[1] More often than not, the special circumstances indicate circumstances that were common rather than special, calmly noting the death, illness, or disappearance of parents, only hinting at a story that the census enumerator could not recount and that, in its

Application for Admission, Hebrew Orphan Asylum, 1903. Courtesy of the Collection of American Jewish Historical Society.

bare outline, was all too familiar to the asylum official filling out the application for admission.

On Application for Admission No. 3132, Lena's application, recorded on March 2, 1903, next to "Special Circumstances of the Case" the registrar writes: "Husband dead 2 yrs." The story told in my family about the death of my grandfather's father was not much longer or more detailed than "Husband dead 2 yrs." As I have reported, it went like this: My grandfather and his brothers were sent to an orphanage after their father died and their mother could not support her children. There was a slightly longer version: After my grandfather's (unnamed) father died around the time the sixth child in the family was born, my grandfather's mother, known to us as Grandma Marshall, was unable to support and care for her two girls and four boys, one of whom was a baby, so she sent the three older boys to the orphanage and kept the two girls and baby boy at home. As my father told my sister Cindy in an interview: "My father was born in 1892. . . . His father died just before his brother Harry was born. Dick was maybe nine or ten when Harry was born. What happened was his mother was widowed. The three oldest boys, my father, Ruby, and Irving, all went to an orphanage. . . . They basically spent a few years in an orphanage or home because she couldn't take care of them. The two sisters, Daisy and Millie, were at home with the baby, and I don't know what happened from there."[2] Adele's recollection (passed on from Millie and presumably Lena) that Harris Warshawsky died after collapsing in his factory was never mentioned by my father or grandmother. Even in the longer version of the story, the death of the father is basically a subordinate clause.

Harris Warshawsky is not named on the application for admission. Like Harry's birth certificate, which names the father as "no father," the application for admission erases him. Many other applications note the name and birthplace of the missing or deceased parents. Harris Warshawsky is not even referred to as a father; he is alluded to only as "Husband." The "special circumstances of the case" outline Lena's story, a forgotten story that in some ways eclipses Harris Warshawsky's story yet at the same time hides behind his forgotten story. Although my narrative is about the search for a missing father, it also tells the story of a mother—who, although present in traces of family memories as well as some documents, is also missing. Her story, too, must be read between the lines as we try to reconstruct the special circumstances of the case. In erasing her husband's story, she seems to have erased part of her own story as well.

We know that six months after Harris died, the Warshawsky family no longer lived at 151 Norfolk Street. The birth certificate that the midwife, Sarah Manson, filled out on August 26, 1901, following Harry's birth on August 17, 1901, states that Harry was born and the family then resided at 130 Suffolk Street. Why did the Warshawsky family move to 130 Suffolk Street? Perhaps they no longer could afford the apartment at 151 Norfolk Street. According to the census of 1900, at 130 Suffolk Street there was a Russian immigrant named Warshow who operated a butcher

"Street Peddler on the Lower East Side, New York City." Courtesy of the Picture Collection, The New York Public Library, Astor, Lenox and Tilden Foundations.

shop. Given the metamorphosis of names at the time, it is possible that the butcher Warshow was a Warshowsky and a relative. The Rudermans don't seem to be living with the Warshawsky family on Norfolk Street, and it is possible that they were living on Suffolk Street. On Harry's birth certificate, the words "Milk Store" are written on the line next to "Occupation," which follows the lines indicating father's name, residence, birthplace, and age; but next to "Father's Name" the midwife writes: "no father"; "Milk Store" is no doubt meant to refer to Lena's occupation.

The New York City Directory confirms that in 1902 Lena lived at 130 Suffolk Street and sold milk with her younger brother, Abraham Ruderman, at 132 Suffolk Street. In 1900, according to the census, Samuel Shapiro, a twenty-four-year-old Russian immigrant, lived at 132 Suffolk Street and had a milk store. This is may be the store that Lena and her brother were operating in 1902. When Lena visited her sons at the Hebrew Orphan Asylum on March 29, 1903, she brought with her Miss Katie Held, identified as a "friend," who lived at 132 Suffolk Street. According to the 1900 census, the father of the then twenty-year-old Kathrin Held was a janitor, presumably the janitor for that building. Katie probably helped take care of Lena's children; she is the only visitor accompanying Lena who was not a member of the Ruderman family. The vast majority of residents at 132 Suffolk Street were garment industry workers, but the neighbors also included a cigar maker, a briar pipe maker, an ironworker, a tobacco cutter, a horseshoer, a barber, a fruit peddler, and a man who had a soda water stand. My grandfather was personable, gregarious, and a good salesman. I picture him at ten years old greeting these neighbors by name as he worked behind the store's counter after school.

Abraham Cahan's novella, *Yekl: A Tale of the New York Ghetto*, published in 1896, contains a long description of Suffolk Street. Walking down the street on a sultry summer evening, Cahan's protagonist

> had to pick and nudge his way through dense swarms of
> bedraggled half-naked humanity; past garbage barrels rearing
> their overflowing contents in sickening piles, and lining the

streets in malicious suggestion of rows of trees; underneath tiers and tiers of fire escapes, barricaded and festooned with mattresses, pillows, and featherbeds not yet gathered in for the night. . . . Suffolk Street is in the very thick of the battle for breath. For it lies in the heart of that part of the East Side which has within the last two or three decades become the Ghetto of the American metropolis, and indeed, the metropolis of the Ghettos of the world. It is one of the most densely populated spots on the face of the earth—a seething human sea fed by streams, streamlets, and rills of immigration flowing from all the Yiddish-speaking centers of Europe. . . . Nor is there a tenement house but harbors in its bosom specimens of all the whimsical metamorphoses wrought upon the children of Israel of the great modern exodus by the vicissitudes of life in this their Promised Land of today.

One can picture Lena Warshawsky in Cahan's description of the "Jews born to plenty, whom the new conditions have delivered up to the clutches of penury" *and* the "Jews reared in the straits of need, who have here risen to prosperity."[3] Reversals of fortune were frequent at this time. Perhaps Harris's coat factory left Lena with money in the bank; yet a contractor's shop would disappear without the contractor,

"A scene in the ghetto, Hester Street," c. 1902. Courtesy of the Library of Congress, Prints and Photographs Division.

and without his income the family would have been without any obvious means of support. It seems likely that Lena took the death benefits that she would have received from Harris's membership in a lodge or mutual benefit society—what was essentially a life insurance policy—and opened a store with her brother. In Yezierska's *The Bread Givers*, Zalmon the fish-peddler boasts that he "got a thousand dollars from two lodges for my wife's death"; when Reb Smolinsky asks Zalmon for "a little money to start myself a business" after offering his daughter in marriage to him, Zalmon estimates the need to be "only a matter of a few hundred dollars."[4] In 1902 and 1903, Trow's Directory lists "Ruderman & Warshawsky, grocers" at 130 Suffolk Street. It seems that the milk store expanded to become a grocery store. There is an article in the *Daily People* on September 19, 1901, with the headline "Sold Impure Milk," which reports that five people were arraigned on the previous day "in the Essex Market Police Court on charges of selling impure milk." Among them is "Abraham Rudman, of 132 Suffolk Street." The article concludes, "They were all held for examination."

Sold Impure Milk.

Inspector Johnson, of the Board of Health, arraigned yesterday in the Essex Market Police Court on charges of selling impure milk, Hymen Blumenfelt, of 301 East Third street, Mendel Scholetes, of 224 Second street, Abraham Rudman, of 132 Suffolk street, Sarah Brigenbaum, of 88 Suffolk street and Joseph Freedman, of 224 Second street. They were all held for examination.

"Sold Impure Milk," *Daily People*, September 19, 1901.

I have found no information about the outcome of this arraignment. An article that appeared in the *Daily People* a year later, on September 23, 1902, reported that thirty "milk dealers" were fined a total of more than $1,000 for "selling adulterated milk." The paper notes fines of $75, $150, and $250 to individuals, ranging from a wholesale dealer to a driver. The New York papers at this time periodically reported efforts on the part of health officials to stop the practice of watering down milk.[5] Perhaps selling groceries was safer, or more profitable, than selling milk. Lena, Abraham Ruderman's older sister, gets equal billing with her brother in the store's name; she must have been a partner with a financial stake in the store.

"The Adulteration of Milk—An Inspector Testing Milk at a Grocery on the East Side, New York City," *Frank Leslie's Illustrated Newspaper*, December 10, 1887. Courtesy of Corbis Images.

In *Out of the Shadow: A Russian Jewish Girlhood on the Lower East Side*, a 1918 autobiography that describes this period, Rose Cohen recounts how her father, a tailor, is excited because the family of his prospective son-in-law owns a grocery story on Broome Street: "His opinion of businessmen was high. It was his dream some day to lay down his needle and thread and perhaps open a little candy store or a soda water stand. But up to this time it had been no more than a dream. For when could he hope to put away fifty or seventy-five dollars! Now, however, with the prospect of having a son-in-law in business the dream looked nearer reality."

Although the marriage does not take place, Cohen's father did eventually open a grocery store on Cherry Street in 1902 with $100 in savings, and the family lived in two rooms behind the store.[6] Between February of 1901 and March of 1903, Lena Warshawsky seems to have become a businesswoman. (In later years, my father and his cousin Adele recounted that Lena had a candy store, but this must have been close to a decade later. The 1910 census identifies Lena as "a retail merchant, confectionary.") "Ruderman & Warshawsky, grocers" would have provided mother and six children with an income and presumably a place to live—not to mention groceries—and Lena would not have needed to leave home to go to work. Perhaps the grocery store was prosperous, at least for a while, allowing Lena to support the Warshawsky family after the demise of her husband's coat firm.

By the time that Lena Roshafsky (Warshowsky) submits the application for admission to the Hebrew Orphan Asylum for her three sons on March 9, 1903, where we read "Husband dead 2 yrs." under "Special Circumstances of the Case," her address is still 130 Suffolk Street, but her occupation is listed as "Washing, etc." There is no mention of a store. In answer to the question, "Was any money left to the applicant or the Children from Lodges or Societies?" the space is blank. Any benefit money they received would have been spent by 1903. I picture Lena telling a long story to the registrar at this point in the intake interview; there is no yes-or-no answer to this question. In the 1905 New York State census, which finds the Warshawsky and Ruderman families on 418

Hopkinson Avenue in Brooklyn, where presumably the rent was cheaper than in Manhattan, Abraham Ruderman's occupation is listed as "tailor," like his father's, and Lena's occupation is "home work," like her mother's. Lena seems to be out of business and back in the garment industry, at the lowest level. Twelve family members are living together in the apartment, including Lena's two sisters and two young granddaughters of Meyer and Anna Ruderman. Shop work, whether in or outside of the home, would have been a step down from the business of a grocery store.

It is possible that in 1903 Lena had to understate her means of support to get her sons admitted to the Hebrew Orphan Asylum, but it does not seem likely that she would have sent David, Ruby, and Isi off to an orphanage if she were able to take care of them. The two-year interval between her husband's death and her decision to commit her sons could indicate either a precipitous decline after a period of prosperity, or a gradual descent, or perhaps a stubborn resistance to economic reality. In a brief reminiscence that he wrote, my father described his father in this period as being in a condition of "near poverty beginning as one of eight [sic] children with a young widowed mother."[7] Most of the children admitted to the Hebrew Orphan Asylum had a living parent who could not take care of the children after the death (or desertion) of a spouse. The typical workday was ten to twelve hours, at a minimum. It cannot have been an easy decision for Lena to send away her young children, especially her oldest son.

I have found evidence that Lena's older brother Isaac sent his two young sons, Nathan and Reuben, to the Brooklyn Hebrew Orphan Asylum in 1896 following the death of his wife, then withdrew them in 1897 when he remarried, and then sent them back in 1898 for the rest of their childhood. Nathan Ruderman, who stayed in the Brooklyn Hebrew Orphan Asylum until he was discharged to his uncle at the age of eighteen, remained close to the Ruderman/Warshawsky/Marshall families for decades afterwards. As Lena and the Rudermans agonized over how she would support her children in the winter of 1903, Isaac's sons Nathan and Reuben Ruderman, then inmates at the Brooklyn Hebrew Orphan Asylum, would have provided a precedent for her half-orphan sons.[8]

My grandfather's sister Millie told a story to her daughter Adele about how she had carried her baby brother Harry out of their apartment during a fire. A young child herself, Millie was a heroine, and Adele's voice still conveys Millie's pride in repeating the story. Might this have been on Suffolk Street? According to the January 1903 *Annual Report of the Committee on Fire Patrol to the New York Board of Fire Underwriters*, there was a fire across the street in a grocery store at 131 Suffolk Street on February 10, 1902, another in a paper box store at 133 Suffolk Street on August 9, 1902, and another in a bakery at 136 Suffolk Street on October 8, 1902. Any one of these fires might have caused smoke and commotion in Millie's building. On May 16, 1902, at 1:15 P.M., there was a fire in a grocery store owned by Solomon Hartman at 124–128 Suffolk Street. Apparently the building was on the corner of Suffolk and Rivington, and it also had entrances at 148–150 Rivington Street; there is a small grocery store on that corner today, and another at 122 Suffolk Street, in a building that was constructed in 1900. Since most buildings in this neighborhood were adjoined, a fire at 128 Suffolk Street is likely to have been experienced as a fire at 130 Suffolk Street, especially if there were smoke, firemen, and people shouting, "Fire!" Millie was eight years old and Harry was nine months old on May 16. According to the *New York Times*, there was $500 worth of damage to Solomon Hartman's grocery store, which suggests a serious fire. According to the 1900 U.S. census, Solomon Hartman lived at 130 Suffolk Street, the building where the Warshawsky family lived and where Katie Held's father was a janitor. He was a neighbor of Mr. Warshow, the butcher.[9]

I do not know if the fire in Solomon Hartman's grocery store on the afternoon of May 16, 1902, was the fire that Millie told Adele about many years later, or whether there was any relation between Solomon Hartman's grocery store at 128 Suffolk Street and "Ruderman & Warshawsky, grocers" at 132 Suffolk Street besides their proximity. I do know that among the stories that were not passed down (at least in my family) about what life was like for the Warshawksy family between February of 1901 and March of 1903 is the story about what happened in their neighborhood on May 16 and in the days after. May 16 was the beginning of a boycott of kosher meat organized by women on the Lower East Side that led to mass rallies with up to twenty thousand people and what was repeatedly described in the press as riots by hundreds of women in mobs that fought in the streets with a thousand policemen. Upset by steep rises in the price of meat passed down to local butchers by a "meat trust," the women initially supported the butchers as they protested the increase. Then, when the butchers gave in to the wholesalers and raised their prices, the women called for—and at times violently enforced—a total boycott of kosher meat and some fifteen hundred East Side butcher shops.[10]

The May 16, 1902, headline in the *Daily People* read: "EAST SIDE RIOT, Indignant Women Make it Hot for Kosher Butchers. Rush Madly Through the District, Invading Shops and Mobbing Butchers Who Dared to Open for Business. Many Arrests Made." Portraying the "several hundred women" as if they were frenzied bachantes, the article described "angry women" who were "nearly crazy with excitement, shrieking and weeping, . . . laughing, shrieking hysterically, gesticulating madly, and threatening all who refused to comply with their demands."[11] According to the *New York Times*, "Not alone were the proprietors of the butcher shops attacked, but those who patronized them also met with the mob's fury. The meat which they had bought was taken from them, thrown in the gutters, and stamped upon. Water, kerosense oil, and according to some of the butchers, carbolic acid was poured upon the meat by the maddened women who from early morning till late in the afternoon beseiged the hundreds of little butcher shops."[12] The Hornell, New York, *Evening Tribune* described "a pushing, scrambling mob of hundreds," and pictured women and girls who "went into the tenement houses" at supper time and "threw all the meat they could lay their hands on out the windows."[13]

In its long narrative account of May 17, the *New York Times* described "angry, yelling mobs that thronged the streets for miles" and retraced the events of the battles between the mobs and the police in almost Homeric terms: "Time and time again the mobs surged on, and were repelled by the policemen. At one minute there would be an advance from Essex Street followed by a rush, a mixed scream of women, fierce curses, and at last comparative quiet. Hardly was one rush over when another would begin." Bricks and other "missiles" were hurled from windows and rooftops; police, after initially hesitating, clubbed women in the back with their nightsticks, and carried them to prison in horse cars that were chased by the crowd.[14] According to the *Times*, "The Hebrew newspapers . . . characterized the outbreak as little short of a revolution, and compared it to the revolutions of this kind which have occurred in Paris in times past."[15] An angry *New York Times* editorial, portraying the events in more prosaic terms, complained about "women tearing the buttons and badges from the uniforms of policemen and trampling them under foot."[16] Some ninety people (seventy of whom were women) were arrested, arraigned, and fined between $3 and $10 at the Essex Street Market Court, where a large crowd gathered to demand their release. Describing "The revolt of the women of the east side" under the headline, "MOB TRIES TO STORM JAIL FOR WOMEN," the *World* reported that "Policemen Beat Back A Crowd of Two Hundred Men" shouting, "Release the women!"[17] The *Times* reported: "At one time it was estimated that 3,000 persons were in the streets."[18] The boycott lasted until June 5, when the price of meat was lowered.[19]

Where were Lena, David, Daisy, Ruby, Isi, Millie, and Harry during these riots? I earlier pictured the Warshawsky family in the middle of the 1894 Tailors' Strike, which affected almost all of their neighbors and filled the streets surrounding their apartment. In March of 1902, when David was ten years old and Millie was eight, their neighborhood (according to all of the newspapers) was turned into a battle zone. "Ruderman & Warshawsky, grocers" at 132 Suffolk Street was on the front lines. Not only were there fifteen hundred small butcher shops in the area; there were twenty-seven shops on Suffolk Street alone, including Robert Pincus at 126 Suffolk Street and David Prager at 131 Suffolk Street. The Hornell *Evening Tribune* article that described the "pushing, scrambling mob of hundreds" reported "police lines in Broome, Norfolk, Essex, Ludlow and Suffolk streets between Delancy and Grand" and noted that "everybody was kept out of those streets."[20] The newspapers emphasized the presence of children in the clashes with the police. On May 18, reporting a resumption of the riots, the *New York Times* wrote: "A teacher in School 75, on Norfolk Street, said last night that nearly half of the boys in her class bore some marks of the rioting. Several of them had teeth knocked out and nearly all had bruised faces or scalps. The Hebrew boys do not as a rule play 'hookey,' but for the last few days have staid away from school."[21] Either David and his brothers and sisters were told to stay inside and hide, venturing outside only to run to school, or they were in the middle of the commotion, along with the children of the mothers who participated (willingly or unwillingly) in the boycott.

Although the inflamed and inflamatory rhetoric of the newspapers depicted mobs of angry, hysterical women, the historian Paula Hyman describes careful and strategic community organizing by mature "house-wives with children," "mothers of large famlies" who formed neigh-borhood committees, made appeals in synagogues, distributed printed statements, and lobbied elected officials.[22] Was Lena a petty bourgeois shopkeeper who sided with the butchers or a desperate and solidaric single mother struggling to feed her children, or both? The boycott would have disrupted business, but it also might temporarily have been good for business; there was an increased demand for milk, eggs, bread, fish, vegetables, and other foods.[23] Indeed, the fire in her neighbor Solomon Hartman's grocery might temporarily have been good for business.

It is unclear whether it was just a coincidence that this fire occurred on May 16. On May 17, the *Times* reported arrests of "would-be incen-diaries" who made two "attempts" to "ignite" the kerosene they had poured on meat and on the floors in a butcher shop. On May 20, the *Daily People* reported on "a small-sized panic" caused by a fire at 30 Essex Street, where a store on the ground floor was "occupied by Israel Cohen as a butcher shop." Although it was assumed that "some one care-lessly left a candle in the cellar," the article reports that three policemen had been in Essex Street "looking out for possible trouble between the people and the butchers on account of selling kosher meat."[24] A May 24 *New York Times* editorial declared: "It will not do to have a swarm of ignorant and infuriated women going about any part of this city with petroleum destroying goods and trying to set fire to the shops of those against whom they are angry."[25] The *Annual Report of the Committee on Fire Patrol* gives the address of the fire at Solomon Hartman's grocery store as 124–128 Suffolk Street, but the 1902 Trow's Directory lists 128 Suffolk Street as the address of Solomon Hartman's grocery store, and 126 Suffolk Street is listed as the address of Robert Pincus's butcher shop.[26] Perhaps this fire was related to the kosher meat boycott after all.

We do not know what effect these disturbances had on Lena's business, but the accounts of the 1902 kosher meat boycott and riots confirm that this was an economically precarious and volatile time in which mothers had to take matters into their own hands to take care of their families. We can wonder how the mother who posed her children in vaguely Victorian garb for formal portraits in an Essex Street photographer's studio less than a decade earlier imagined her children's future as her neighbors, customers, and their children fought with police in the streets. In any case, it does not appear that the grocery store at 132 Suffolk Street was successful. According to the Hebrew Orphan Asylum records, between March 9, 1903, when she filled out the admissions application for David, Ruby, and Isi, and March 29, 1903, when she first came to visit them, Lena moved from Suffolk Street to Essex Street with the Rudermans. When he visited his nephews on April 17, 1904, Abe Ruderman also was living at 82 Essex Street. The grocery store had failed. By 1905, according to the Register of Visits, the whole family had moved to Brooklyn, except for David, Ruby, and Isi, who remained in Manhattan in the orphanage.

After his discharge from the orphanage in 1906 at the age of fifteen, David appears to have lived with his mother until he was married in 1922 at the age of thirty-one. Economics kept families together, and perhaps he did not want to marry until he had achieved financial independence, but one can imagine that Lena's oldest son was dedicated to the mother from whom he was forced to separate at the age of eleven. The circumstances must have required great strength and determination on her part. From what I can tell, the Ruderman family was close.

Census records alone indicate that Meyer and Anna Ruderman were at the center of a multigenerational, extended family of children, grandchildren, nieces, and nephews for most of their almost fifty years in America. This cannot have been only for economic reasons. As Lena visited her sons in her four annual visits between 1903 and 1905, traveling first the length of Manhattan and later the distance from Brooklyn, she brought a different relative with her each time: their sister, grandmother, grandfather, aunt, and uncle. This may be a sign of strong familial bonds, but it is also a sign of a conscious effort to maintain familial bonds after the boys were sent to the orphanage.

Sometime between 1906 and 1910, Lena acquired the candy store. The census enumerator Nahuni Greenberg identifies her as a "retail merchant" with a "confectionary" on April 21, 1910, and less than four months later, Reuben and Isadore are discharged from the Hebrew Orphan Asylum in care of Mrs. Roshafsky. Meyer Ruderman is still working as a tailor in 1910 (when he is reported to be sixty-eight) and in 1915 (when he is reported to be seventy-three). In 1920 (when he is reported to be seventy-five but was probably eighty), he has no occupation, and neither does Lena (who is reported to be fifty). In 1917, when he registers for the draft, in answer to the question asking whether a relative was "solely dependent" on him, David wrote: "Mother to support," and in answer to the question, "Do you claim exemption from draft?" he wrote: "Support of home and mother." Isadore, or Irving, who along with his brother Ruby was an automobile mechanic at the American Motor Service at 2119 Bergen Street, wrote: "Part support of mother." Reuben married in 1915. At the time both David and Irving still lived with their mother, as did Harry. (Lena lived with Harry for the rest of her life, even after he married. I am not aware that she ever lived alone.)

I have no idea how my grandmother Jeanette got along with her mother-in-law after her marriage to my grandfather in 1922; they lived with or across the street from her parents for almost all of my father's first nineteen years. I do not know whether she kept up with Lena after my grandfather's death. In general, according to my mother, with the exception of Millie and her family, my grandfather does not seem to have been close to his siblings after his marriage, or at least by the time my mother knew the family. Yet in the two decades after her husband's death, Lena must have been the center of gravity in this family as it reconstituted itself in Brooklyn.

The last time that the name of Harris Warshawsky appears on any document that I have found is on Daisy's 1912 marriage certificate. She is Daisy Warshawsky, about to be Daisy Braverman, and next to "Father's Name" is written "Harris Warshawsky." On Reuben's 1915 marriage certificate, he is Reuben Marshall, and next to "Father's Name" is written only "Harold"—the last name inferred and effaced by the single Americanized Christian name. Millie's 1919 marriage certificate records "Harris" as Mildred Marshall's father, as does David Henry Marshall's 1922 marriage certificate. Harris Warshawsky has disappeared.

Certificate and Record of Marriage, Herman Braverman and Daisy Warshawsky, New York City Department of Records.

Certificate and Record of Marriage, Reuben Marshall and Minnie Goldberg, New York City Department of Records.

Lena appears on their marriage certificates as "Lena Ruderman," "Lena Rudderman," "Lena Rudman," and "Lena Anderman"—signs, perhaps, of careless clerks or hard-of-hearing rabbis, but also of the fading story of the fourteen-year-old girl who came to New York City from Minsk, married Harris Warshawsky at the age of twenty, and was left a pregnant widow with five young children after eleven years of marriage.

This simple plot is all that was passed down. The specific circumstances—how Harris Warshawsky died, when he died, and what happened before and after his death—were forgotten, or withheld, along with the family name. It was not until I started asking questions about the family name that I learned that my grandfather's parents were named Harris and Lena. When Harris died in 1901, David was almost ten years old; two years later, he entered the Hebrew Orphan Asylum, fatherless. By

Certificate and Record of Marriage, Isador Levine and Mildred Marshall, New York City Department of Records.

Certificate and Record of Marriage, David H. Marshall and Jeanette Levitt, New York City Department of Records.

the time that David's oldest son (my father) was ten years old, an age that might have caused him to look back upon his own experience as a ten-year-old boy, to think about a momentous event in his own childhood, Harris Warshawsky had been dead for thirty-three years. By the time that I was ten years old, Harris Warshawsky had been dead for almost sixty-three years. No one knew the "special circumstances of the case."

Reading the Death Certificate

I searched obituaries and the lists of deaths that were published regularly in the New York City and Brooklyn newspapers, scanning the names for Warshawsky, Warshafsky, Roshofsky, and other variations, including Harris and Marshall. There were no men of the right age by any of these names. Eventually, I found the list of Queens Vital Statistics published in the small *Newtown Register* on February 28, 1901, which listed the death notice: "Astoria—Harris Warshawsky, 36 years." Eventually I located in the New York City Municipal Archives the certificate and record of death for Harris Warshawsky. There is only one official record of a death in 1901 in New York City for a Harris Warshawsky. No other record corresponds to the biographical facts that are known. The death certificate explains why the death of Harris Warshawsky appears in the list of deaths in Queens County, and not in New York City.

The handwriting on the death certificate—the flow of the thick ink still palpable in the photocopy provided by the New York City Department of Records and Information Services—is difficult to read. It took me a long time to decipher and interpret this document. I returned to read it over and over again, studying the handwriting, comparing the letters, until all of the words took shape; eventually, research

Certificate and Record of Death, Harris Warshawsky, New York City Department of Records.

and cross-referencing allowed me to decipher and identify the names of people, places, and diseases recorded there. As these names became legible, they posed more questions than they answered. If the discovery of the death certificate confirmed the date and indeed the fact of my great-grandfather's death, and provided more information, it also opened up mysteries, and called for more stories. It inscribed Harris Warshawsky in other people's stories—not just the stories of my grandfather and his mother—that themselves provided keys to their stories. The death certificate became one of the key texts in the story of naming, renaming, and unnaming that I was trying to read, reconstruct, and tell.

Certificate No. 382, the "State of New York Certificate and Record of Death" recording the death of Harris Warshawsky, is dated February 14, 1901. It lists the date of death as February 14, 1901, and the date of burial as February 17, 1901. According to this record, filled in by hand on a printed form, Harris Warshawsky was a thirty-six-year-old, white, married tailor who was born in Russia. The biographical facts— age, occupation, national origin, marital status, and, of course, name— match the information in census records, birth certificates, naturalization papers, city directories, and family accounts.

There are blank spaces on the form next to "How long in U.S. if foreign born," "Father's Name," and "Mother's Name." These blank spaces suggest that no family members were present at the end to provide these details. The "Direct Cause of Death" is listed as "Cardiac Failure." Next to "Place of Death" is written "River Crest Sanitarium." Next to "Last Place of Residence" is written "88 Watkins St Brooklyn," which is described next to "Class of Dwelling" as a "Tenement." (A tenement is defined as "a house occupied by more than two families.") Next to "Place of Burial" is written "Machpelah," followed by two letters (initials that I first read as NW) and the word "Field."

So the death certificate places Harris Warshawsky in three places at the end of his life: 88 Watkins Street, River Crest Sanitarium, and Machpelah Cemetery. Not all of these and other entries on the form were legible to me at first as I studied the attending physician's hand-writing in the photocopy I obtained from the New York City Municipal Archives. At first the certificate seemed to raise more questions than it answered; in its entries I found both dead ends and signs pointing toward discovery. These signs seemed to point to a story, if I could just learn to read them, even as they spoke of more secrets.

The "last known place of residence," for example, "88 Watkins St Brooklyn," does not match the 151 Norfolk Street residence of the

Warshawsky family reported in the 1900 U.S. census. This entry on the death certificate is written by a different hand from the other entries. Unlike the forceful slant of the doctor's handwriting, this is a shaky, horizontal hand. Presumably, 88 Watkins Street was added after the rest of the record was filled out by the attending physician. Who added this address, which is not connected to Harris Warshawsky in any other document that I have located? Where does this address place him before his death? Watkins Street, in the Brownsville section of Brooklyn, is not far from where the Ruderman and Warshawsky families would relocate in 1905, but it is not near the Lower East Side Manhattan neighborhood that (according to all other records) they inhabited throughout the last decade of the nineteenth century. What was Harris Warshawsky doing there?

Near a fire station that is still in operation, a public library, and a school, this narrow street was part of the rapidly growing and changing Jewish neighborhood of Brownsville at the turn of the century, what a columnist for the *Brooklyn Daily Eagle* deplored as "Brooklyn's Ghetto" at the end of 1899.[1] If one can judge by the location of the fire station (which was located at 107–109 Watkins Street as early as 1903),[2] 88 Watkins Street would have been close to the intersection of Pitkin Avenue, a major commercial thoroughfare. At the end of 1899, the Hebrew Educational Society constructed a new building at the corner of Watkins Street and Eastern Parkway. Classes and clubs met at the Hebrew Educational Society Institute at the corner of Pitkin Avenue and Watkins Street. In the first years of the new century, the *Brooklyn Daily Eagle* is filled with notices of edifying lectures being offered at its Watkins Street building, often in Yiddish. An article in the *Brooklyn Daily Eagle* in May of 1900 stated that the new building was "for the use of the workers in Brownsville."[3]

It is difficult to trace building numbers for a neighborhood that was then and is still in flux. Contemporary directories for this neighborhood often give cross streets rather than building numbers for addresses, suggesting that the construction (and perhaps the destruction) of buildings outpaced any numbering system. Brooklyn was still a new frontier at this time. *The Rise of David Levinsky* describes the frenetic real estate construction and speculation in Brooklyn that was "intoxicating a certain element of the population" in this period.[4] According to Wendell E. Prichett, manufacturers in search of cheap, non-unionized labor developed their own housing in this area, most of it rental housing. "By 1900 almost twenty-five thousand people lived in Brownsville, most occupying wooden frame, 'double-decker' houses designed for two families," although these were soon subdivided. "While the Lower East Side was once an area of single-family houses, Brownsville was 'born' a tenement community." Large portions of the neighborhoods that this Brooklyn "real estate 'boom'" (as Cahan called it) first created have been razed, although some buildings from the turn of the century remain today. What have been described as "the lost synagogues of Brooklyn" are now homes to tabernacle faith churches.[5]

The death certificate identifies the last place of residence as a tenement, but apartments could have housed factory shops, especially since Brownsville represented a less-regulated frontier of the garment industry. There were a great many tailors in the vicinity in tenement apartments and clothing firms. According to Trow's Directory of 1899, the United Brotherhood of Tailors, Local Branch 21, had its meetings on Watkins Street, north of Pitkin Avenue. A Louis Hawer, a tailor, had a firm at 106 Watkins Street. At 138 Watkins Street was one Henry Teplizky. The *Thirteenth Annual Report of the Factory Inspector of the State of New York*, published in 1899, lists Henry Teplizky as a clothing manufacturer and Louis Hawer as a manufacturer of pants in its inventory of factories in Brooklyn. Teplizky employed twenty-two males and nineteen females, while Hawer employed only three males and one female, suggesting that this was a tenement shop. The former had five code violations reported while the latter had six.[6]

On December 15, 1899, the *Brooklyn Daily Eagle* ran a story with the headline "Preparing to Cleanse Brownsville Ghetto" reporting on inspections conducted by "Health Officer Black and a Sanitary Committee" in which they visited "sweat shops on Watkins street." Despite "nests of filth" caused by "dusts and clippings" swept under benches, "the doctor indicated that he was well satisfied with the

improvements that had been made." Noting that the "sanitary conditions in almost every instance were very bad," the article notes: "When
the sewer connections are all made the municipal officials will issue
orders for paving the streets." Indeed, most of the references to Watkins
Street in the paper at the turn of the century are notices of sewer and
asphalt projects. The article notes that most of the property owners are
"non-residents."

For years I searched for 88 Watkins Street in directories and census pages, neither of which can be searched by street address.[7] I tried
to cross-reference census listings with factory owners and shopkeepers
that I came across with Watkins Street addresses, and with anyone with
a Watkins Street address who was mentioned in newspaper articles in
the hope of getting to the neighborhood of 88 Watkins Street in the
census pages. These were typically victims or perpetrators of crimes. I
found an April 19, 1901, article about a "saloon at 34 and 36 Watkins
street" where the owner, Aaron Finkelstein, was arrested and charged
with "selling beer to a boy on Sunday, March 17."[8] Using directories,
electoral districts, assembly districts, and census listings, I walked up
and down Watkins Street in 1900 page by page, only to be frustrated
when the census enumerator abruptly turned the corner just as he was
approaching the block where No. 88 would be located. I am fairly certain
that no 88 Watkins Street is listed in the 1900 census. It may not have
had a numbered address until the following year. With the exception of
children, wives, and the occasional shop owner, servant, or schoolteacher,
virtually everyone living on Watkins Street in 1900 was a Russian Jewish
tailor or involved in some aspect of the garment industry. I found an 88
Watkins Street in the 12th election district and 21st assembly district of
Kings County in the 1905 New York State census. It seems to be a small
building, housing only eleven families and forty-seven individuals. The
neighborhood resembles the Watkins Street neighborhoods that the 1900
U.S. census enumerator visited, but the Russian tailors have been joined
by Italian day laborers and their families; the wives mostly do "house
work."[9] This may or may not be the building that stood at this address
in 1901, but it indicates that the neighborhood was still in transition.

At a time when many contractors were expanding into Brooklyn because of cheaper labor, Harris Warshawsky might have set up shop on Watkins Street. If, in Cahan's account, "Small tradesmen of the slums, and even working-men, were investing their savings in houses and lots," and "Jewish carpenters, house-painters, bricklayers, or instalment peddlers became builders of tenements or frame dwellings, real estate speculators,"[10] surely a successful contractor might have pursued a construction project there, perhaps investing in a new tenement house. Perhaps he set up one of the Watkins Street sweatshops described by the *Brooklyn Daily Eagle*. Might this be where, according to the story conveyed to me by Millie's daughter, Harris collapsed in his factory at the end of his life? We know that Harris Warshawsky's coat-manufacturing shop at 191 Broome Street was visited by the factory inspector sometime between November 30, 1899, and November 30, 1900, but he might have relocated his business to Brooklyn sometime between that visit and February of 1901, either because he was so successful, or because he wasn't successful and could pay less in wages and rent by setting up a shop in Brooklyn. As I have noted, the average firm in the men's clothing trade at the time lasted only seven years. In the six months between June 11, 1900, when the census enumerator Joseph Bissert visited the family at 151 Norfolk Street and February of 1901, Harris might have moved the entire family to Watkins Street in Brooklyn, part of a growing Jewish immigration from the Lower East Side to Brownsville. Harry was born on August 17, 1901, at 130 Suffolk Street, but his widowed mother and his family might have returned to their old neighborhood on the Lower East Side, where presumably the Rudermans still lived, in the six months after his father's death.

One could imagine another sort of story: the desertion of families by husbands was a growing social problem at the time. The *Jewish Daily Forward* published letters from deserted wives with photographs in a "Gallery of Missing Husbands." In 1905, over 14 percent of the relief funds distributed by the United Hebrew Charities went to deserted women.[11] Lena's March 2, 1903, application for admission to the Hebrew Orphan Asylum for her three sons is the twenty-second application of the year. Of the twenty-one applications submitted before hers, beginning January 1, 1903, a third of them note that the father had "absconded." Under "Special Circumstances of the Case," we read: "Applicant's father absconded 6 months ago" (No. 3122); "Applicant's father absconded two months ago" (No. 3123); "Husband absconded 9 months ago—Whereabouts unknown" (No. 3125); "Husband absconded 9 months ago" (No. 3126); "The children's father deserted them" (No. 3115); and even, "Father absconded last August, whereabouts unknown. Mother also absconded about six weeks ago, whereabouts unknown" (No. 3121). Of the twenty-four applications that were received during the rest of the month of March, a third noted that the father had "absconded" or "deserted" his family. Harris Warshawsky may not even have known that his wife was pregnant in the first weeks of 1901. When his death certificate was filled out, no one was present who knew the names of Harris's father and mother or the number of years he had been in the United States. Did he die alone?[12]

There were an unusual number of Jewish social, educational, and charitable organizations appearing in this Watkins Street neighborhood at the turn of the century. The Society for the Aid of the Poor Sick rented a store nearby at Thatford and Pitkin avenues in the late 1890s, and then "bought a small house on Watkins Street, into which the dispensary was moved."[13] The East New York Dispensary, related to the Help for the Sick Poor Society of Brownsville, received a license from the State of New York on July 11, 1900, and was located at 128 Watkins Street.[14] If the 88 Watkins Street address links Harris Warshawsky with these charitable institutions, this could indicate that he had fallen on hard times, that he was away from his family, and that the medical benefits most men in his community and social class would have received through a lodge or a *landsmanshaftn* organization were inaccessible. In ordinary circumstances, someone of his apparent social and economic status would have been very reluctant to be associated with the "sick poor."[15]

The death certificate identifies the undertaker as "Jos. Wiener," residing at 155 Rivington Street, a few doors down from 176 Rivington Street, where the Warshawskys lived before moving to 151 Norfolk

Street, in the Lower East Side neighborhood they inhabited throughout the 1890s. This suggests that whether or not Harris was working or living in Brooklyn in 1901, his family was still in the old neighborhood, and this is where the body was sent. Why would a Lower East Side undertaker be retained if the body were to be transported from Astoria to a residence in Brooklyn or a cemetery in Queens? In 1901, before the professionalization and licensing of undertakers and funeral homes, undertakers were basically drivers hired to transport corpses. As the Lower East Side Tenement House Museum explains, "in the late 19th and early 20th centuries, one hired an undertaker as one would hire a cab today. Many funeral parlor proprietors began their careers as cartmen with horse-drawn carriages."[16] According to the 1901 Trow's Copartnership and Corporation Directory, the Wiener Brothers (Samuel and Harry) were in the wagon business at 305 Rivington Street. Joseph Wiener, an undertaker, is listed in the 1905 New York State census as living at 72 St. Marks Place. It is possible that the death and funeral benefits that Harris Warshawsky would have obtained through a lodge or fraternal society included a specific undertaker, who would have been dispatched to Astoria whether his body was brought home to Watkins Street or to Norfolk Street. Yet the most significant question here is how Harris Warshawsky got to the River Crest Sanitarium in Astoria.

Reading the Death Certificate

The Place of Death

The "Certificate and Record of Death" lists Harris Warshawsky's place of death as the River Crest Sanitarium in Astoria, Long Island. The certificate is filled out and signed by Dr. W. Alfred McCorn, who, I discovered, was the resident physician at River Crest in 1901. Both the words "River Crest" and the doctor's signature were illegible to me as I first studied the death certificate; it was only after I had located River Crest on a list of sanitariums in New York at the turn of the century, and then located Dr. W. A. McCorn on a list of physicians there, that the letters took shape and became legible. River Crest (sometimes written Rivercrest) Sanitarium, I then learned, was established by Dr. John Joseph Kindred in 1896 on a thirty-acre property known as the Walcott estate, just across the East River from 108th Street in Manhattan. Kindred, a prominent developer as well as a doctor, opened several institutions; he also served in the U.S. Congress between 1911 and 1913 and between 1921 and 1929. River Crest seems to have operated until about 1960. A Catholic high school now occupies the site where it stood overlooking the East River.

In the New York Public Library, there is a twenty-two-page brochure (with photographs) from the River Crest Sanitarium from the 1890s in which River Crest is described as: "A Private Sanitarium for

New York City Office
616 Madison Ave.
Corner of 58th St.
Telephone 1470 Plaza.
Jno. Jos. Kindred, M. D.,
Consultant.

RIVER CREST SANITARIUM,
ASTORIA, L. I., N. Y. CITY.
Established 1896
by Jno. Jos. Kindred, M. D.

Office hours
at New York City Office.
3-4 daily.
Sanitarium Telephone 820-821 Astoria.
Wm. Elliott Dold, M. D.,
Physician in Charge.

Postcard, River Crest Sanitarium.

the care and treatment of mental and nervous diseases and selected cases of alcoholic and drug habituation." According to the brochure, the "Physicians have had the advantages of many years' experience in the best institutions at home and abroad." John Joseph Kindred, M.D., and Wm. Elliott Dold, M.D., have a long list of prior affiliations with prominent institutions ranging from the Royal Asylum in Edinburgh, Scotland, to the Bloomingdale Asylum in New York. The sanitarium is said to have a brick building "planned and arranged for the scientific treatment and care of mental cases. . . . Three distinct classifications of patients are strictly maintained in this building." Narcotic patients are described as being both "habitués and voluntary patients."

Although the brochure advertises "very reasonable rates for care and treatment," it highlights the sort of amenities that a resort would advertise: "It is designed to conduct the establishment on a *liberal* scale and no expense or pains have been spared to make the accommodation, table, attendance, and all apartments of a high order and suited to the better class of patients." The medical facilities—the "brick building is planned and arranged for the scientific treatment and care of mental cases" and the "basement is devoted to Hydrotherapy, with its Baruch system of baths, given by trained attendants"—are juxtaposed with "bowling alley, lawn tennis, croquet courts," and a "herd of cows" outside, as well as a house with "cheerful parlors, large well ventilated and handsomely furnished sleeping rooms, an inviting dining-room, library, billiard and smoking-rooms, office." The brochure emphasizes the "lack of institutional features" and "the homelike air." In addition: "All of the buildings are lighted throughout by *Electricity*, are steam-heated and provided with hot and cold water, baths, et. in accordance with improved modern ideas." Although it features "quiet and secluded" grounds that "suggest to the tired neurasthenic, the rest and comfort of a quiet nook in the Catskills," the brochure also underlines the "view of New York City" and "the satisfying impression of the near proximity of the city." If River Crest Sanitarium was "just 35 minutes from the heart of New York City," it seems another world from Essex, Norfolk, Rivington, and Suffolk streets on the Lower East Side. None of the Warshawsky residences would have had such luxurious amenities.[1]

An advertisement that appeared in the 1898 *Medical Record* also juxtaposes medical facilities with country club amenities. Noting that the sanitarium was "Duly Licensed by the State Commission in Lunacy," offering treatment "For Mental and Nervous Diseases. Alcoholic and Drug Habitues," it also boasts a "physician's elegant home," "private care," and "splendid views," adding: "Every facility provided for the proper care and amusement of patients. Conducted liberally, all appointments being suited to first-class patients."[2] In 1900, the River Crest Sanitarium was advertised in the *Medical News* as an institution "For Mental and Nervous Diseases." An advertisement in the *Alienist and Neurologist* in January of 1901, one month before Harris Warshawsky died, declares: "FOR MENTAL AND NERVOUS DISEASES. Separate detached building for Alcoholic and Drug Habitues."[3]

There is evidence that River Crest was something like a contemporary celebrity rehab clinic. There were numerous stories in the *New York Times*, the *Brooklyn Daily Eagle*, and other papers at the turn of

Left: *Medical Record*, 1898.

Below: *Standard Medical Directory of North America*, 1902.

the century about famous and wealthy inmates who either entered River Crest voluntarily or had been committed: reports of family estate battles, lawsuits against doctors, inmates who contested certificates of lunacy, and inmates who escaped. A popular musical theater actress named Della Fox, who suffered from drug and alcohol abuse and mental instability, was committed and released in 1901. The actor Maurice Barrymore, father of Ethel and John Barrymore, was sent to River Crest in April of 1901 from Bellevue Hospital. Several articles detailed the sad descent into insanity of William Steinitz, the former world chess champion, who also was transferred from Bellevue to River Crest.

In 1902, a New York merchant's wife named Mrs. Rachel Richman, who was declared insane after being charged with the theft of $25,000 in valuables, was sent to River Crest. In 1900, a court ordered the release of a thirty-year-old heir named Samuel T. White from River Crest, where he had been committed by his wife for being "mentally unsound" and "an excessive smoker of cigarettes." A man went to court in 1901 to contest the will of his late wife, who had been placed in the River Crest Sanitarium, after she left most of her estate, worth $100,000, to "a negro Pullman car porter." On February 13, 1900, almost exactly a year before Harris Warshawsky's death, the *New York Times* reported the misadventures of one Dr. Wilde, a well-to-do doctor and missionary who was "suffering from fixed delusional insanity" and had escaped from River Crest: "He imagines that he is Capt. Dreyfus and that he is undergoing sentence on Devil's Island."[4] The stories were colorful, but apparently the *New York Times* paid attention to the sort of people who became patients at the River Crest Sanitarium.

How did Harris Warshawsky, a Russian Jewish immigrant tailor, come to cross the East River to die in the private River Crest Sanitarium? According to the *Twelfth Annual Report of the State Commission in Lunacy*, published in 1901, there were then twenty licensed private institutions for the care of the insane in New York. The weekly rate for board at River Crest was $15, which was more than some institutions and less than others. The average weekly household income in New York State in 1901 was less than $13 (or $675 per year), so this was not inexpensive. These rates probably did not include all the first-class amenities described in the advertisements and promotional materials. If River Crest maintained "three distinct classifications of patients," there probably were varying accommodations. The capacity in 1900, according to the *State Commission in Lunacy*, was sixty-seven patients.[5] The 1900 U.S. census records sixty-nine patients at River Crest Sanitarium in June of 1900. (It is not clear whether the census enumerator, John F. Evers, included every patient in residence on June 22 and June 23, or whether only patients who had been committed and were actually "living" there on June 1 were included. The sanitarium would have had patients passing through for stays of varying durations.) Also in residence are John Kindred, the owner, and Dr. W. Alfred McCorn, the resident physician, and their families, as well as a nurse and twenty-seven servants. There are also four boarders, two of whom are actors.

It is difficult to get a sense of who these patients were from the pages of the census. Thirty-three of the sixty-nine patients were female. The enumerator noted the occupation of only sixteen patients. (Was this information provided by the staff, or did he try to interview the various patients institutionalized for insanity, drug addiction, or alcoholism?) The patients include an actress—the same Della Fox whose troubles were chronicled in the newspapers—and an artist, a physician, a lawyer, a schoolteacher, a salesman, and a merchant. They also include a shipping clerk, a barber, a carpenter, a coat maker, a midwife, a bookkeeper, a tailor, and a "Gents. Tailor." One would know only from the *New York Times*, however, that Samuel White, the bookkeeper, was the heir who was committed against his will by his wife for being "mentally unsound" and "an excessive smoker of cigarettes." Of the sixty-nine patients, thirty-one were born in New York or New Jersey, six were born in Ireland, two were born in England, twelve were born in Germany, two were born in Bohemia, and one in Italy. No patients were born in Russia, according to the enumerator, but six were said to be from Finland, and I am guessing that John F. Evers, like his colleague Joseph Bissert on Norfolk Street, wrote Finland instead of Russia. There are very few Jewish names on the list, but the ones from "Finland" are more likely to sound Jewish—for example, Samuel Freedman, a "Finnish" tailor who had been in the United States for less than a year. More than half of the patients were born in the United States, Ireland, or England. This does not seem to have been the melting pot that one sees in the public Manhattan State Hospital asylum at Ward's Island.

The Manhattan Chess Club had to raise $1,200—a substantial sum—to get the chess champion William Steinitz transferred from the public Manhattan State Hospital asylum at Ward's Island to the private River Crest Sanitarium. The *Brooklyn Eagle* obtained an interview with the chess champion "for the express purpose of ascertaining the condition of the man concerning whose fate the entire chess world is at present anxious." According to an April 5, 1900, article, "The reporter was very courteously received by Dr. W. A. McCorn"—the physician who signed Harris Warshawsky's death certificate—who stated his opinion that the "probationary period" allowed by "state authorities" was "entirely too brief for a proper study of the case." An April 11, 1900, article in the *Oswego Daily Times* describes how, "through the intervention of friends," Steinitz was transferred "to River Crest sanitarium, where he was comfortably quartered in a cottage annex" and "he practically had the freedom of the grounds." According to the article, Steinitz left in April after a stay of several weeks.[6]

Despite the efforts of his friends and admirers, when Steinitz had a relapse, he ended up back at Ward's Island because his family could not afford a private sanitarium. On June 13, 1900, nine days before John F. Evers visited River Crest, the census enumerator recorded "Wm. Steinitz" among the patients at Ward's Island. His occupation is listed as "Chess Champion." The list of patients at Ward's Island takes up more than ten pages. The private estate of River Crest Sanitarium, where Steinitz held forth to reporters from a cottage, was obviously a more desirable location than this large public institution for the insane.[7]

How did Harris Warshawsky find his way to the commanding hills of Astoria from the tenements, shops, and factories of either Norfolk Street on the Lower East Side or Watkins Street in Brownsville? Why wasn't he at the Manhattan State Hospital at Ward's Island with William

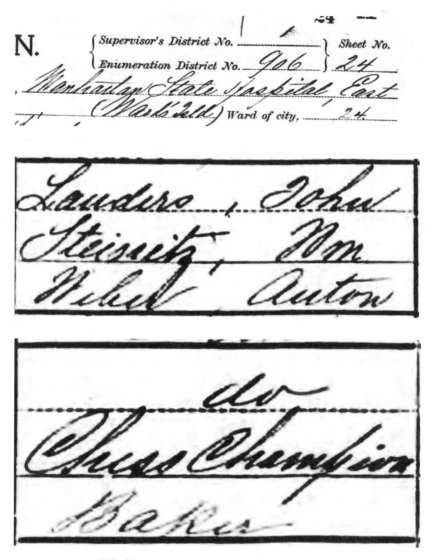

US Census, 1900. Courtesy of *Ancestry.com*.

Steinitz and hundreds of other inmates? Even if Harris Warshawsky had become a successful contractor or factory owner who could afford the first-class accommodations at River Crest, even if there were some patients from humble professions in less expensive accommodations, his presence still seems to constitute a social and cultural leap.

There are several related questions here. What medical condition had brought him to River Crest? The advertisements for River Crest Sanitarium in both promotional materials and medical journals highlight the treatment of both "mental and nervous diseases" and alcoholism and drug addiction. This pairing was common in most advertisements for sanitariums at the time; "alcoholic insanity" was discussed in the medical literature, and alcoholism and insanity were considered to be related, yet of course there were psychiatric conditions that had no relation to drugs or alcohol. Furthermore, even if in February of 1901 (or earlier) he could afford this treatment, why would he have gone to this institution in particular? Was there a special route that had brought him—or people like him—to River Crest? What were the special circumstances of the case that would have led him to this particular private institution and to Dr. W. Alfred McCorn?

11

---◆◈◆---

Reading the Death Certificate

The Name of the Physician

According to the "Certificate and Record of Death," Dr. W. Alfred McCorn attended Harris Warshawsky from February 11 to February 14, the date of death and the date that Dr. McCorn filled out and signed the certificate. McCorn himself died at the age of forty-five, almost exactly three years after he signed Harris Warshawsky's death certificate, on February 18, 1904. In an obituary in the medical journal the *Alienist and Neurologist,* the editors mourned the loss of an "alienist and neurologist of promise, perseverance and ability." Born in 1859 in Newfield, New York, McCorn graduated from Cornell University in 1879, and he received his medical degree from the University of Buffalo in 1882.[1] The April 1904 *Medical Record* noted that McCorn was "connected with New York State hospitals for the insane, and with the Kankakee, Ill., Hospital."[2] In 1901 he was the resident physician at River Crest Sanitarium.

In the last year of the nineteenth century, McCorn attained more notoriety than the most colorful patients at River Crest when he accidentally shot and killed a boy named Clifton White who was stealing cherries on the grounds of the sanitarium. The story was reported extensively in both the *New York Times* and the *Brooklyn Eagle* for months, as well as in other newspapers. According to the *Brooklyn Eagle*, on June 23, 1899, McCorn shot a .38 caliber revolver at a group of boys at close range "in order to frighten them away as the sanitarium people had been much annoyed by raids upon the cherry trees." The *Eagle* reported that after the shooting, McCorn, although a physician, went back inside and had an attendant call the police, sending "a blanket out to be put over the wounded boy." According to the article, "No effort was made, the police say, to take the boy to the sanitarium." Several articles suggest his indifference, if not negligence, after the shooting, as well as his reckless-ness in firing at a group of boys stealing cherries. The *Daily Star*, which notes that McCorn "waited until he was about one hundred feet from the boys before opening fire," describes the doctor as "tall and spare, with slightly stooping shoulders. His face is smooth shaven and thin, the check bones are prominent, his eyes are of a cold gray color, and his skin sallow. He wears glasses." The article reports that McCorn "did not look at all pleased when he was escorted to a cell," and suggests that he had "regarded his position as anything but serious." In contrast, "Dr. Kindred of the River Crest Sanitarium was at the hospital nearly all of the night to aid in every way to save the boy's life."[3]

Arrested for assault, McCorn spent the night in jail. The boy was able to make a statement before he died the next morning, and McCorn was arraigned, first for murder and then later for manslaughter. On July 7, a coroner's jury ruled the shooting accidental, and on July 17, bail was set at $10,000 and McCorn was released. He told the *Eagle* that his "health had been greatly impaired by his confinement in the jail." On September 15, the *Eagle* reported that a grand jury dismissed "the charge of homicide against Dr. William McCorn, superintendent of Rivercrest Sanitarium, Astoria," stating that it "was shown at the autopsy that McCorn fired a bullet from a pistol which struck a stone under the tree. The ball then ricocheted and entering the lad's side, caused his death."[4]

It is Dr. McCorn's position as a physician and medical researcher that is relevant to the story of Harris Warshawsky's death, and to the question of how Harris Warshawsky might have ended up at River Crest

YOUNG CLIFTON WHITE
DIED THIS FORENOON.

Shot Down While Stealing Cherries Near the River Crest Sanitarium in Astoria.

DR.WILLIAM MC CORN ARRESTED

It Is Likely That He Will Be Charged With Manslaughter When Arraigned Monday.

"Dr. McCorn Released," *Brooklyn Daily Eagle*, June 24, 1899.

Sanitarium. It is difficult to ascertain the status and character of River Crest, beyond the impression one gets from advertising and newspaper accounts that make it seem like a high society insane asylum and celebrity rehab clinic. McCorn himself seems to have been a reputable specialist and researcher with some prestigious affiliations and associations.

"Dr. McCorn Acquitted," *Brooklyn Daily Eagle*, September 15, 1899.

He was a medical officer at the New York City Asylum for the Insane (part of Manhattan State Hospital) in 1888, not long after he completed medical school. This is his affiliation when he writes a note for the *Medical Record* in 1888. An article that was reprinted in regional newspapers in July and August of 1888 noted: "Dr. W. A. McCorn, of the New York City Asylum for the Insane, has found hyoscyamine, subcutaneously administered, a very useful remedy in quieting mania." He was appointed first assistant physician at the Milwaukee State Hospital for the Insane in 1888 or 1889, and in 1893 he appears to have been the prison physician at the Wisconsin State Prison.[5] By 1895, McCorn was listed on the payroll at the Illinois Eastern Hospital for the Insane. In 1898, the *Medico-Legal Journal* referred to McCorn as "Neurologist and Assistant Physician at the Illinois Eastern Hospital for the Insane" and "an observer of high rank."[6] It is at Illinois Eastern Hospital that he became acquainted with one of the most prominent figures in American psychiatry, Dr. Adolph Meyer, who spent most of his career at the Johns Hopkins University hospital and medical school in Baltimore.

Meyer's papers in the Johns Hopkins archives contain ten letters from McCorn to Meyer, written between 1897 and 1901. One gets the impression from the letters that McCorn would have liked to have been—yet was not quite—a protégé of Meyer, who was known as a generous mentor.[7] The first letter (dated October 19, 1897) asks Meyer to endorse a translation that McCorn has completed of "Scholz's Textbook on Insanity," and the second (dated November 23, 1897) requests professional advice about similar projects translating German psychiatric works into English. However, subsequent letters contain complaints (and what McCorn calls "gossip") about professional, personal, and political tensions at Eastern Illinois and increasingly plaintive requests for Meyer's assistance in finding McCorn another position. The only record of Meyer's responses is a draft of a letter that he wrote to McCorn on July 24, 1900, while McCorn was at River Crest, politely but firmly declining McCorn's offer to assist *him* in securing a position at the Pathological Institute after the removal of a Dr. Van Gersow.[8]

In 1898, McCorn moved from Illinois Eastern Hospital to McClean Hospital, formerly the McLean Asylum for the Insane and today a prominent psychiatric hospital affiliated with Harvard University. Meyer worked at McClain, and perhaps he helped place McCorn there in what appears to have been a temporary position. McCorn seems to have moved from McClain to River Crest Sanitarium. An article in the *New York Times* on December 30, 1900, about a patient's suit against Dr. J. J. Kindred identifies McCorn as "the resident physician at River Crest Sanitarium." An article in the *Brooklyn Daily Eagle* about a lawsuit against McCorn by the family of the boy he shot describes him in December of 1901 as "formerly house physician at the River Crest Sanitarium."[10] In 1901 and 1902, Dr. McCorn was listed as physician in charge at the Grand View Sanitarium for Mental and Nervous Diseases in South Windham, Connecticut, a large private facility. A June 14, 1901, letter to Meyer written on Grand View Sanitarium letterhead begins, "You may be somewhat surprised to find me up in this vicinity and I am at myself, for I was never fooled greater or more smoothly in my life." It goes on to describe ethical and professional concerns about being asked to use a certain untested treatment on alcoholics, as well as personal altercations with the owner of the sanitarium, one of which ends when Mrs. McCorn "knocked [the owner] down and had him put in a restraint sheet." This event leads McCorn to consider a position in Hartford, where, he tells Meyer, he would "take up the study of alcoholism" with a Dr. Crothers "with the purpose in view of devoting the rest of my life to the work." In a subsequent letter dated July 21, 1901, which is not on letterhead, McCorn tells Meyer that he has decided against taking the Hartford position and is back in New York without a job. Noting that it is "a bad time of the year to find anything," McCorn states that he is "ready for anything that is honorable" and asks Meyer if he knows of any openings.[11] The 1904 issue of the *Alienist and Neurologist* identifies McCorn as "Supt. Elizabeth General Hospital, Elizabeth, N.J.," and the *Journal of the American Medical Association* in its obituary identifies him as "formerly superintendent of the Elizabeth (N.J.) General Hospital."[12]

I am not sure how to read Dr. McCorn's career trajectory. At least some of his appointments were prestigious and represented positions of responsibility, but he moved institutions frequently, and it is not clear that his positions matched his academic ambitions and intellectual engagement. His letter to Meyer about his almost-comic adventures at the Grand View Sanitarium suggests that Meyer will be surprised that he is there, and that he is concerned with the academic standing of the doctor with whom he would work in Hartford. To understand McCorn's role in Harris Warshowsky's story, we need to recognize that he was more than a physician or clinician. He was engaged in intellectual, scholarly, and scientific work as well as clinical work. His translations from German of Richard von Krafft-Ebing, Carl Wernicke, August Hoffmann, Alfred Hoche, Theodor Tiling, Havelock Ellis, and others appeared in academic and professional journals, including the *Alienist and Neurologist* and the *American Journal of Insanity* (which in 1921 changed its name to the *American Journal of Psychiatry*). His first article in the *American Journal of Insanity*, "Degeneration in Criminals as Shown by the Bertillon System of Measurement and Photographs," was published in 1896.[13] In 1901, he published the lead article in this prominent journal, an essay about hallucinations.[14] On November 19, 1899, the *Brooklyn Daily Eagle* announced that he would be delivering a paper, "Insanity in its Medico-Legal Aspects," before the Queens-Nassau Medical Society.[15] In 1901, the *Medico-Legal Journal* noted his research and described his work in complimentary terms: "Dr. McCorn's paper shows research, and is of high value as a reference."[16] When, in 1902, Arthur MacDonald submitted to the U.S. Congress *A Plan for the Study of Man with Reference to Bills to Establish a Laboratory for the Study of the Criminal, Pauper, and Defective Classes,* McCorn is listed among the fifty-five American specialists who wrote in support of the project, most of whom had prominent scholarly or institutional affiliations.[17] McCorn had academic connections and genuine credentials as a researcher.

I have asked how Harris Warshawsky, a Russian Jewish immigrant tailor from the Lower East Side or Brooklyn, found himself at a private sanitarium for the care of the insane and the addicted that advertised facilities "suited to first-class patients" and catered to celebrities and social-ites. We don't know if he had arrived at River Crest or resided there before the last four days of his life when Dr. McCorn, according to the death certificate, attended him, from February 11 to February 14. These dates could refer to the period that he received specific medical attention, that is to say, when he was dying of the cardiac failure noted on the death certificate as the "direct cause of death," and not to the entire time that he was a patient at the sanitarium. When I first read the words "cardiac failure," it made sense to me; Harris's son David, my grandfather, would die of heart disease in 1952 at the age of sixty-one, and Harris's grandson Stephen, my uncle, would die of heart disease in 1982 at the age of fifty-six. Yet it does not seem likely that Harris Warshawsky collapsed after a heart attack in Brooklyn (or the Lower East Side) and was immediately transported to the River Crest Sanitarium in Astoria, even if he could afford the best care, or even if River Crest took some patients who might have gone to state hospitals. Patients with heart attacks would not have been sent to the River Crest Sanitarium for Mental and Nervous Diseases, Alcoholic and Narcotic Habitues, to be attended to by Dr. McCorn.

McCorn's signature on the death certificate suggests a reason for Harris Warshawsky's presence there, beyond his role as the resident physician who was required to fill out a legal form. I believe that Harris Warshawsky's admission to River Crest, which in its brochure advertised its "scientific treatment and care of mental cases," is in fact related to McCorn's presence there. River Crest was not a research hospital, of course, but McCorn's scholarly and medical research interests seem to be more than a sideline or a footnote. The presence of Dr. W. Alfred McCorn at Harris Warshawsky's death is a key to understanding what brought Harris Warshawsky to River Crest Sanitarium. The story here might begin to explain why the Warshawsky name was left behind, why the traces of the father were erased.

———❖———

Reading the Death Certificate

The Name of the Disease

In 1901, the year of Harris Warshawsky's death, an article was published in the *Proceedings of the American Medico-Psychological Association* (later the American Psychiatric Association) entitled "Notes on the Hebrew Insane," by Dr. Frank G. Hyde of Ward's Island, the major state psychiatric facility in New York City. The paper analyzes information about patients admitted to the Manhattan State Hospital East between 1871 and 1900 and considers the "enormous increase in Hebrews in recent years," owing in part to the rise in immigration. Dr. Hyde writes that many of these immigrants, "predisposed to psychoses, unable to cope with the unequal conditions, break down and eventually find their way to the hospital. The men who are admitted are largely drawn from those who are employed in sweat shops and as hucksters; these on the one hand laboring many hours a day in close, ill-ventilated shops with little or no exercise, and closely packed in squalid tenements at night—constantly ignoring the law of cleanliness—are thereby placed in the most suitable surroundings to bring out hereditary tendencies toward insanity. The Hebrews as a race are hysterical and neurasthenic."[1]

Around the turn of the century, in articles such as Hyde's "Notes on the Hebrew Insane," "The Insane Jew," by M. Beadles, and "Some

Observations on Insanity in Jews" by Harvey Baird (the latter two both published in the *Journal of Mental Science*), medical researchers discussed the increase of Jewish patients and the causes of insanity in Jews.[2]

If some form of insanity landed Harris Warshawsky in the River Crest Sanitarium for Mental and Nervous Diseases, his family was no doubt less concerned with the scientific theories that traced a genetic disposition toward insanity among Jews to the Old Testament than with popular beliefs that insanity was hereditary. In "Notes on the Hebrew Insane," Dr. Hyde writes, "By those who are associated with Hebrews in hospitals the men are looked upon as neurotic. It is difficult in many cases to obtain satisfactory histories of this class of patients owing in part to the suspiciousness of friends of patients and on the other to their unwillingness to admit hereditary influences." Hyde also suggests that patients were taken home prematurely "[o]n the first show of returning reason" so they could "resume their struggle for riches, with the result, in a great many cases, of prompt return to the hospital."[3] It is possible that Harris Warshawsky, like many psychiatric patients, had more than one visit to River Crest, or some other facility, in cycles of psychosis and improvement. We can presume that only extreme behavior and symptoms that could not be ignored would have brought him to River Crest Sanitarium. In any case, his ultimate demise in an institution licensed to care for the insane, especially if a certificate of commitment or what were called "lunacy papers" had been filed, would not have made a story that a family would want to share; it was certainly not a story that a widow would want to pass on to her children or a story that a child would want to recount.

David Roshafsky (Warshawsky) would have found little consolation in the fact that fourteen-year-old Joseph Kerner had applied for admission to the Hebrew Orphan Asylum the day before David had because his mother was in the "insane pavilion of Long Island State Hospital," or that two weeks later, David, Nathan, and Celia Weiss (ages twelve, ten, and six) had been brought there by their stepmother because their mother was dead and their father was "insane," or that some six weeks later a Russian tailor named Sam Kroll had arrived with his children

Annie, Herman, and Sarah (ages ten, seven, and five) because their mother was "insane and an inmate of Ward's Island." If he had spoken with his fellow orphan asylum inmate Mary Jacobowitz, who was born in 1892, is it likely that she mentioned that her mother had died in Bellevue Hospital because she "was insane & committed suicide"?[4] (Long Island State Hospital, Ward's Island, and Bellevue Hospital, were all public institutions.) It is possible that these children did not even know the true story that had brought them to the Hebrew Orphan Asylum. However, whether David, the oldest son, did not know that his father had died at River Crest Sanitarium, or whether he was complicit in hiding the shameful story, he would have been witness to the behavior that brought his father to River Crest, witness to the symptoms of whatever "mental and nervous diseases" had brought him to an institution for the care of the insane.

I have mentioned that "cardiac failure" is written on the death certificate as the direct cause of death. For a long time I had trouble reading the handwriting on the next line, the entry for "Indirect Cause of Death." The word "Exhaustion" was legible, but the other two words were difficult to decipher. Eventually, as I studied Dr. McCorn's handwriting and looked up different spellings, I realized that the full phrase was: "Exhaustion General Paresis." On the top of the form, where the doctor certifies "to the best of my knowledge and belief, the cause of his death was as hereunder written," McCorn writes: "Cardiac Failure in Exhaustion of General Paresis." Once I deciphered it, the name of this disease spoke volumes. "Paresis" was used as a sort of catchall term in popular discussions of insanity at the beginning of the twentieth century. Also called "general paresis of the insane," or "general paralysis of the insane," it was an increasingly specific clinical diagnosis of insanity in the late nineteenth and early twentieth centuries at a time when psychiatry was still undergoing professionalization as a medical practice and field of research. Paresis eventually referred to a now very rare form of neurosyphilis or infection of the brain caused by syphilis. It was a frequent and important topic in medical research and clinical accounts of insanity, but it was only at the turn of the century that syphilis was recognized as the cause of this deterioration of the brain, and the link was definitively established only in 1914.[5] The popular use of the term paresis did not necessarily imply a relation to a sexually transmitted disease.

Although alcohol and sexual dissipation were associated with paresis, and the condition was said to have "a syphilitic taint," so were urban life and excessive work; an 1890 newspaper article referred to paresis as "The Disease of Overwork."[6] Most common in men between the ages of twenty and forty, it could be dormant and unrecognized for fifteen or twenty years and occur in the absence of obvious syphilitic symptoms. The manifestations of paresis range from dementia and loss of memory and motor function to hallucinations, mood changes, mania, violence, and symptoms that today we would describe as psychotic. It was a form of insanity especially associated with delusions of grandeur and manic behavior. An 1895 article in the *New York Sun*, reporting on a recent study by Dr. Louis C. Pettit of Ward's Island, describes a typical progression from "mild mental deterioration with some confusion of ideas or apathy" to "a short period of depression, during which homicidal or suicidal tendencies develop," to "delirium of grandeur, the condition where the victim imagines himself some great person, or perhaps the Almighty."[7] A summary that appears in the 1901 *Twelfth Annual Report of the State Commission in Lunacy* notes that a paretic could "live seven or eight, or even ten years after the disease has become well marked." According to the report, "Paresis at first hyperstimulates the ambition; afterwards it seems to destroy it, and to render the victim unable to cope with the duties and responsibilities of ordinary life."[8] Based on the extensive medical literature at the time, including Dr. McCorn's own publications, we can imagine what symptoms led McCorn to diagnose "General Paresis" in Harris Warshawsky at the time of his death at the age of thirty-six.

On March 28, 1901, just six weeks after he signed Harris Warshawsky's death certificate, Dr. W. Alfred McCorn read a paper before the Brooklyn Society for Neurology on dementia and brain syphilis.[9] The paper was subsequently published as an article in the *Brooklyn Medical Journal* with the title, "The Clinical Differation of Brain Syphilis and

MEDICAL MEN MEET.

The regular meeting of the Brooklyn Society for Neurology was held last night in the building of the Medical Society of the County of Kings. The programme was an especially interesting one and included a paper on "Tetanus," by T. C. Fair, and another on "Paretic Dementia and Cerebral Syphillis," by W. Alfred McCorn.

"Medical Men Meet," *Brooklyn Daily Eagle*, March 29, 1901.

General Paresis," in February of 1902, one year after Harris Warshawsky's death. (In 1898, McCorn, then assistant physician at McLean, translated an article by Dr. Theodor Tiling on alcoholic paresis.)[10] By the time the *Brooklyn Medical Journal* article was published, McCorn was affiliated with Grand View Sanitarium in Connecticut, but the article opens with a brief case history based on McCorn's own clinical experience at River Crest Sanitarium.

McCorn begins: "On October 5, 1900, R.H. was admitted to River Crest. He was 37 years of age, single, salesman by occupation, born in Germany of healthy parentage, and came to this country thirteen years ago. He was a capable business man until about a week prior to his admission, when he seemed to lose his interest in affairs, complained of headache and insomnia, soon became incoherent and irrational in his statements with respect to time and place and appeared to be greatly confused and very stupid."[11]

McCorn goes on to describe the symptoms and treatment of the patient he calls "R.H." This thirty-seven-year-old successful businessman who immigrated in about 1887 has been seen by "three specialists" at River Crest, who declared the man to be "unquestionably a paretic," as well as by "another eminent neurologist of New York." The point of McCorn's paper is to distinguish the symptoms of "general paresis" from those of "brain syphilis," which are said to be often confused. McCorn constructs the narrative of his argument by presenting what he calls "clinical pictures," focusing on an extended profile of the symptoms and typical history of someone suffering from general paresis. McCorn traces the "typical course" of the disease and offers "a detailed description of the more common symptoms."

Drawing upon his clinical experience, as well as the medical literature, McCorn states that he believes that many patients who deny that they ever had symptoms of a venereal disease are sincere since these symptoms can be invisible and since in paresis "ten to fifteen and even more years may lapse since the infection before the disease may manifest

---

THE CLINICAL DIFFERATION OF BRAIN SYPH-ILIS AND GENERAL PARESIS.

BY W. A. M'CORN, M.D., GRAND VIEW SANITARIUM, WINDHAM, CONN.

Read befoae the Brooklyn Society for Neurology.

On October 5, 1900, R. H. was admitted to River Crest. He was 37 years of age, single, salesman by occupation, born in Germany of healthy parentage, and came to this country thirteen years ago. He was a capable business man until about a week prior to his admission, when he seemed to lose his interest in affairs, complained of headache and insomnia, soon became incoherent and irrational in his statements with respect to time and place and appeared to be greatly confused and very stupid.

"The Clinical Differation of Brain Syphilis and General Paresis," *Brooklyn Medical Journal*, 16.2 (February, 1902).

itself." He continues: "My own experience shows that a period of twelve to eighteen years to be most common." "Mental stress seems to be an essential factor in the generation of paresis," writes McCorn. He notes that "at one time the votaries at shrines of Venus and Bacchus were regarded as especially prone to paresis," yet he again cites "my experience" to state that, on the contrary, "paretics are hard workers instead of hard dissipators." The article then offers a case history of an individual that is really a composite portrait of a man suffering from general paresis, a series of "clinical pictures" that detail not just the symptoms of the condition but the common chronology of "progressive" symptoms, the narrative of the patient overtaken by the painful plot of paresis.

"The first manifestation of paresis usually recognized by the friends of the patient," begins McCorn, "is an outbreak of violence or extreme irritability, which renders their care of him at home extremely hazardous, if not impossible." Also common at this point is "his lavish expenditures for useless articles or in absurd quantities, for instance the purchase of ten bicycle suits, as was recently done by one of our patients just before his admission." McCorn suggests that "if the relatives are requested to hark back they will be able to call to mind little eccentricities in his conduct, trifling neglects in his manner of dress, the failure to keep appointments," and uncharacteristic behavior, such as bad table manners and "a multitude of other little indiscretions and breaches of good breeding." Headaches and "attacks of vertigo with periods of abstraction" are common, as well as depression and hypochondria. According to McCorn, this behavior "may be of only a few months' duration or extend over a year or so. But sooner or later the true character of the disease is manifested by the appearance of exaltation, delusions of absurd grandeur, hesitancy or slurring in speech, eye symptoms, violence, disorientation as to time and place and the characteristic physical symptoms."

Simultaneously offering character studies of both the disease and the typical patient, McCorn recounts a narrative in which the paretic patient can manifest "a gradual improvement in the general physical and mental conditions" during which he "gives up many of his absurdly grandiose ideas, becomes quiet and fat"; during this stage, "even to members of his own family he appears nearly well." Yet "careful examination is able to elicit however a weakness of memory, a blunted condition of all the former ethical and aesthetic feelings and the presence still of many, if not all, the physical signs. It is at this time or during the fatty state, so-called, by some, that the patient's relatives insist on removing him to his home, where ordinarily under the conditions of excitement attending his return, perhaps later being foolishly allowed to take up business again, he soon has an outbreak of excitement or does some absurd thing, which renders his return to the institution imperative."

McCorn notes that even in the "early stages" of the disease, "manifestations of pure frenzy" can be dangerous: "the patient is constantly in motion, talks continually and so rapidly that he has true flight of ideas and is therefore often incoherent in the expression of his extravagant ideas; his violence at this time is one of blind rage, strikes, bites and kicks at those who come near him, however kindly their intentions, destroys everything within reach, bangs and bruises himself unmercifully and may even inflict fatal injuries upon himself or die of heart failure in his struggles, and it is this condition of excitement which renders these patients the dreaded ones in institutions, for they are almost universally those in which death often ensues suddenly and thus bring blame upon the employees and officials of our hospitals for the insane, when in reality no fault should be attached to them." In other words, the patient could be in and out of institutions over a period of months or years as the neural degeneration progresses, or in the early stages of excitement, and then appear in an institution and suddenly die of heart failure.

In any case, according to McCorn, "Paretics as a rule have a marked euphoria from the onset of the disease, accompanied by absurdly extravagant delusions," which accompanies a "progressive mental enfeeblement, which is manifest in the earliest stages of the disease, when the finer feelings, the ethical ideas particularly, are blunted." There is a change in character: "The individual becomes careless in his deportment and does things which are noticed by his friends and those intimately acquainted with him to be foreign and unusual to his character and the man in general. The person, who has always been sedate and reserved, becomes somewhat frivolous, extravagant, uncouth in his manner and perhaps even licentious, the careful business man a reckless speculator, spendthrift and profligate. . . . His interest in his family and their welfare is early lost, so that he is irritable and fault-finding in his home and almost impossible to live with, even if he does not become actually violent." (In an article that McCorn translated in 1901, "The Physician's Duties in Committing Insane to the Hospital," Alfred Hoche describes how insane patients are "dangerous to the community," including "many cases of general paresis, in whom it consists chiefly in the patient squandering his property and ruining his family's reputation and standing.")[12]

Eventually, writes McCorn in his case study, the paretic's "judgment becomes so defective that he commits the most glaring violations of propriety and good breeding, if not of common decency, that he can no longer be tolerated at large, and this defect not alone concerns the ethical, but the intellectual functions as well, for instance patients well-to-do steal trifles, indecently expose their person on the street, etc."

In McCorn's clinical pictures and narratives of the progression of paresis, in his stories and scenarios of the paretic patient, we can read Harris Warshawsky's story. The diagnosis of "general paresis" that McCorn records for Harris Warshawsky on the death certificate may or may not be correct—perhaps today he would have been treated for schizophrenia or bipolar disorder—yet the diagnosis explains why he ended up at an institution for the care of the insane. It provides us with an inventory of symptoms that McCorn must have catalogued to reach his diagnosis; it reads as an anthology of vignettes that allow us to imagine the last chapters of the history of the life that ended with Dr. W. Alfred McCorn signing Harris Warshawsky's death certificate. The declaration of the cause of death sums up the story that led to Harris Warshawsky's arrival at that point, that endpoint, that place of death.

13

———❖———

The Case of H. W.

Let us call him "H. W." On February 11, 1901, H. W. is admitted to River Crest Sanitarium in Astoria, New York. He is thirty-six years of age, married, a contractor in the coat business by occupation, born in Russia of Hebrew parentage, and come to this country thirteen to fifteen years ago. In Dr. McCorn's experience, a period of twelve to eighteen years is most common between the infection and the manifestation of paresis. H. W. has been married for eleven years, having arrived in New York about three to five years before he was married; his wife is unaware of any prior syphilitic infection. Perhaps, like R. H., H. W. "was a capable business man until about a week prior to his admission," when he started to exhibit symptoms of paresis. Perhaps he was one of the patients that doctors dread, who appear at a hospital for the insane in a condition of excitement, become violent, and then "die of heart failure," leaving the institution's staff and officials to be blamed. McCorn attended H. W. from February 11 to February 14, before the patient died of "cardiac failure."[1]

It is more likely, however, that H. W. has exhibited disturbing symptoms for months, or even years, that this is not his first time in the hospital or sanitarium. A hard worker, not a hard dissipater, a victim of the disease of overwork, he becomes more and more manic; he exhibits manifestations of pure frenzy, delusions of absurd grandeur. He dresses like a millionaire. There is nothing beyond the scope of his possession or ability to accomplish. He moves his coat factory from Broome Street to Watkins Street where he can rent more space and get cheaper labor— why not a become a coat manufacturer?—in the burgeoning Brownsville garment district. He has recently moved his family from their Rivington Street apartment to a new, modern building on Norfolk Street, and now he wants to move them to Brooklyn. He invests in Brooklyn real estate. The careful businessman becomes a reckless speculator, spendthrift, and profligate. Soon he is squandering his property and ruining his family's reputation and standing. His death will leave them with benefit payments from his lodge, but also with debts. His wife's family will help, but within two years his wife will have to take in washing and then send her sons (ages eleven, ten, and seven) to the Hebrew Orphan Asylum.

Or worse: H. W. begins to lose his motor skills (in other words, his livelihood) and suffers more and more from headaches, blackouts, vertigo, periods of abstraction. After what is first seen as irritable and increasingly eccentric behavior, making him almost impossible to live with, he loses his interest in his family and their welfare; he becomes careless and dirty in his deportment, loses his sense of ethics and decorum, and then becomes violent: kicking, biting, and striking out in a blind rage. Dr. McCorn paints a distressing portrait: "He destroys his clothing, soils his bed and becomes extremely troublesome and rapidly emaciates, yet notwithstanding his staggering gait, the general incoordination of all muscular efforts and general debility, he possesses that euphoria so characteristic of the general paretic." His wife only recently has realized that she is pregnant. She already has five children under the age of eleven. She is appalled by his "absurdly extravagant grandeur" and "egotistical character" and sacrilegious delusions. As Dr. McCorn writes: "he not only has half a dozen wives, but fifty thousand; he is not only the possessor of millions, but of untold billions; he is not only the greatest personage that ever lived, but the Emperor, God, the Ruler of the universe, however abject his actual condition may be at the time."

H. W.'s wife locks the door to him, sends him away, flees with the children to her family. He ends up alone in Brooklyn, having alienated everyone, destitute, disowned, insane, sick. As the *New York Sun* reported in 1895, few paretics actually die of this disease: "They are carried off by exhaustion from maniacal excitement or frenzy or by malnutrition or by insomnia and by other current diseases."[2] The Society for the Aid of the Poor Sick, which, along with the Hebrew Educational Society, has recently established a presence in the Watkins Street neighborhood of Brownsville, tries to help. (Dr. McCorn is well known in Brooklyn medical circles and in the Medical Society of the County of Kings.) The association with both the Society for the Aid of the Poor Sick will add insult to injury as far as his family's reputation is concerned, but at first the family doesn't even know what has happened to him.

Or, perhaps H. W. is still in Manhattan, on the Lower East Side. He behaves erratically, making wild accusations against his wife, barely three months pregnant. She has not had a child in five years. Who is really the father, he demands. His behavior causes his in-laws and the neighbors to summon the police. He is taken from his home, or from his factory at 198 Broome Street, and brought to Bellevue Hospital, which is located on 26th Street between First Avenue and the East River. Recalling a coworker at their previous coat shop, H. W.'s father-in-law remembers the time just two years earlier when (as reported in the *New York American*) "Moses Sternam, a Russian tailor, of No. 84 Suffolk street, was taken from the 'L' station at One Hundred and Seventy-seventh street and Third avenue to Bellevue Hospital, violently insane."[3]

Bellevue Hospital is the Ellis Island of insane asylums in New York City: although it is legally possible for someone to be committed to what we would today call a psychiatric facility without first entering Bellevue, almost everyone enters here. A large inscription, "Pavilion for the Insane" is written on the outside of the building. Within a year, a new superintendent will remove this inscription, considering that it might unnecessarily disturb patients or their friends, and change the name to the "Psychopathic Pavilion," but H. W. must enter under the sign of madness.[4] H. W. is evaluated and, like chess champion William

Steinitz, who also suffers from paresis and was transferred from Bellevue to River Crest in 1900, and the actor Maurice Barrymore, another victim of paresis, who was transferred from Bellevue to River Crest Sanitarium in 1901,[5] he is sent to Dr. McCorn, who, in consultation with other specialists at River Crest and another eminent neurologist of New York, is engaged in a study of paretics. Within days, however, H. W. is dead, apparently from heart failure due to the exhaustion following the state of excitement so common in general paresis. No family members are present when Dr. McCorn fills out the death certificate.

14

—◆—

The Pavilion for the Insane

One way or another, wherever he lived, unless he voluntarily entered River Crest on his own, it is likely that Harris Warshawsky entered the Pavilion for the Insane at Bellevue Hospital, where the "alleged insane" were evaluated and processed before being sent to public or private facilities. The pavilion was at the cutting edge of public health care when it was opened on June 21, 1879. Between October 1, 1900, and October 1, 1901, 2,463 people (1,320 men and 1,153 women) passed through the Reception Pavilion for the Insane at Bellevue Hospital. A *New York Times* article published on March 8, 1896, reported that it was "overcrowded by double the number of patients for which it has accommodation." According to the October 1901 *Twenty-Ninth Annual Report of the New York Visiting Committee of the State Charities Aid Association for Bellevue Hospital and Other Public Institutions*: "All supposedly insane patients" are brought to the Pavilion for the Insane "for examination and observation before being sent to State or private institutions."

"Legally," the report notes, "the alleged insane are wards of the city until examined, adjudged insane and committed to a State or private institution. This procedure requires five days." The report adds that it was "not generally known that persons alleged to be insane may be examined at their homes" without passing through Bellevue.[1] The author of the report of the Manhattan State Hospital contained in the State Commission in Lunacy's 1901 annual report complains that despite the possibility that patients could be committed to the hospital directly from their homes, "not one single patient has been received in this way during the year covered by this report."[2]

Perhaps an examination leading to "lunacy papers" was not something a family wanted to share with neighbors, boarders, and extended family, or even with the physician hired by the fraternal lodge or benevo-

State of New York State Commission in Lunacy Twelfth Annual Report, 1901.

lent society in which they (and their friends, fellow congregants, or business associates) were members. In *Out of the Shadow*, Rose Cohen writes about her stay in a hospital: "It was not an easy thing for my people to send me to the hospital. For the very word filled us with fear. How could a helpless sick person be trusted to strangers! Besides, it was quite understood that in the hospital patients were praticed upon by hardened medical students and then neglected. Whenever we saw any one miserable, dirty, or neglected, we would say, 'He looks like a "hegdish" (hospital).' And so we saw our neighbors all about us borrow and pawn but keep their sick at home. And when once in a while we saw a person taken to the hospital we looked after him mournfully as if he were already carried to the burial grounds. It was also an open acknowledgement of the direst poverty."[3]

Obviously, a visit to a psychiatric hospital—that is to say, an insane asylum—would have been even more shameful, but it is likely that the character of the patient's illness and the manifestation of its symptoms would have been even more disturbing and embarrassing than a visit to a hospital, and finally too much for a family to treat at home. It is possible that, despite his background as a Russian immigrant tailor, Harris Warshawsky was successful enough to have both the resources and the social contacts to check in to the private River Crest Sanitarium on his own. It seems more likely, however, given his diagnosis, that he passed through Bellevue in the weeks or months preceding February 11, 1901, especially if his arrival at River Crest was precipitated by some violent or extreme behavior. Few patients entered Bellevue Hospital voluntarily.

February of 1901 would not have been a good time to pass through Bellevue's Pavilion for the Insane. The Visiting Committee, which in its 1900 report deplored the fact that the resident physician had not been replaced after his resignation, noted a year later: "Largely as a result of the public sentiment awakened by the abuses at the Pavilion for the Insane at Bellevue during the latter part of 1900," two physicians recently had been appointed and various reforms instituted.[4] In December of 1900, a Frenchman named Louis H. Hilliard died of asphyxiation after being admitted to the Pavilion for the Insane, and his death was witnessed by a newspaper reporter who was feigning insanity in order to investigate abusive conditions. On February 1, 1901, ten days before Harris Warshawsky died, the *New York Times*, which provided extensive coverage of the trial of the nurses prosecuted after the death, detailed the scathing report of a grand jury, which described "inexperienced and incompetent" attendants who had been appointed because of political connections, and facilities that included "Iron handcuffs, anklets, straitjackets, and other forms of mechanical restraint [that] are used to subdue the insane patients, although such appliances were long ago discarded, the jury says, by the majority of the other State asylums."[5]

A summary of the "gross abuses which characterized the management of Bellevue Hospital" in the *Medico-Legal Journal* in 1901 described the "unlimited and unrestricted use of mechanical restraint, that seems to have been in vogue in Bellevue" as "a disgrace to our civilization." It continued, "Out of 700 patients in Bellevue in 1900, 250 were wounded and bruised, and beaten by the attendants. The number killed cannot be reported."[6] The 1902 report of the Visiting Committee describes numerous reforms and improvements that were put in effect after the investigation and the trial, including the abolition of mechanical restraints "except when ordered by the medical officers."[7] If Harris Warshawsky entered Bellevue in January or February of 1901, he arrived exactly when this scandal was playing out in the newspapers.

Of the 2,473 people admitted to Bellevue between October 1, 1900, and October 1, 1901, most (1,453) were transferred to Manhattan State Hospital, Ward's Island. According to the discussion of the admission process in the 1901 *Twelfth Annual Report of the State Commission in Lunacy,* "Where the patient or his friends or relatives are in circumstances to meet the actual costs of his support and treatment—set by the authorities at $3.50 per week—they are expected to do so, and where their means are such as to permit of larger expenditure, the latter are expected and encouraged to send the patients to duly licensed private asylums, and thus save the State not alone the cost of maintenance, but undue over-crowding from inmates who can be elsewhere provided for."[8]

Presumably Harris Warshawsky fell into this category. A relatively small number of patients (eighty-nine) were transferred from Bellevue to other state hospitals. Only three private institutions are listed by name in the State Commission in Lunacy report: seventeen patients were transferred to the Long Island Home in Amityville; five patients were sent to the Bloomingdale Asylum in White Plains; thirty-two patients (twenty-five men and seven women) were sent to the River Crest Sanitarium.[9] Harris Warshawsky may have been among them.

I have speculated about Harris Warshawsky's ability to pay the $15 weekly minimum fee at this private sanitarium, which was considerably more than the $3.50 per week cost at Ward's Island expected from those who could afford it. The other two private hospitals to which Bellevue transferred patients, the Long Island Home and the Bloomingdale Asylum, each charged $10 a week, and the Bloomingdale Asylum of New York Hospital, according to the 1901 Commission in Lunacy report, "receives and treats, gratuitously, a small number of indigent insane, and receives a considerable number of acute and hopeful cases, which pay only part of their expenses."[10]

Perhaps the coat business was lucrative enough that Harris (or his family) could afford the best care, although it is difficult to conceive how his work as a contractor, and his entire firm, could continue making coats in his absence, given the ways in which the contracting business operated, and the central role that the contractor himself typically played in the production process. Ward's Island regularly had patients transferred to it from private facilities when they "ceased to be able to pay, or have paid for them, the costs of their support in private hospitals."[11] Perhaps the medical benefits provided by the Order of B'rith Abraham or some other mutual benefit association or a Minsk *landsmanshaftn* organization helped the family with these expenses. Perhaps there was a wealthy and well-connected relative who intervened.

However, the statistics in the report are surprising. River Crest may have taken the crème de la crème, the actors, doctors, society matrons, businessmen, and heirs who could afford the spa-like accommodations expected by the "first-class patients" that River Crest sought to reach in its advertisements. Yet, according to the reports, between October 1, 1900, and October 1, 1901, eighteen patients were transferred to River Crest, while only one was sent to Bloomingdale and only eight were sent to Long Island Hospital. (1,483 patients were transferred to the primary state facility, Ward's Island.) Bloomingdale had a capacity of 330 patients and Long Island had a capacity of 114 patients, while River Crest had a capacity of only sixty-seven patients. Between October 1, 1899, and October 1, 1900, fifty patients were transferred to River Crest, compared to twenty-six to Bloomingdale and eighteen to Long Island. The 1890 brochure for River Crest describes a brick building "planned and arranged for the scientific treatment and care of mental cases," noting that "Three distinct classifications of patients are strictly maintained in this building." Perhaps River Crest had second- and third-class patients as well as first-class patients.

I puzzled over these numbers for a long time as I tried to figure out how Harris Warshawsky ended up at River Crest Sanitarium, and then I found an article in the New York newspaper, *Daily People*, published on December 28, 1900 (about six weeks before Harris Warshawsky was treated at River Crest), with the headline, "Further Revelations of the Workings of the Bellevue Insanity Trust." The subtitle reads: "River Crest Sanitarium Received Nineteen More Patients From Bellevue Than All the Other Sanitariums Put Together." The article addresses the allegation (indeed it alleges) that "the examiners in lunacy" at Bellevue were "'railroading' patients to River Crest Asylum" since "last year more 'able to pay' insanity patients from Bellevue Hospital" were sent there than were sent to "all the rest of the private asylums near the city together." Dr. Kindred, the proprietor of River Crest, is revealed to have "formerly occupied an office with Dr. Allen Fitch, the chief examiner of insane patients at Bellevue," and it is suggested that through this connection he has "established a virtual monopoly in the care of the private insane." (The article notes in particular Kindred's "home for inebriates" and the "many well-to-do inebriates, who are willing to pay almost any sum to escape from the hospital" at Bellevue.)

This was the period in which private physicians were paid a fee to examine patients who were transferred from the Bellevue Pavilion of the Insane to private institutions—a practice that was ended after the Hilliard case and the other scandals at the end of 1900 and the beginning of 1901.[12] Dr. Kindred insisted that his relations with Bellevue were "entirely proper" and that "no physician attached thereto has any interest, financial or otherwise, in my hospital."[13]

Whether or not there were conflicts of interest in patient transfers, I cannot say. River Crest does seem to have had some sort of institutional relationship with Bellevue, but I believe that the key figure here would have been Dr. McCorn. As the resident physician at River Crest, McCorn would have had professional colleagues and contacts at Bellevue. He had been a Medical Officer at Manhattan State Hospital, the New York City Asylum for the Insane, as early as 1888. In 1900, after having been associated with numerous prominent public and pri-

FURTHER REVELATIONS

OF THE WORKINGS OF THE BELLEVUE INSANITY TRUST.

River Crest Sanitarium Received Nineteen More Patients From Bellevue Than All the Other Sanitariums Put Together. Mrs. Johnson's Experience.

"Further Revelations of the Workings of the Bellevue Insanity Trust," *Daily People*, December 28, 1900.

vate institutions, this "alienist and neurologist of promise, perseverance and ability," this "observer of high rank," was engaged in some sort of research project on the symptoms of general paresis, based on his own clinical experience, apparently in consultation with specialists and an "eminent neurologist of New York."

It is possible that Harris Warshawsky or his family had the connections as well as the financial means to get him to River Crest Sanitarium, but I imagine that in February of 1901, and in the months before that, Dr. McCorn let it be known to the staff at Bellevue (and perhaps other institutions) that he was interested in patients with certain symptoms because he was conducting a study of brain syphilis and general paresis. Perhaps McCorn himself served as one of the private examiners who helped process patients at Bellevue. He would have been doing both the Jewish tailor from Russia and himself a favor by arranging for his transfer to River Crest to be part of what was in effect a sort of clinical study.

We cannot know for certain, of course, whether Harris Warshawsky contributed to the composite portrait of a man suffering from general paresis that Dr. McCorn outlined in his article, or whether any of Harris's symptoms were represented in the series of "clinical pictures" that Dr. McCorn drew from his clinical experience. As I have suggested, we cannot know whether Dr. McCorn diagnosed Harris Warshawsky's symptoms correctly; perhaps today he would have been treated for some recognizable form of bipolar disorder or schizophrenia or psychosis. We can conclude, I believe, that whatever physical symptoms or psychological behaviors Harris Warshawsky exhibited, they were consistent with what Dr. McCorn called "general paresis." We may infer from the diagnosis the behavior and symptoms that led to the diagnosis. The family would not have seen the death certificate. They probably never met Dr. McCorn. They may have been unaware of the specific medical diagnosis or its implications. They probably didn't know what "general paresis" meant. If they did, it is not clear that they would have been aware of the then still-debated neurosyphilitic origins of the disease or understood that there was a "syphilitic taint" associated with the disease. What would have been all too clear was the insanity itself. What would have brought shame and left a sense of stigma was the behavior that was character-ized as insane, the actions that would have led to a diagnosis of general paresis and residence in an asylum for the insane.

We cannot know whether Harris Warshawsky was in and out of institutions for months or years, in cycles of improvement and relapse; whether his behavior was limited to rude and uncharacteristic behavior or full-blown manifestations of mania and violence; whether he made a fortune in a manic period of overwork, or whether he ruined his family finances, perhaps by opening a shop or factory on the new frontier of Watkins Street; or whether it was just one incident of shocking behavior that caused him to be committed to River Crest, or a succession of dis-turbing events. Whether he was there for some time before his final days when Dr. McCorn attended him in his capacity as resident physician, or whether, to the dismay of the doctor who knew he would be blamed, Harris's excitement and exhaustion caused him to die of cardiac failure just four days after his arrival, we cannot know. Whatever the special circumstances of the case, whether the culmination of a traumatizing series of events at home or at work, or merely sudden and uncharacter-istic behavior, whether his actions were violent or merely embarrassing, this would not make a good family story. It would be better to tell the children that their father had collapsed after a heart attack on the floor of his factory, and hope that they would forget the circumstances leading up to his death. According to Harris Warshawsky's granddaughter Adele, who heard many stories from her mother Millie and her grandmother Lena, they did not like to talk about him.

The Place of Burial

Machpelah

The blanks on the death certificate suggest that no family member was present at Harris Warshawsky's death to provide the names of his mother and father, or to count the years it had been since he left Russia, and the years he had resided in the United States and in New York City. Of course, if his family knew he was at River Crest, they might not have expected his stay to be so brief; nor would he have been sent there if his death had been expected. Perhaps he was that dreaded patient to whom Dr. McCorn alludes in his article, the paretic who dies suddenly of heart failure in his struggles and brings "blame upon the employees and officials of our hospitals for the insane, when in reality no fault should be attached to them."

How did the Warshawsky family learn of his death? Who retrieved the body? Who sat with the body? Harris died at 3:00 P.M. on February 14, 1901, which was a Thursday. The family probably couldn't have heard the news before Friday. Although, according to Jewish law, burial is supposed to take place within twenty-four hours, they wouldn't have been able to bury him by Friday afternoon, and burials were not allowed on the Sabbath. Harris Warshawsky would have had to be buried on Sunday, February 17; this is the date listed next to "date of burial" on the death certificate.

Next to "Place of Burial" on the death certificate is the name "Machpelah," which is the name of a cemetery in the large territory of adjoining and overlapping cemeteries in what is today the Ridgewood area of Queens. Machpelah Cemetery is best known today as the location of Harry Houdini's grave. Houdini was buried there in 1926 after an overeager fan punched him in the stomach and ruptured his appendix; visitors gather at his grave on Halloween looking for ghosts. Machpelah is a popular name for Jewish cemeteries. The name evokes the tomb of the patriarchs, the double tomb in the burial cave purchased by Abraham: the burial place of Abraham, Isaac, Jacob, Sarah, Rebecca, and Leah. All the patriarchs and matriarchs were said to have been buried there, except for Rachel, who died in childbirth.

The Book of Genesis tells us that Abraham bought the burial cave from Ephron after Sarah died so he could bury his wife. When Jacob dies in Egypt at the end of Genesis, he instructs Joseph: "I am to be gathered unto my people: bury me with my fathers in the cave that is in the field of Ephron the Hittite." He continues, "In this burying place, they buried Abraham and Sarah his wife; there they buried Isaac and Rebecca his wife; and there I buried Leah." Joseph gets permission from the pharaoh to return his father to the cave of Machpelah. When Joseph dies, he is embalmed and buried in Egypt, yet he commands his brethren to "carry up my bones" when God comes to "bring you out of this land unto the land which he sware to Abraham, to Isaac, and to Jacob." According to the Book of Exodus, when Moses led the Hebrews out of Egypt, he "took the bones of Joseph with him." After Joshua dies, the bones of Joseph are buried "in a parcel of ground which Jacob bought."[1] The name Machpelah, which etymologically points to the Hebrew word for double, evokes the alpha and omega of genealogy, the ultimate end-point that embodies all origins. The lost grave of the mother and father represents the end of the line, the primal scene of death.

Machpelah Cemetery is described in late-nineteenth- and early-twentieth-century directories and guidebooks as a Hebrew cemetery adjoining Cypress Hills Cemetery, as well as other cemeteries. An essay titled "Our Hebrew Cemeteries" published in the *Brooklyn Daily Eagle* in

1886 includes "the Union Field, the new Union Field, the Machpelah, the Maimonides, the Mount Hope," as well as cemeteries owned by New York City synagogues and "private cemeteries" among "the Jewish cemeteries around the Cypress Hills." In 1901, 209 people were interred in Machpelah Cemetery. There were 128 interments in New Union Fields Cemetery and 132 in Mt. Neboh Cemetery, both of which then adjoined Cypress Hills, where there were 104 interments.[2] According to the *American Jewish Yearbook* of 1899–1900, Machpelah had "83 component societies and 160 lot-owners; the whole cemetery contains about 1,400 family lots."

Aside from social reasons, death and funeral benefits that would ensure members a proper Jewish burial among Jews were among the main reasons that people joined *landsmanshaftn*, lodges, or mutual aid societies. According to the author of "Our Hebrew Cemeteries," "as a rule the Jews are as desirous as the Roman Catholics to sleep in ground consecrated to their own religious faith, and they are far more anxious than any other denomination to preserve in death the relations of consanguinity and family relationship."[3] The historian Daniel Soyer writes: "To ensure that the dead remained part of the community, landsmanshaftn maintained their own cemeteries. The societies bought lots from the commercially maintained Jewish cemeteries in the New York area, and allocated the graves as needed to their members."[4] With gated entryways marking distinct cemetery sectors that formed small neighborhoods, these societies often reunited landsmen with fellow immigrants and exiles from their home town after their death, demarcating a literal and symbolic common ground, a return to origins. Other societies simply guaranteed a grave and proper burial. Death benefits would include not only burial expenses and a cemetery plot but also the transportation of the body to the cemetery according to traditional funereal practices.

The temperature in New York City on Sunday, February 17, 1901, was between 28 and 37 degrees Fahrenheit, with brisk winds.[5] If Harris Warshawsky was returned by Joseph Wiener of Rivington Street to his family's home on the Lower East Side sometime between the Thursday that he died and the Sunday he was buried, David might have watched, that Sunday, like the young David in Henry Roth's *Call it Sleep*, a "line of black carriages" on the street in front of the house, one "square and black with windows in its sides" and "black plumes on the horses." He might have seen the drivers standing in the street by the horse-drawn carriages, "a small group of men, all dressed alike in long black coats and tall hats." He might have watched as "the doors in back of the strange carriage were thrown open. Inside the gloomy interior metal glimmered, tasseled curtains shut out the light." He might have seen four men labor to place "a huge black box" into the carriage as a "soft moan came from the crowd."[6]

Tradition required the funeral procession to take a circuitous route and make stops along the way for reflection, but there was no way to avoid a long and complicated journey from the Lower East Side. Some lodges required members to accompany the funeral procession as far as the "ferry or bridge."[7] According to the 1900 *Brooklyn Daily Eagle Almanac*, Machpelah Cemetery and the neighboring cemeteries on Cypress Hills Street could be "reached by Brooklyn Elevated Railroad, by Jamaica and Brooklyn electric line from all ferries and bridges," but this would have been difficult for a funeral procession. The Williamsburg Bridge, entered from Delancey Street, several blocks from 151 Norfolk Street, was still being constructed in February of 1901. The 1903 *Manhattan Guide Greater New York Red Book* recommended getting to the Cypress Hills Street cemeteries by the Grand, Roosevelt, or Fulton ferries.

According to Jewish law, the five Warshawsky children were too young to be mourners and sit *shiva*, so they probably were spared the cold trip to the cemetery. David, the oldest son, was not yet ten years old. Did the Ruderman family accompany Lena, who was then about two months pregnant? Who said the Mourner's Kaddish for David's father at the funeral, and in the synagogue for the next eleven months, as custom required? Was Jack Warshafsky or Samuel Warshafsky still alive and living in New York? Or did Harris Warshawsky burn his bridges when he crossed the East River to go to either 88 Watkins Street or the River Crest Sanitarium? Did his body lie at River Crest unattended until he could be buried? My father was never brought by his father to visit the grave of the grandfather he never knew. If he had been there, he would have remembered, unless he had been a very young child at the time. Did his father (my grandfather) ever visit the cemetery where his father was buried? Did my grandfather (either as David Warshawsky or as David Marshall), the grandson of David Warshafsky, read the name of his father chiseled on a headstone? For most of his life, after leaving the Hebrew Orphan Asylum, my grandfather lived in Brooklyn within five miles of the cemeteries on Cypress Hills Street. Did he know where his father was buried?

I was never taken to see my grandfather's grave. The first time I remember seeing it is when we went to a small Marshall family plot in Mount Lebanon Cemetery on Long Island for the funeral of my uncle, Harris Warshawsky's grandson Stephen. I was twenty-nine years old. I remember being taken aback to see the name "David Marshall" inscribed on the headstone. Like Wordsworth facing "the view/ Of a blind Beggar" with "a written paper, to explain/ The story of the Man and who he was . . . I look'd/ As if admonish'd from another world."[8] I picture Lena standing there in January of 1952, standing before the grave of her oldest son, her mind returning to another trip to a Long Island cemetery after her husband died half a century earlier. How could she not have thought about the death of her husband at the funeral of her son?

My father, Harris Warshawsky's grandson Arthur, was cremated. At times this undertaking has felt like an act of filial piety, an effort to return my father's ashes to the tomb of the patriarchs, the grave at Machpelah. Finding Harris Warshawsky's place of burial was no easier than finding his name. Although the name "Machpelah" is recorded on his death certificate as the place of burial, it was difficult to confirm this and to locate his grave. Like the last known residence, 88 Watkins Street, it seemed another dead end. Some of the cemeteries in the cities of the dead that spread across Long Island, Queens, and Brooklyn now have online, searchable databases that demarcate virtual plots in cyberspace, but it is difficult to find records for cemeteries that were all but abandoned, and even more difficult to find records for burial societies, *landsmanshaftn*, or synagogues that disappeared years ago, long after they had purchased plots at the turn of the last century.

I scrolled through reels of microfilm and carefully unfolded hand-written cemetery maps in the Center for Jewish History; many of the records are in Yiddish, which I cannot read. In the course of a century, some cemeteries changed borders, changed names, incorporated other cemeteries. Others went bankrupt. There is a website filled with hundreds of angry exchanges about Jewish cemeteries in this area that have been subjected to neglect and worse: vandalism and desecration, grave robbers in search of brass, satanists in search of skulls. One reads of bitter lawsuits and defensive rabbis. Some years ago, a *New York Times* article reporting on the annual vigil for Houdini's ghost described Machpelah Cemetery as "utterly deserted and forgotten" with grave sites "overgrown" and headstones "in disrepair or toppled or covered in ivy."[9]

Machpelah is one of the cemeteries that went into receivership after years of neglect. The current owner, who manages several cemeteries, has offices on lower Broadway in New York. The woman who answers the phone is sometimes sympathetic, as if one were calling about a relative who had recently died, and sometimes the Cerebus figure who blocks the gates of the underworld to those who might discover that the grave of a great-grandfather has fallen into disrepair. It took three phone calls before I was able to engage her in my story. She speculated about a possible match based on the date of burial; complaining about the parchment-thin paper of an almost illegible map that she had claimed, moments before, did not exist, she gave me a location, B-35, and gave me directions from Houdini's grave. The plot was associated with a synagogue, B'nai Adam, which I discovered in an 1896 directory of charitable organizations to have been located on Norfolk Street. I was hopeful.

On a dark Friday morning in November, I descended underground to take the A train from lower Manhattan to Euclid Avenue in Brooklyn. Going under the East River, passing stations in Brooklyn where I imagined my grandfather and father once stood waiting, I recalled a *New York Times* article about an abandoned Brooklyn subway station that had been closed for years. The photographs revealed not a ruin but rather

Machpelah Cemetery.

Machpelah Cemetery.

Machpelah Cemetery.

a perfectly preserved tomb of the pharaohs: as if suddenly discovered, brightly colored paint and jewels glimmer in the torchlight. As I waited for the B-13 bus at Euclid Avenue, children arrived at P.S. 159 Isaac Pitkin, a large elementary school with an imposing staircase in a neighborhood where the melting pot had recently been stirred. A restaurant window advertised a menu of Canadian fried chicken, curry, and pizza.

Several cemeteries wind up the hill of Cypress Hills Street, some with large gates and domed temples, some with more modest gatehouses designed to receive those who came to bury or visit the dead. Machpelah Cemetery has no attendant on the premises, and the main gates are locked.

Machpelah Cemetery.

I slip in next to a small two-story building, erected in 1928; now empty, the windows are boarded up. I am the only mourner, if I am a mourner, on the sloping picturesque grounds. A groundskeeper cleans up branches from a wild storm that recently swept through New York and tore down trees. He cuts the branches and assembles bundles of sticks to carry away. Some gravestones and monuments are toppled, like children's blocks built too high, the sprawl of stone and statue a gesture of the structure that once stood there. Small slabs sit isolated. One lies flat on the ground; I clear away the grass growing over its edges to feel the Hebrew letters, as if they were Braille. Some Marshalls are buried in a special parklike section

Machpelah Cemetery.

with the Strauss family, the patrons of the cemetery when the reception house was built. If we have a family plot, it lies elsewhere.

On one small monument, which leans sideways like the tombstones in the Jewish cemetery of Prague, is a reclining figure of a young girl at rest, as if quietly reading on her bed; her head leans on her arm on a pillow as she lies on her side. Time has worn down clarity, blurred the sculptor's edges, giving the figure an almost juvenile look, as if the girl herself had made the figure in clay: a self-portrait, affecting and precocious but not yet refined. It reminds me of Pompeii, the figures frozen in time by lava and ash; but here there is an almost lazy tranquility, not a grimace of pain. The inscription, written on tablets, is also worn away, illegible, like so many of the smooth slates remaining: Hebrew or English letters worn down to a suggestion; or wiped clean, like a page of writing that has been erased until only a blank sheet remains.

Houdini's monument has a strangely affecting sculpture of a woman, a mourner kneeling on the steps next to the double inscription of Houdini and Weiss. Weiss was his real name, the name of his father, a rabbi. Leaning on a benchlike ledge with one hand on her forehead, in grief or in shock, her bare shoulder is exposed as a neglected strap, in a trope of classical drapery, slips in a sign of grief. Every Halloween people come here to see if Houdini's ghost will make an appearance. Buried in the coffin he used in his act, he has not escaped. His wife, not allowed a grave in Machpelah because she was not Jewish, eventually gave up waiting for his spirit. Harris Warshawsky is nowhere to be found. Taking the subway back to Manhattan, I think of Orpheus: too much looking back can leave you empty-handed on your return.

16

———◆◈◆———

Saying Kaddish for a Ghost

So I picture him standing there on May 30, 1906: David Roshofsky, alias David Warshawsky, son of Harris Warshawsky or Aaron Warshawsky, grandson of David Warshafsky, receiving the Bible that will name him David Marshall. Imagining the Shabuoth ceremony in the magnificent Hebrew Orphan Asylum synagogue, celebrating the delivery of the tablets to Moses in the consecration of Israel's youth to the faith of their fathers, I think about Kaddish, the mourner's prayer that is included in all Jewish services. Kaddish (a prayer in Aramaic that dates from the Middle Ages) is supposed to be said three times daily for a deceased parent in the eleven-month period of mourning following the death, and on the *yarhzeit* or anniversary of the death. Most of the children who were inmates of the Hebrew Orphan Asylum would not have been expected to recite this prayer of mourning, even on the *yarhzeit* of a mother's or father's death. The ritual of Kaddish traditionally was restricted to boys, and only after their bar mitzvah. How many orphans, most of whom had been admitted at a very young age, even knew the date on which their parents had died?

Yet the mourner's prayer—sometimes called the "Orphan's Kaddish"—must have resonated in a synagogue with a thousand orphans.

The Mourner's Kaddish does not name death or the dead; not a prayer *for* the dead, it praises the name of God and calls for resignation. In contemporary services, the mourners in the assembly are called upon to say aloud the name of the dead for whom they mourn. As Kaddish was recited in the weekly services at the Hebrew Orphan Asylum, perhaps most of the children stood silently, yet wouldn't each child recall the name of the dead—or recall that the name of their dead was unknown to them? Would David, at this moment, newly called to the Torah as David ben Ahron, David son of Aaron, have been called upon to say the name of his father? Called as the son of his father, named as the son of his father, hearing his father's name, he would have been called upon to think about his father, to think the name of his father.

In the Jewish tradition (as described in the 1906 *Jewish Encyclopedia*), the son is required to say Kaddish to redeem the soul of the dead parent: "a son or grandson's piety may exert a redeeming influence in behalf of a departed father or grandfather."[1] According to legend, as recounted in a religious manual of 1898, the great sage Rabbi Akiva rescued from the Hell-like fires of Gehenna an evil man whose spirit he met in a grave-yard carrying a heavy load of branches. Responding to the rabbi's offer of help, the ghost lamented that "there was no help for him, unless, as he heard, something should happen that was clearly impossible, namely, that a son of his would give out 'Bless ye' in the Synagogue, and the people would respond." Rabbi Akiva sought out the man's widow and discovered "a posthumous son uncircumcised and wholly untaught." He circumcised him and forcibly taught him to read the Torah until finally the son stood before the assembly and "recited the Bareku and the Kaddish and released his father" from his tortures.[2] Later rabbis worried that focusing on the sins of the deceased father three times daily for an entire year was unseemly; they reduced the mandated period of mourning in which the son said Kaddish from twelve to eleven months because "it was considered unworthy of the son to entertain such views of the demerit of his parents."[3] If the son was called upon to redeem his father's soul, he should not spend so much time remembering why his father needed redemption.

In thinking of his father, perhaps David remembered him saying Kaddish in synagogue, on Yom Kippur or perhaps on the *yarhzeit* of David's grandfather's death when Ahron ben David, father of David ben Ahron, said the name David, the name of *his* father. Surely in his confirmation training David would have learned about the responsibility of the son to honor his father by standing before the assembly, to redeem the soul of his father by reciting Kaddish. He would not have been able to do this before; he was nine years old when his father died. What would David have thought about his father at this moment in 1906, as he was called upon to recall his father's name? It was five years and three months since his father had died, in a death that might have been the culmination of a trauma, and perhaps the beginning of a trauma. Leon Wieseltier writes: "*Bera mezakeh aba.* The son acquits the father. Or, the son vindicates the father. Or, the son vouches for the father. Or, the son shows merit in the father. This is the principle on which the mourner's kaddish is founded."[4] As he thought about his father's death, about the events leading up to his death, would David have felt called upon to acquit him, to finally enable his release, his respite, his repose?

I mentioned that the names Aaron and Harris are echoed in the names and middle initials of Harris Warshawsky's children (Harry, David Henry, Daisy H., Reuben Harold) and grandchildren (Harold, Arnold, Arthur, Adele). I noted that the Hebrew name of my father, Arthur, was Ahron or Aaron. My father signed his name Arthur K. Marshall; the *K* stood for Kay, the middle name that is listed on his birth certificate. This puzzled and amused me when I was young, since *K* seemed to be an initial that stood for itself, or nothing. As a child, I imagined that my grandmother had been influenced by the tales of the Knights of the Round Table, since King Arthur's brother was Sir Kay. Years into my research and my search for the name of my great-grandfather, my sister Cindy reminded me that my father said that his Hebrew name was Aaron Kaddish. I must have known this and forgotten. I was astounded. Knowing now that the *K* in Arthur K. Marshall stood for Kaddish, not for nothing, I saw another story. I had imagined what my grandfather felt on February 25, 1924, just eleven days after the twenty-third *yahrzeit* of his father's death, as his first child and first son was named Aaron after his late father, just as he, also a first son, had been named David after his father's late father. Now I tried to imagine what it meant that the Hebrew name Aaron Kaddish was hidden behind Arthur Kay. Naming a child Kaddish (it often was given as a first name, even in English) is presumably a custom that derives from the idea that the son *is* the Kaddish. It was not uncommon for a father to sometimes call his son, "my Kaddish." The son represents Kaddish, embodies Kaddish, stands for the possibility of Kaddish: the one who will recite Kaddish for his father and redeem his soul.

I later discovered that on the marriage certificate of my grandmother Jeanette's parents, the name of her paternal grandfather is recorded as "Kadesh Levitt." Arthur was named for his father's father and his mother's grandfather in a dutiful, double homage to lost fathers. By all accounts, David H. Marshall was not a religious man. Despite the religious training he received at the Hebrew Orphan Asylum, he was, according to my mother, an atheist. Yet in fulfilling his filial duty by naming his son after his dead father, in identifying his son as Aaron Kaddish, how could my grandfather not think about Kaddish? Would not the name have resonated as he thought about sons and fathers, and fathers and sons? He was thirty-three years old; his father had died at the age of thirty-six. Did he think of himself, anticipating a death that one day would call upon his son to say his name, to stand and recite Kaddish? Or, in recalling his forgotten father's name in his son's name, in naming his father's death in his son's name, in invoking, pronouncing, or at least *hearing* Kaddish in his son's name, was he completing a long-deferred act? Did this naming atone for an unfulfilled obligation? Did his father require more redemption? Whose Kaddish was Aaron Kaddish? Would Aaron Kaddish—the great-grandson, grandson, and son—acquit Aaron, his unknown grandfather, Kadesh, his unknown great-grandfather, and, one day, David, his father?

In some versions of the story of Rabbi Akiva, it turns out that the name of the ghost in the graveyard seemingly doomed to perpetual punishment is Akiva, a strange doubling that suggests the stakes in the identification of mourning. In another version, when Rabbi Akiva asks the spirit for his name, he replies: "I do not know, because the guilty of Gehenna do not remember their names. . . . I am a guilty Jew, and the wardens of Gehenna will not tell me my name."[5] Part of the punishment is to have his name forgotten. Redeeming the father from Gehenna would require recalling his name. My grandfather, David ben Aaron, recalled his father, Aaron ben David, by naming his son Aaron ben David. Yet in this act of naming, both the naming of Aaron Kaddish and the naming of Arthur K. Marshall, did David H. Marshall recall the moment that he gave up the name of his father and grandfather?

Standing there on May 30, 1906, looking ahead, does David Warshawsky know that he will be discharged from the Hebrew Orphan Asylum on September 9, leaving his brothers behind, three years and six months after being committed there? Visiting days took place on the first Sunday of January, April, July, and October, so the last time he could have seen his mother would have been April 1, 1906, two months earlier. He knows that when he leaves he won't be returning to Suffolk Street or the Lower East Side, the scene of struggle for his twenty-nine-year-old mother, a working widow with six young children, including a baby born with "no father," in the two years after his father's death. Looking back, he would remember the painful events that led to his father's demise and death, and the difficult aftermath: moving apartments, the birth of his brother Harry, the failure of the milk and grocery stores, his mother forced to take in "washing, etc.," her inability to provide or care for the six children, the move from a crowded tenement apartment to an institution with a thousand other inmates, where, when he first arrived, children lost their names and were assigned numbers. As the Bible bearing the words "David Marshall" is delivered to him on Shabuoth, I imagine that he is ready to leave the story of his father behind.

Soon after he is discharged on September 9, 1906, the New Year will be observed. On Rosh Hashanah, on September 20, 1906, he will attend services with his family in Brooklyn. The congregants will recite the lines of the service asking God to inscribe their names in the book of life: "write us down in the book of life . . ." and "O write down for a happy life all the sons of thy covenant" and "May we be remembered and written in the book of life." Yom Kippur, the Day of Atonement, will be on September 29, 1906. In the last service, those assembled will say: "seal us in the book of life" and "may we be remembered and sealed."[6] On Shabuoth, May 30, with his new name inscribed in and on his Bible, he is ready to leave the name of his father, the name of his grandfather, behind: to look forward. He wants to be released. He wants his period of mourning to be over.

17

———◆———

Picturing a Future

As he left the orphanage on September 9, 1906, I imagine that it felt like a liberation. We know that even during these years of moderate reform and liberalization, discipline at the Hebrew Orphan Asylum was militaristic and family visits were strictly limited. David's brothers would remain until 1910, when (according to the 1910 U.S. census) Isadore was fourteen and Ruby was seventeen. Ruby was on the "free list" on January 1, 1909, when (according to HOA records) he turned sixteen and was no longer eligible for state or city support. Did Ruby stay for so long to watch out for Isadore? Why did David leave in September of 1906, at least a year before (according to one record) his commitment to the orphanage expired?[1] In this period at the Hebrew Orphan Asylum, there was an effort to relocate children with their families and even provide subsidies to help support them. Did David feel called upon, or did he feel obligated, to go to work and help support his family? The age at which minors could obtain working papers had risen from twelve to fourteen in 1903.[2] In September of 1906, David was one month away from his fifteenth birthday, as measured by the October 4, 1891, birthdate on his birth certificate—but one month away from his fourteenth birthday as measured by the October 5, 1892, birthdate he always listed as an adult. Did Lena and the Ruderman family decide that it was time for David to come home so he could supplement the family income? Or did he plead with his mother on visiting day: "*You* went to work when you were fourteen . . . *you* came to America from Russia without your family . . . *you* worked in a shop so you could send your family money. . . ." Or did he not know his mother's story? David was the eldest son; did he feel, in 1901, when his father died, that he became the "man of the house" at the age of nine? After leaving the orphanage, he would live with his mother until he married at the age of thirty-one.

Yet had he stayed behind, he would have attended high school, or received further vocational or professional training, like many of the inmates, including his brothers. My father recalled that after leaving the orphanage his father had "finished a program at high school." My parents and grandmother described my grandfather as very well spoken and as someone who valued education and intelligence. His typewritten letters to my father during World War II are well written and self-assured. My father, describing his father as "worldly and knowledgeable about a lot of other things," said that he "had a lot of education" but "a lot of it was [his] own self-worth," by which he meant, I assume, that his education and confidence came from autodidactic self-improvement.[3]

Education and vocational training were central tenets of the Hebrew Orphan Asylum philosophy. Children followed a rigorous course of studies in the institution's own elementary school, which was an official New York City public school, and then (around the sixth or seventh grade) attended public schools in the neighborhood, and sometimes high schools and vocational schools in New York City. (In 1903, nine hundred children attended public schools: 150 in Public School No. 43 and 750 in the asylum's home school, which was known as Public School No. 192. In 1906, 115 boys attended P.S. 5 and sixty-two girls attended P.S. 43.)[4] There was (according to the HOA annual reports) a good and well-used library.

The annual reports in this decade always included a photograph of well-dressed boys reading studiously in the "reading room." A library catalogue printed in 1878 and a supplement printed in 1881 list a wide variety of classics. In the annual report of 1905, Superintendent Coffee proudly reported a "very important" gift from Judge Newburger of a "collection of 800 works from the Progress Library." The *Chronicle of the Hebrew Orphan Asylum Published by the Literary Society of the Institution*, a short-lived literary magazine produced by the children, announced this gift in its 1904 issue, noting that the collection included "works of the greatest of the modern masters" and "translations from the masterpieces of the different European writers."[5] In 1917, a report following an inspection by the New York City Department of Public Charities stated: "It may be said here that the library of the institution, splendidly equipped and furnished, is patronized liberally by the children." Annual reports listed regular contributions (in books and funds) to the library. In 1906, the asylum contracted with the New York City Board of Education to offer a course of ten lectures on subjects that

"Reading Room," *Eighty-Third Report of the Hebrew Orphan Asylum of the City of New York*, 1906. Courtesy of the Collection of the American Jewish Historical Society.

included "Life in the Philippines," "A Talk on the Government of the United States," "Life Among the Esquimeaux," "Benjamin Franklin," and "Real Success in Life."

Students were placed in trade and technical schools, and the asylum offered its own courses in stenography, typewriting, bookkeeping, and the promising field of telegraphy. There was also "manual training" in woodworking and other trades. In another 1904 issue of *The Chronicle of the Hebrew Orphan Asylum*, an article entitled "Our Business School" describes training in typewriting, stenography, and bookkeeping, including "methods of keeping business books, as for example, the call book, journal, ledger, etc." I imagine that David Roshafsky, alias David Warshawsky, was among the thirty-six boys and girls who attended business class on Sunday mornings between 8:30 and 10:30.[6] In 1904, *The Menorah: A Monthly Magazine for the Jewish Home* printed a report on the National Conference of Jewish Charities in which Superintendent Coffee made a presentation entitled "What Becomes of Our Graduates." According to the article, "The majority of the graduates entered business life either as clerks, salesmen and salesladies or some of them were even proprietors of their businesses. Thirty per cent of the graduates were either electricians, plumbers, stenographers or engineers. Five were ministers, four physicians, seven lawyers and eleven public school teachers. The present graduates were particularly attracted to civil and mechanical engineering."[7] In 1917, seven years after they left the asylum, Ruby and Isadore were both auto mechanics. David went into business.

The orphan asylum's Emanuel Lehman Industrial and Provident Trust Fund provided special funding for thirty-four inmates in 1906. Three students were sent to the College of the City of New York and three to the Normal College. The others were sent to trade and technical schools. Beneficiaries were placed in institutions that would "prepare them for industrial or mechanical life." According to the committee's April 15, 1906, report, "Only such inmates of the Institution as have shown special aptitude and talent will be placed in institutions preparing for professional activities." Some were sent to trade schools "with a view to their becoming fitted for active mercantile and trade life at the earliest reasonable opportunity." Superintendent Solomon Lowenstein explained that the Lehman Fund Committee demanded "proficiency and aptitude for professional work, in addition to high mental ability, before extending the benefits of this Fund to those children desiring to enter professional careers. It has been further deemed advisable that with all other than cases of exceptional ability, the course of education should not be too prolonged, and the time of entering upon wage-earning not too distant, and therefore preference has in most instances been given to mercantile rather than to professional training."

I do not know what David Warshawsky did to merit the Kate Kleinert Memorial Prize, awarded to him on June 3, 1906. According to the headline in the *New York Times*, the annual award ceremony honored "Bright Pupils at Asylum." The prize suggests that David was a boy of some accomplishments, that he was noticed among 1,020 inmates.[8] Although the $10 prize was not among the largest awarded, $10 was the equivalent of more than $250 today. Efforts were made to place children or to assist them in their life after the orphanage. In 1906, eleven discharged boys were given small allowances to assist them in "entering business life" until their experience could qualify them to earn greater pay. We don't know whether David received such assistance when he left the orphanage. Presumably he received a new set of clothes from the Ladies Sewing Society of the Hebrew Orphan Asylum. According to a pamphlet that it published in 1903, the Ladies Sewing Society supplied thirty-nine boys who left the institution with shirts, shoes, stockings, drawers, suits, handkerchiefs, nightshirts, hats, and caps, among other items.[9]

What were David's plans in 1906? One can imagine a New York story of self-invention. I picture David (or Dick) in the Hebrew Orphan Asylum library reading Horatio Alger novels, such as *Ragged Dick*, about orphans worse off than those in the Hebrew Orphan Asylum. (Alger's *The Mad Heiress*, in which the male protagonist is named Henry Marshall, probably wouldn't have appealed to an adolescent boy, unless the part about the heroine being sent to an insane asylum caught his attention.)[10] What did he want to become in imagining himself David Henry

Marshall? My grandfather's niece Adele told me a story that I had never heard from my father or my grandmother: she said that my grandfather had changed the name to Marshall because he wanted to go to West Point, and he wouldn't have had a chance with a Jewish name like Warshawsky. I immediately dismissed this story as preposterous, as my father would have done. Aside from the fact that I had never once heard even a hint that this was a motivation for changing the name, it seemed out of character and inconsistent with what I knew about him. My grandfather did serve in the army. As legally required, he registered for the draft in 1917, under the name David H. Marshall; he claimed an exemption on the grounds of "Support of home & mother." He was drafted and assigned to a desk job on Governors Island, which was then a supply base, in the Finance and Accounting Division of the Army Transport Service. I found it hard to believe that the boy who would become an unimposing, unathletic, bespectacled accountant would have planned to attend the United States Military Academy at West Point as he left the Hebrew Orphan Asylum for Brooklyn.

However, when David, Ruby, and Isi arrived at the asylum in March of 1903, it had a very well-known cadet corps and military band. In fact, the cadet corps, which was divided into military companies and drilled twice a week, had been formed in 1877. The atmosphere of military school discipline was evident even in dormitory life, where older boys acted as "monitors" and daily inspections were carried out. The cadet corps attracted national attention when it participated in the George Washington Centennial in April of 1889, when President Benjamin Henry Harrison came to New York for a military parade and reenactment of Washington's inauguration. The Hebrew Orphan Asylum cadets won a competition, and the blue banner that they were awarded was presented to them by General William Tecumsah Sherman. When Sherman died in February of 1891, the cadet corps and band marched in his funeral procession. According to Hyman Bogen, the cadet corps and band were at the time "the only Jewish paramilitary units of their kind in America, if not the world."[11]

This paramilitary culture was consistent with the culture of Americanization that prevailed in the Hebrew Orphan Asylum. In 1896, the *American Hebrew* published an article called "Jewish Cadets," which quoted at length from a Memorial Day speech delivered by the Honorable Ferdinand Levy to a cadet corps formed by the Hebrew Institute. After a performance by the Hebrew Orphan Asylum Military Band, as he presented the cadets with an American flag, Levy described himself as an "American citizen who is proud of his citizenship, who is an honor to our own race and creed," and declared: "Your parents, my young friends, came from a land where freedom is known only as a longing of the heart to which even expression may not be given. With them the love of country could not develop. Only freemen have a country; slaves have but a birthplace. . . . You will grow up here to enjoy the full rights of citizenship, to enjoy all the benefits of our free institutions, to feel that you are the equals of every man, free sovereigns in a free land." The ceremony ended with the singing of "America." The article begins not with Joshua and David but rather with "Phinehas, the grandson of Aaron," who was "the first to organize young Israelites into a band of cadets."[12]

During the years in which David Warshawsky was an inmate at the Hebrew Orphan Asylum, this culture of Americanization was embodied by the cadet corps, which continued to attract public attention and won two consecutive high-profile competitions. The superintendent's report in the 1903 HOA annual report, published in the year that David Warshawsky arrived, proudly stated: "On the 22nd of March our battalion of cadets enjoyed the honor of being reviewed by the City Superintendent, Dr. William H. Maxwell, who was highly pleased with their magnificent discipline and the precise execution of their marches and evolutions." The 1906 annual report, published in the year that David was discharged, boasted: "A company of our Cadet Corps, in a competitive drill with Cadet Corps of other Institutions, held at the 12th Regiment Armory, succeeded in two successive years in winning banners given by Companies G and E of the 12th Regiment, demonstrating in a most signal manner its right to be known as one of the best drilled battalions in the city. The great success attending the Review and Exhibition Drill of the entire Battalion, held at the 7th Regiment Armory two years ago, has induced your Board to repeat the same this year."

Major General Frederick D. Grant, the son of Ulysses S. Grant, was the reviewing officer. The cadet corps and band are discussed in five separate sections of the 1906 annual report. Superintendent Lowenstein states: "The excellent condition of the Cadet Corps has been manifested by the Public Drill given on the evening of April 21, 1906, and by the fact that our boys have already carried off a prize in one special competition and are hopeful of repeating their victory in another, to take place in the near future, when they will come into competition with all the institutional and military school battalions of the City."[13]

An article in the *New York Times* on November 30, 1906 (less than three months after David's discharge), reports that Governor-elect Charles E. Hughes "reviewed the cadet corps of the Hebrew Orphan Asylum yesterday," watching five hundred boys perform military exercises. Under the headlines, "Hughes Reviews Cadets; Both are Delighted. Hebrew Orphan Lads Show Their Military Prowess," the article describes the cadets "lined up in battalions at either end of the ground" executing "manoeuvres of every character, by battalions, by platoons, by companies, and by columns of fours." The band is described as "one of the remarkable juvenile musical organizations of the city."[14] A photograph in the 1906 annual report shows boys in uniform "in battalion formation." This photograph, as well as a photograph featuring the cadet corps and the band, was regularly included in the annual reports of this decade.

The 1907 annual report detailed these activities and noted that "Governor-Elect Hughes kindly consented to act as reviewing officer at the drill and dress parade held by the boys on the grounds of the Institution, and expressed his cordial admiration of the soldierlike bearing and military efficiency of the Cadet Corps." On April 30, 1906, there were 595 boys in residence. It is hard to believe that David was not involved in the cadet corps or unaffected by the pride taken in the Hebrew Orphan Asylum military culture during the years in which he

was an inmate. The 1908 annual report indicates that 350 boys participated in the cadet corps. There is a list of excursions that the children
made during the year; the first trip listed is West Point.[15]

A *New York Times* article published on April 26, 1908, "400
Boys Drill Like Veterans: Fine Exhibition by Corps of Hebrew Orphan
Asylum in Seventh Regiment Armory," begins: "Four hundred boys,
between the ages of 10 and 13, of the Hebrew Orphan Asylum proved
themselves able to compete with regular soldiers in parade manoeuvres
last night in the Seventh Regiment Armory." The exercises culminated
in "a 'rally 'round the flag' which ended with the 400 boys, some flat
on their stomachs and others on their knees, firing in all directions,
while the flag waved in the centre."[16] In 1909, there were 386 boys in
the cadet corps. As we have seen, the fiftieth anniversary celebration in
1910 held in the New York Hippodrome featured the cadet corps firing
rifles while performing "Rally 'Round the Flag."[17] The cadet corps was
more than a small club. The majority of boys were actively involved.

It is feasible that the fourteen-year-old David Warshawsky was
caught up in the military culture of the asylum and perhaps even excelled
in the cadet corps activities. Perhaps he read *The History of the United
States Naval Academy*, by Edward Chauncey Marshall, in the Hebrew
Orphan Asylum library. Originally published in 1862, it describes in
detail the nomination and application procedures ("Candidates must be
over fourteen and under eighteen years of age at the time of examination for admission") and explains that acting midshipmen receive $500
per annum. In addition to history and biographical sketches of naval
heroes, it includes an account of the typical routine and "daily division
of time" of naval cadets that in many ways resembles the daily schedules
and routines of the Hebrew Orphan Asylum.[18]

During the 1907–08 school year, a boy named Warshawsky was
on the prize-winning rifle team of Stuyvesant High School, then a
trade school attended by some Hebrew Orphan Asylum boys. Could
this have been Ruby?[19] In addition to the excitement and attention
that the cadet corps generated between 1904 and 1906, in the years
immediately following David's departure there would be a connection

"Cadet Corp and Band," *Eighty-Third Report of the Hebrew Orphan Asylum of the City of New York*, 1906. Courtesy of the Collection of the American Jewish Historical Society.

with West Point through the Hebrew Orphan Asylum's bandleader. The 1906 annual report praises the "zealous enthusiasm of the leader, Mr. Philip Egner," and notes that a "number of our former inmates have also formed a Military Band."[20] The 1910 annual report, noting that the "Cadet Corps and band continue their excellent work," reports that "Mr. Philip Egner, the former leader of our band, who had successfully conducted it for six years, was appointed band-master at the United States Military Academy at West Point."[21] Indeed, Egner taught music at the U.S. Military Academy from 1909 until 1917, then served in the army, and eventually was the leader of the West Point Band and Orchestra for twenty-five years, becoming a well-known band composer.[22]

If the adolescent David Warshawsky aspired to attend West Point, would it have been even remotely realistic to have had this as a goal? It would have been wise to have planned on applying to West Point with the name of David Marshall rather than either David Warshawsky or David Roshofsky. During the first decades of the twentieth century, there were frequent discussions about anti-Semitism at West Point. There were congressional hearings about hazing and other abuses in 1901.[23] An article in the *Times* on December 7, 1915, with the headline, "SAYS WEST POINT IS NOT ANTI-SEMITIC," reported that Congressman Walter M. Chandler of New York told the secretary of war that "there was a belief prevalent among the Jews of New York that an anti-semitic policy was in force at West Point, and that Jewish cadets were socially ostracized." The congressman asserted: "I have held several preliminary competitive examinations after due notice to all the people of my district to fill vacancies at West Point and Annapolis. Very few Jews have taken part in these examinations. In this connection it has been repeatedly bought to my attention . . . that there is a belief prevalent among the people of this race that it is difficult for a Jew to gain admission to West Point. . . ."[24]

The congressman's statement indicates the path to West Point. Appointments were made based on nominations by congressman, senators, and the president, following rigorous "mental and physical examination before boards of army officers," according to the June 1906 *Official Register of the Officers and Cadets of the United States Military Academy.* Appointments were "required by law to be made one year in advance of the date of admission"[25] and congressmen, like Congressman Chandler, regularly held well-publicized preliminary examinations in their districts that were open to all. Since cadets had to be between the ages of seventeen and twenty-two, and appointments had to be made a year in advance, this means that a candidate might begin the application process as early as the age of fifteen. Despite open and competitive examinations, however, it was well known that many appointments involved political connections as well as merit.

On February 3, 1909, the *New York Times* published a letter to the editor, under the headline, "Failed to Enter West Point," by someone who complained that he could not "secure an appointment" when "Some five years ago I tried hard to enter West Point" because "[f]avorites of the Congressman received both principal and alternate nominations." The letter was signed "WOOD B. SOLJER." On October 12, 1911, Edward W. Stitt, district superintendent of schools, praised congressmen who made selections by "competitive examinations" that were well-publicized in information sent to "the Principals of public, parochial, and private schools" and "notices in the public press" and called for civil service–like exams to be administered by the Board of Education so nominations could be "awarded for merit, and not on account of political influence."[26] Would David Marshall, alias David Warshawsky, have had any political influence?

My father's cousin Adele suggested that Lena "knew people" who would help. No obvious or even likely political connections come to mind. Brooklyn had six congressional representatives in 1910, the year that the census enumerator recorded the Warshawsky family in Ward 26, which was then the Fifth District. (The Rudermans were in the 26th Ward, then in the Fourth District.) From what I can tell, there had been no Jewish representatives from Brooklyn since Mitchell May represented the Sixth District between 1899 and 1901, when his campaign biography noted that he was "a member of the Hebrew Orphan Asylum" and the "Hebrew Benevolent Association."[27] Representatives from all parties had to pay attention to their Jewish constituencies, given the demographics of Brooklyn at the time. A few doors down from the Warshawskys' apartment at 441 Hopkinson Avenue in 1909, at 432 Hopkinson Avenue, was the Junior Democratic League. Would the Warshawsky family have had any political connections?

A decade earlier, on October 26, 1899, the *New York Times* reported on a political meeting in which the notorious Tammany Hall politician "Silver-Dollar" Smith was nominated for the assembly the day after being acquitted (implausibly, in the opinion of the *Times*) of bribery and corruption charges. The *New York Herald*'s account of the meeting in Walhalla Hall on Orchard Street, with the ironic headline, "Distinguished Citizens of the East Side Insist that Indicted Officials Are Worthy of Their Suffrage," includes among the "distinguished citizens" in attendance one "Harris Warshawsky." Smith, who died at the end of 1899, lived on Essex Street in the Warshawskys' neighborhood and ran the infamous Silver Dollar Saloon on Essex Street.[28] Lena's connections, if she had any, in the years between 1906 and 1912 probably would have been more respectable. We know from the 1910 census that about this time she had a candy store (a "confectionary"), although we don't know where. Might she have talked about her son, or introduced her son, who might have worked at the counter, to a prominent customer? In fact, in these years polling places were located in stores and shops. The November 6, 1905, issue of the *City Record* provides the official Board of Elections list of polling places for the election of November 7. Thirty-seven candy stores and four confectionaries are listed.[29]

It seems just as likely that David would have hoped that his Hebrew Orphan Asylum connections would open doors for him. Besides the prominent members of the board of trustees, the cadet corps had attracted the notice of the mayor and the governor, among others. He might have received encouragement or assistance from various quarters, including Philip Egner. Of course, even if he were a star cadet, a leader among his peers, the idea of applying to West Point might have been naive. Indeed, on May 30, 1906, as he entered manhood in the Jewish tradition, at about the age of fourteen, David would not know that when he would register for the draft on June 5, 1917, at the age of twenty-five, he would be only five feet three inches tall. The draft registration card calls for the registrar to report not the registrant's actual height but only whether he is "tall, medium, or short"; however, David H. Marshall's actual height is recorded. (Reuben is identified as "medium," and Isadore is identified as "tall" on their registration cards.) The registrar writes in David's height: *5 ft 3"*. To be admitted to West Point, candidates had to be at least "five feet four inches in height at the age of seventeen, or five feet five inches in height at the age of eighteen and upwards."[30]

Detail, World War I Registration Card, 1917.

In 1906, David would not have known that he didn't stand a chance, regardless of his name, religion, or martial prowess, of being admitted to West Point. Yet whether he was realistic or delusional, it is conceivable that he left the Hebrew Orphan Asylum with a plan to attend night school and take the preliminary entrance exams. For this future, and indeed for other futures, he would have needed a different name. One can imagine that in later years, in retrospect, this dream would have seemed naive, and that this story would have been one of the stories from the orphan asylum days that my grandfather would not tell to his wife and sons. At the same time, it is a story—an explanation of why the name was changed, if not of what it was changed from—that both Lena and Millie would have remembered and repeated to Adele. If the story seems unlikely, it is also unlikely that someone would have made it up.

18

---◆◇◆---

Picturing a Past

Whatever David's plans and aspirations were when he left the
Hebrew Orphan Asylum in September of 1906, one month
before his birthday, he continued his schooling and started to work.
According to my father, my grandfather had "a number of different jobs"
while going to "accounting school or business school at night" in order
to become "an accountant."[1] Lena's brother, Michael Ruderman, who was
about eight years older than David and must have been like an older
brother, would have been a role model. He became a bookkeeper and
then an accountant, but during the 1898–99 school year, when he was
about fifteen years old, he was enrolled in the College of the City of
New York in the sub-freshman class, scientific course.[2] Tuition was free,
but it must have been a high priority for the Ruderman family to send
their son to City College, even to the equivalent of high school. In *The
Rise of David Levinsky*, Cahan's protagonist writes: "The majority of the
students at the College of the City of New York was already made up of
Jewish boys, mostly from the tenement-houses. . . . The East Side was
full of poor Jews—wage-earners, peddlers, grocers, salesmen, insurance
agents—who would beggar themselves to give their children a liberal
education."[3] In 1906, David could not follow this path, either because

he did not have the educational preparation, or because he needed to work to help support his family.

In the eleven-year period between my grandfather's discharge from the Hebrew Orphan Asylum in 1906 and his registration for the draft in 1917, when (like Michael Ruderman) he lists his occupation as "accountant," there is only one official document, the 1910 U.S. census, that tells us what he was doing. (The Rudermans are listed in the New York State 1915 census but neither the Warshawsky family nor the Marshall family appears.) According to the 1910 U.S. census, in April of that year, four years after he left the orphan asylum, David Warshawsky, reported to be age seventeen, was an "office boy" in a jewelry store. An office boy was below a clerk but nevertheless a desirable entry-level position in an urban economy increasingly relying on clerical skills. Newspapers at the time alternated between describing the office boy as a comic character who wielded enormous power despite his laziness and bad habits, and as an inspiring character from a Horatio Alger story. (Alger's novel, *Silas Snobden's Office Boy*, was published in 1899.) Biographical narratives and obituaries throughout most of the twentieth century adhered to the formula of the successful executive who first entered his establishment as an office boy. On the other hand, according to an article published in the *New York Times* in 1906, "the office boy as the world and the comic papers know him" was "a haughty man of affairs in miniature, keeper of the boss's ink well, guardian of the sanctum portals, connoisseur in creepy literature and the weed, master of reformed spelling and the unwritten languages."

The *Times* describes a large-scale effort by the Young Men's Christian Association to "reform the tribe" by training office boys in character and manners as well as skills, reporting in its headline, "500,000 Employers Stand Ready to Seize the Graduates and Put Them to Work." Describing the "General Outline" printed by the YMCA, the *Times* reports that a graduate of the school will "evince no desire to carve his illustrious initials in mahogany, or to manipulate an absent stenographer's typewriter with his feet. . . . 'We are going to make industrious, willing boys of you,' promises an Assistant Instructor at the 57th Street Branch on the first night of classes, 'and there is no reason why you should not rise to be great men.'" According to a 1908 article in the *American Educational Review*, which took this vocational enterprise more seriously than did the *New York Times*, the YMCA's night course for office boys and junior clerks focused on "business arithmetic, correspondence and commercial geography, business etiquet [sic] and slangless English." The article provides an inventory of the other duties expected of office boys: "They are drilled in the right way of handling mail matter, letter copying, manifolding and mimeographing, filing, indexing of books and cards, answering desk calls, telephoning and other kindred duties. They are schooled in cheerfulness and politeness."[4] David Warshawsky would have acquired many of these skills in the Hebrew Orphan Asylum business classes, but it seems likely that he took this sort of vocational course between 1906 and 1910.

My father, who reported that his father succeeded in "breaking away from a near poverty," said that he "put himself through school and a night business college while taking jobs as a runner on Wall Street and a copy boy at the old *N Y World*."[5] Being a runner on Wall Street would have been an education in itself. Runners, who delivered market orders and stock certificates between brokers and traders, were, like office boys, at the bottom of the ladder, yet many brokers began their Wall Street careers on the runners' bench. In 1906, the *New York Times* reported that a West Point and Harvard football star, who recently had become "associated with Mills Brothers & Co.," was "one of the long line of college men and scions of financial magnates who have had their introduction to the Street by way of the runners' bench in a broker's office."[6] A 1908 article, under the heading "Many Youthful Tipsters," describes how "youngsters who would be treated with scant consideration in any other business" become "the speculative advisers of gray-haired traders" by sharing information with a "stipulation that 50 or 100 shares be carried for them on the side." Even if they didn't get a cut of trades in exchange for confidential information, in good years the runners and office boys expected to receive generous Christmas bonuses.[7] In 1906, the Dow Jones Industrial Average closed at over 100 for the first time, yet this period also saw the Panic of 1907 and the instability caused by the beginning of the First World War.

My grandfather also would have received an education working as a "copy boy at the old *N Y World*." (My father was not sure which newspaper his father worked for; recalling that his father "worked on a newspaper," my father remembered "the *New York World* or *Sun* or something like that."[8]) In 1946, the newspaper columnist Franklin P. Adams published a column with this recollection: "Years ago there was an office boy, David Warshowsky, on the New York Evening Mail. He was the author of that unforgettable—to me—couplet: *If Donlin only joins the Giants,/ The fans will drink his health in pints.*" The reference to New York Giants outfielder Mike Donlin places this story at about 1910 or 1911; fans chanted these lines at the Polo Grounds at the time to persuade Donlin to return to the team after an absence. (Adams, a legendary columnist who worked at the *New York Evening Mail* between 1904 and 1913, himself wrote one of the most famous sports poems, "Baseball's Sad Lexicon," first published on July 10, 1910, as "That Double Play Again" with the refrain, "Tinker to Evers to Chance.") There might have been two boys named David Warshawsky working as office boys at New York daily papers, but the office boy that Adams recalled thirty-six years later might have been the David Warshawsky who would become David Marshall.[9] Working at a New York City newspaper as a copy boy and an office boy in those years would have provided a remarkable education in city politics, world affairs, and even arts and letters.

There is a classified ad in the "Work Wanted" section of the *New York Daily Tribune* published on October 6, 1909, three years after my grandfather left the Hebrew Orphan Asylum and right after his (supposedly) seventeenth birthday: "ASSISTANT BOOKKEEPER: By intelligent young man; can also make himself generally useful; experienced, with a three-year recommendation. Warshawsky. 21 East 117th st." When I first found this ad, I couldn't see how the address was consistent with the contemporary records I had for David Warshawsky, but then I discovered in the 1908 annual report that the Hebrew Orphan Asylum held the mortgage for 21 East 117th Street.[10] Might David have been placed in an office there through an HOA connection, or was an office in that building helping to place Hebrew Orphan Asylum alumni in positions? In an advertisement in the February 6, 1906 *Daily People*, a Mrs. Stodel offered a furnished room, with or without board, at 21 East 117th Street.[11] David might have rented a room in this building, but in any case he was likely working his way up in an office.[12] The 1915 Trow's Directory locates a "David Warshawski, bkpr" at 453 W 43rd Street.

If David was on a path to become an accountant, following in the steps of Michael Ruderman, he was pursuing an upwardly mobile professional career. Although Isadore and Reuben were allowed to continue their education at the Hebrew Orphan Asylum for four years after David began to work, they appear to have been given the vocational training that was typically provided for the boys. On his 1915 marriage certificate, Reuben lists his occupation as "chauffeur," and both Rueben and Isadore identify themselves as automobile mechanics working at the American Motor Service when they register for the draft in 1917. In 1922, Irving Marshall advertised in the "Situations Wanted" section of

"Work Wanted," *New-York Daily Tribune*, October 6, 1909.

the *Brooklyn Daily Eagle*: "CHAUFFEUR mechanic; all cars; private or commercial; long experience; best reference."[13]

Michael Ruderman offered a different model. When he was naturalized in 1905, his occupation was "manager." In 1910, at age twenty-seven, he is reported in the U.S. census as a "bookkeeper, Cloaks and Suits." In the same 1910 census, Daisy, listed as age eighteen, is reported to be a bookkeeper in a clothing factory. Lena's father and older brother Isaac are tailors, and her brother Abraham is an operator in a shop. Although Daisy and Michael are still associated with the garment industry, like the rest of their family, they represent an upwardly mobile "white collar" alternative to working in a shop. In 1917, when they register for the draft, Michael Ruderman and David H. Marshall are each associated with a firm in the garment industry, but each lists his occupation as "accountant."[14] In the 1920 census, Lena's two nieces (the granddaughters who were raised by her parents and are then living as "roomers" with her married sister Fannie and her family) are identified as accountants. New York State was the first state to license certified public accountants (CPAs) after passage of the Wray Bill in 1896. Michael and David may not have been CPAs, but in the first decades of the twentieth century accountants also were undergoing professionalization.[15] Becoming an accountant also served as an entry into business and entrepreneurship. By the 1930 census, Michael Ruderman is a "manufacturer of silk"; he and his wife and two children have a nineteen-year-old English "servant" named Barbara Gamson living with them.

When David H. Marshall registered for the draft in 1917, he was employed as an "accountant" for a man who had a women's clothing firm on 37th Street in Manhattan called "La Mode de Demain"—the fashion of tomorrow. On August 1, 1918, the *Brooklyn Daily Eagle* and the *Brooklyn Daily Standard Union* listed the names of men from Local Board No. 83 who were called up to report for duty. David H. Marshall of 408 Saratoga Avenue was instructed to report on August 5 to the "Finance Division, Quartermaster Corps, N.Y.C." on Governor's Island, where he was assigned to the Army Transport Service.[16] He was assigned to the Finance and Accounting Division of the Army Transport Service on Governor's Island. I have three small snapshots from around this time, which must have been saved by either my grandfather's mother or his sister Millie. In one photo, he stands smiling in a suit and tie, leaning against a brick building with his arms folded and his legs slightly crossed. This reminds me of a snapshot that we had from a later time on which someone wrote "Smilin' Dick." The other two snapshots must have been taken immediately afterward since he stands in front of the same building but wears a khaki uniform, with a round, wide-brimmed ranger hat. In one photograph, he wears the hat, smiling and leaning forward; in the other, he holds the hat, arms crossed, and poses sternly with a cigar in his mouth. These photos seem to have been taken on

David H. Marshall, 1918.

David H. Marshall, 1918.

the day he was inducted. On the back of the smiling picture is an inscription, dated September 8, 1918, "To The Kid—Knock em all Dead—Get me—Huh!! Dick." I am guessing that this was inscribed to Millie. On the back of the other, inscribed on the same day, is: "To my Dear Brother Isadore--- Good luck and God Speed. Dick." (Isadore is not yet, or not here, called Irving.)

There is also a formal studio portrait, printed as a postcard, showing my grandfather standing in a drab uniform with a high, buttoned-up collar. He is serious, almost pensive, but more impassive than pensive, as he poses for posterity, or wherever such postcards were meant to be sent. The genre of these photographic portraits of men in uniform goes back to the beginnings of photography. One did not know, when the portrait was taken, whether years later it would illustrate a chapter in life's adventures to share with one's children, or whether it would mark the moment before loss. I wonder how he felt, at age twenty-seven, putting on a uniform for the first time in twelve years. This wouldn't have been how he pictured becoming a soldier when he was in the Hebrew Orphan Asylum cadet corps. He was bound for a desk job at Governors Island in New York City.

Another formal portrait shows Dick and Isadore together, taken at Sussman's photographic studio at 1703 Pitkin Avenue in Brooklyn, a three-minute walk from Watkins Street. In this photograph, Isadore, seated, is in uniform and has a military-style haircut, closely cropped on the sides. An article titled "Men Picked from Draft to Go First to

David H. Marshall, c. 1918.

Yaphank" in the *Brooklyn Daily Eagle* on September 7, 1917, included Isadore Marshall on a list of men called to report for duty at Camp Upton, the same boot camp that Irving Berlin was sent to a year later.[17] Dick, not yet drafted, wears an elegant, pinstriped, three-piece suit with a watch chain on his vest and a floral tie; he has his arm around his younger brother's shoulder. Both look straight ahead. This photograph reminds me of the studio portrait of Harris and Lena. Harris would have been around the same age. Did my grandfather think of this portrait, which perhaps, during the family's good years, hung in a parlor? Did he remember the time he posed in a photographer's studio on Essex Street?

Dick and Isadore, c. 1917.

Articles in the *Brooklyn Daily Eagle* in 1919 and 1920 indicate that after being discharged from the army David H. Marshall was the treasurer of two American Legion posts. An article in the *Brooklyn Standard Union* in 1920 about an American Legion post fundraising drive to secure $25,000 for a "monument in honor of the fallen heroes of the section" noted: "David H. Marshall, treasurer of the post, reported a bank balance of $5000."[18] He was always keeping track of the finances, it seems. In 1918, articles in the *Brooklyn Standard Union* and the *Brooklyn Daily Eagle* identify "David H. Marshall" and "D. H. Marshall" as an officer and "chairman of the financial committee" of the Huron Club, a men's social club that organized dinners, dances, charitable events, and events for soldiers.[19] In 1919, the *Brooklyn Standard Union* described the Huron Club as "one of the leading social organizations of the Brownsville section." The article describes the club's plan to "entertain the Republican local and country candidates at a meeting to be held in the clubhouse, 48 Thatford avenue."[20] An October 27, 1919 *Standard Union* article, "Huron Club Dance a Success," included among the officers of the club "David H. Marshall, financial secretary" and "D. H. Marshall, editor." The club's board of directors also included "D. H. Marshall."[21] In 1920, in a *Standard Union* column that reported news of local residents (such as vacation and honeymoon trips) the lead item was: "Dick Marshall, of the Huron Club, is as active as a bee. He is busy every night attending to his many duties necessary for the coming Huron ball, which will be held at Arcadia Hall on Oct. 16."[22]

In the years before he was married, my grandfather seems to have been active in several organizations, perhaps to meet a wife (there is a story that he was introduced to my grandmother in a club) or perhaps to make business contacts, as his father and his father's fellow immigrants did in the 1890s. In 1921, David H. Marshall, age twenty-eight, of 408 Saratoga Avenue in Brooklyn, became a member of the Joseph Warren-Gothic Lodge No. 934 of the Free and Accepted Masons, which met (and still meets) at the Masonic Hall at 71 West 23rd Street in Manhattan. His occupation was listed as "manager." He received his first Masonic degree on November 11, 1921, his second on December

7, 1921, and his third (at which point he became a Master Mason) on February 1, 1922. Although this was a secular lodge in Manhattan, most of the names on the page of the 1923 lodge roster booklet that lists him as residing at 1276 Union Street appear to be Jewish.[23] It seems that my grandfather remained a member of this lodge for many years since he had his adult sons join as well. One of the three January 23, 1952 *New York Times* death notices for my grandfather is a notice placed by "Gothic Lodge, No. 934, F. and A.M.," regretting the "passing of Brother David H. Marshall, father of Brothers Arthur K. and Stephen E. Marshall" and requesting Brethren to attend "Masonic Services."[24] There is also a notice placed by the "officers and members of the Hebrew Mutual Benefit Society," regretting "the loss of their esteemed member," which (judging by the frequency of such notices) probably was included in the burial insurance policy provided by the society and did not indicate active participation in what was one of the oldest Jewish philanthropic organizations in New York.

On March 12, 1922, the *New York Times* published this announcement under the heading "ENGAGED": "LEVITT—MARSHALL—Mr. and Mrs. Louis Levitt, 1,276 Union St., Brooklyn, N.Y., announce the engagement of their daughter, Jeanette, to Mr. David H. Marshall of Brooklyn, N.Y." My grandparents were married on November 12, 1922. My grandmother was twenty years old, more than ten years younger than my grandfather; her father, a Russian immigrant who began as a shoemaker on the Lower East Side, became a prosperous manufacturer of children's shoes. He owned a house at 1276 Union Street.[25] I don't know how unusual it was for a family like this to announce the engagement of their daughter in the *New York Times*, nor do I know when my grandmother started to use the name Jeanette. The 1905, 1910, and 1915 censuses name her as "Jennie." Strangely, I cannot locate a birth certificate for my grandmother. My mother's immigrant parents gave their daughters French names: Helene and Estelle.

Jeanette Levitt and David H. Marshall (Mr. and Mrs. D. H. Marshall) were married at the Chateau Rembrandt on St. Marks Avenue in Brooklyn, which opened one month after they were engaged. An advertisement in the 1922 *Brooklyn Blue Book and Long Island Society Register* (which does not include a notice of their engagement or marriage) boasts "a palatial establishment" with "all the luxurious appointments of a first class New York hotel and the grounds of a country estate."[26] The *Brooklyn Daily Eagle* announced its opening, noting the "magnificence" of "an edifice for social functions that is unsurpassed in the greater City." Formerly the mansion of the late president of the Remington Typewriter Company, it was said to be a "monument to modern architecture" with "luxurious furnishings and facilities."[27] My grandmother saved the menu for the "Wedding Reception and Dinner of Mr. and Mrs. D. H. Marshall." It included "Filet de Sole Rembrandt, Chicken Patty Clamart, Royal Squab Jean, and Roast Stuffed Turkey," as well as "Mignardises, Fruits, Demi Tasse, and Beer, Mineral Water, Cigars, and Cigarettes." According to the New York State marriage certificate, Rabbi Israel Herbert Levinthal, a very prominent, Conservative rabbi, author, and Jewish leader, performed the ceremony. Previously the rabbi at Temple Petach Tikvah on Rochester Avenue and Lincoln Place, he had become the founding rabbi of the Brooklyn Jewish Center in 1919. The center, which set out to reach second-generation Jews, had opened its imposing, classical-style, million-dollar building on Eastern Parkway in the last days of 1920. Samuel Kantor, the cantor, signed the marriage certificate as one of the witnesses.[28] Another witness was Alex S. Drescher, a prominent attorney, former Brooklyn alderman, and a congressional candidate who in 1914 had come in third (with 2,884 votes) in Brooklyn's Tenth District, running on the "Anti-Boss" ticket.[29]

The *New York Times* engagement announcement, the wedding at the Chateau Rembrandt, and the presence of Rabbi Levinthal and former Alderman Drescher, suggest that either the Levitt or the Marshall family had (or sought) a fairly high social status. My mother suggested that the Levitts, who owned their house on Union Street, saw themselves as more elevated than the Marshalls, despite their similar immigrant origins. Ten years later, my grandmother's brother Irving (Isadore) would marry the daughter of a prominent Brooklyn judge. (Did the Levitts know that as a small child David had been photographed in a photographer's studio

WE hereby certify that we are the Groom and Bride named in this Certificate, and that the information given therein is correct, to the best of our knowledge and belief.

_____ Groom

_____ Bride

Signed in the presence of

and

It shall be the duty of the clergymen, magistrates and other persons who perform the marriage ceremony to keep a registry of the marriages celebrated by them. * * * * * * * * * * * * * * * * Every person authorized by law to perform the marriage ceremony shall register his or her name and address in the office of the Bureau of Records (Sec. 35, Sanitary Code). It shall be the duty of every person required to make or keep any such registry, of * * * * * * marriage * * * * * * to present to the Bureau of Records a copy of such registry signed by such person * * * * * * * within ten days after the * * * * * * marriage * * * * which shall thereupon be placed on file in the said Bureau (Sec. 33, Sanitary Code). N. B.—Sec. 1249, Chap. 532, Laws of 1905, makes the failure to report within ten days a written copy of the registry of the marriages provided to be registered a misdemeanor, punishable by fine or imprisonment.

Detail, Certificate and Record of Marriage, David H. Marshall and Jeanette Levitt, New York City Department of Records.

in vaguely Victorian dress, and that his father had run a successful coat factory, around the corner from where Louis Levitt, then a shoemaker, lived with his family and two boarders on Attorney Street in 1900, two years before my grandmother was born?)

My mother speculated that my grandfather did not marry before he was thirty because he was struggling to achieve financial security. My grandfather's siblings appear to have been married at home. Ruby and Irving, as I have noted, worked as auto mechanics. On the marriage certificates of both Daisy and Millie, the groom's occupation is listed as "salesman." Millie's husband would later be the proprietor of what the 1930 census called a "dairy store" and employ her brother Irving. Daisy's husband, Herman Braverman, was supposedly a Communist who was disliked by the family; according to Adele, Daisy had once been engaged to David Sarnoff, who later became a pioneer in radio and television and presided over an enormous telecommunications empire that included RCA and NBC. Could this be a family legend, one of those stories about the man she should have married? Sarnoff was a poor Jewish immigrant from a village near Minsk who came to New York in 1900 and got his start as an office boy working in the Marconi Wireless Telegraph Company of America.[30] Maybe Daisy thought he wouldn't amount to anything.

I pictured Lena Warshawsky in the reversals of fortune that Cahan described among the Jews on Suffolk Street, "Jews born to plenty, whom the new conditions have delivered up to the clutches of penury; Jews reared in the straits of need, who have risen here to prosperity."[31]

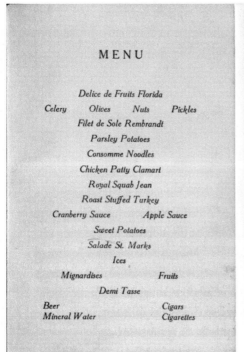
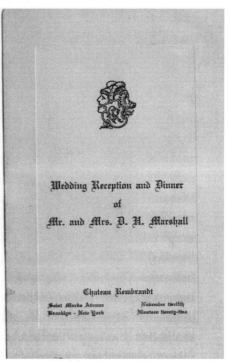

Menu for Wedding Reception Dinner of Mr. and Mrs. D. H. Marshall, 1922.

I imagine Lena Marshall at her oldest son's wedding at the Chateau Rembrandt, dining on "filet de sole Rembrandt" and "parsley potatoes" next to prominent rabbis and politicians. Surely she thought about her own wedding thirty-two years earlier; she was twenty years old, just Jeanette's age, and if her marriage was arranged, as Adele reports, she probably knew her husband only slightly. Adele suggested that Lena didn't care much for him and felt she spent too much time during their marriage being pregnant. After the wedding they lived with the Ruderman family on Essex Street, where their first child was born nine-and-a-half months later; Harris Warshawsky was a tailor and not yet a contractor with his own coat factory. On that evening in Brooklyn in 1922, at the wedding of "Mr. and Mrs. D. H. Marshall," was Lena proud of her son's success, or annoyed by the ostentatiousness of the nouveaux riches Levitts? Twenty-nine years later, on September 23, 1951, a few reversals of fortunes later, she would dine at the Hotel Pierre on Fifth Avenue in New York at her grandson Arthur's wedding. We have a photograph of her from the wedding album, seated next to my parents at a table with Dick, Jeanette, and other relatives. Although she is over eighty years old and has white hair, Grandma Marshall does not look unlike that photograph of Lena Ruderman Warshawsky standing with her husband. As she sat next to her happy grandson, the firstborn son of her firstborn son, surely she thought back not just to the wedding of the son on the dais with her but also, again, to her own wedding more than sixty years earlier. Harris Warshawsky had been dead for half a century. No one spoke his name.

There is a photograph of my grandparents on their honeymoon on the boardwalk in Atlantic City. They are both fashionably dressed; my grandfather has a hat, gloves, and cane. My father described him, perhaps thinking of this picture, as a "dandy" with "his cane and his spats and his hat." Perhaps my grandfather's attire was an echo of his early childhood on the Lower East Side, surrounded by tailors and *la mode de demain,* or the style of his father, who, like other immigrants at the time, displayed his prosperity and Americanization through his clothes. Perhaps it was a reaction to an experience of "near poverty," and to the

Helene and Arthur Marshall with Lena Marshall, Wedding Reception, 1951.

David H. Marshall and Jeanette Levitt, 1922.

coarse institutional uniforms of the Hebrew Orphan Asylum. There is also an engagement photograph of the couple, a glamorous profile pose, as if they were a leading man and lady from Hollywood. According to my grandmother, due to some mishap at the time, they had no wedding photographs. My grandmother told us that they returned from the honeymoon early because she was lonely. At the age of twenty, she was more than a decade younger than her husband.

Jeanette and David H. Marshall, Honeymoon, Atlantic City, 1922.

My father recalled that around the time of his father's marriage in 1922 he "was working as an accountant for some dress manufacturer."[32] On my grandparents' marriage certificate, my grandfather's occupation is listed as "accountant." Two years later in 1924, on my father's birth certificate. his occupation is listed as "credit man." A credit man determined the customers, companies, or manufacturers to which a business should extend credit. The qualities and characteristics of a good credit man were discussed extensively in the business and accounting textbooks of the era. According to a 1917 "Modern Business" series volume, the credit man needed more than knowledge of accounting and business practices: "The position of credit man calls for a person of executive ability" who is "observant" and has a "good memory" and "a thoroly [sic] analytic mind." Moreover, he is "a man of his word" with "high moral standards," "perfect candor," "a spirit of democratic equality and interdependence," and "[s]ocial qualities which enable him to mix readily with all sorts of men and to be liked personally."[33] These social qualities, and the general portrait of a middleman who is an intermediary between management and customer or between manufacturer and distributor, remind me of the qualities described in the garment industry contractor in the 1890s. The description of the credit man as "a sane, normal man" whose "sole aim is to travel the *via media*, the middle road," and who "wants nothing to do with the chronic failure or the flashy success" or "the insidious disease of over-confidence which leads to failures, disaster and panics" makes me picture someone trying to ward off the economic and perhaps the psychic fluctuations that characterized the world of Harris Warshawsky.[34]

Eventually, my grandfather's experience as an accountant led him to a position with the Eugene Company, one of the first manufacturers of the permanent wave machines that changed women's hairstyles in the 1920s. Eugene Suter and Isidoro Calvete created the first permanent wave rollers in 1917. My father recalled that his father started to work for the company in 1926, beginning as an accountant and "controller for this company and actually he got more into everything. Management. Sales. . . ." His father "was one of the early people in the beauty field," he wrote, describing how "they brought in these permanent wave machines with these long spiral curlers." On my laptop computer in the hospital where my father was dying, I found photographs of the original permanent wave machines and some of the products that my grandfather and later my father had sold. My father wrote that my grandfather had "left a secure job as an accountant to jump into a startup company in a new industry in the 1920s—and succeeded." Working for the Eugene Company, according to my father, "he was making what my mother said he used to call 'good money.'"[35] In September of 1926, when my father was about two-and-a-half years old, two months before his brother Stephen was born, my grandmother placed this ad in the "Help Wanted" section of the *Brooklyn Daily Eagle*: "HOUSEWORKER, white; near and competent, in small family. Marshall, 1276 Union st. DECatur 7963." In May of 1929, five years after the Immigration Act of 1924 set quotas that greatly reduced immigration from Eastern Europe, Mrs. Marshall benevolently measured her distance from greenhorns in this "Help Wanted" ad: "HOUSEWORKER, white; no objection to girl just landed. Call Mrs. Marshall, 1276 Union st. DECatur 7963."[36] Just months before the stock market crash, the small Brooklyn family had a housekeeper and a telephone. (According to my father, "Maids weren't that expensive in the late 20s and my father was doing well").[37] In the 1930 census, my grandfather is listed as a "manager," and his business is reported as "machines."

In 1933, the Eugene Company partners broke up and my grandfather bet on the wrong partner; he was out of a steady job for several years. During the Depression, my grandmother opened a dress shop to help support the family—a return, of sorts, to the garment industry. My father remembers that it was in a "poor neighborhood" and that he and his brother went there after school and stayed until the shop closed at 7 or 8 P.M. Later, according to my father, my grandfather "worked hard to rebuild his financial life after the Depression and war had taken away the success he had made in breaking away from a near poverty."[38] Although he lived and worked in a very different world from that of his father, he needed the entrepreneurial energy, resilience, and interpersonal skills required of the contractor in the 1890s, as well as the resilience required when faced with economic instability. Whether by choice or necessity, he took risks, and ended up in business for himself.

For two years between 1932 and 1934, the family lived in Long Beach because of a polio scare, and when they returned to Brooklyn they had to live with my grandmother's parents on Union Street—not in the upstairs apartment, where they had lived before, but in shared quarters. Although this brown sandstone two-family house must have been more spacious than the tenement apartments that my grandfather had lived in on the Lower East Side, as he moved his wife and two sons into an apartment shared with his wife's parents and brother—Dick and Jeanette slept in the parlor, while my father shared a room with his Uncle Jack and his brother shared a room with his grandmother—I wonder if he thought of the years that the Warshawskys and Rudermans lived together, or the years in which the Warshawsky family fortunes had declined so precipitously. According to my father, "We didn't have any money. He

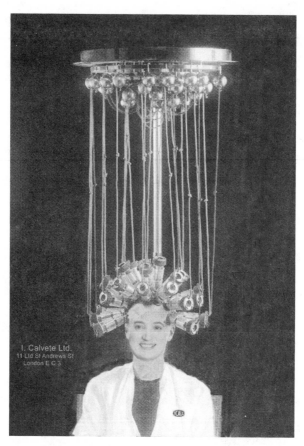

Permanent Wave Machine made by Icall for Eugene Suter, 1923.

didn't have a job."[39] Sometime around 1935, my grandfather traveled the country inspecting beauty supplies manufacturers to enforce codes established by the National Recovery Administration. Around 1936 he and a partner tried to sell some sort of hair curling machine that my father described in incomprehensible technical detail, but a manufacturer cheated them by putting sand in the chemicals and the business failed. My grandfather set up his own company as a manufacturers' sales representative in this industry. My father described him as "a pioneer in the Salon Industries in 1927 and then as a Rep in 1937."

Eugene Suter and early version of Permanent Wave Machine designed by Isidoro Calvete, 1920.

A letter that my grandfather sent to my father when he was in the army, dated April 9, 1943, is on stationery with the heading, in large black letters: "D. H. MARSHALL BEAUTY SPECIALTIES," at 62 West 45th Street in Manhattan. We have a formal photograph of my grandfather from around this time. On the back is written: "Return to D. H. Marshall c/o M. Wahl & Son 41 W 29th St NYC." M. Wahl & Son is listed in the Manhattan telephone directory in 1940 as a business selling beauty parlor equipment ("bty plr equip"); presumably it was a manufacturer that my grandfather was representing from his office on 45th Street (which is also listed in the 1940 directory). The portrait might have been taken a few years earlier; it resembles the portrait taken with Isadore in his World War I uniform more than it resembles the snapshot taken with my father in his World War II uniform. Why M. Wahl & Son wanted a formal portrait of D. H. Marshall (made by Unity Studio, a well-known theatrical photographer) is another mystery.

M. Wahl & Son also had its roots on the Lower East Side: it appears in the "Hair Goods" section of the 1915 Trow's Directory with an address of 131 Essex Street.

My grandfather's business was later called the Marlee Sales Corporation, the name a merger of Marshall and the name of a partner who had quickly disappeared yet left part of his name behind. I found a published record of a patent, filed on June 17, 1947, by David H. Marshall, "doing business as Marlee Sales Co., New York, NY," for "HAIR BRUSHES, AND EYEBROW AND EYELASH BRUSHES FOR APPLYING EYEBROW AND EYELASH PREPARATIONS."[40] My father joined the business in 1947, eventually taking it over after his father died. He recalled how proud his father was when he agreed to

David H. Marshall.

join the business, relating this moment to his pride at escaping financial insecurity twice, first as a child and then after the Depression.

By 1951, the year that my parents married, the business lost a big account and my grandfather and his two sons were struggling. My grandfather had a heart attack. According to my mother, "one of the reasons they felt that he had this heart attack was because business was terrible."[41] Lying in a hospital bed with pneumonia, did he think back fifty years to the death of his father in 1901? When my grandfather died, my grandmother was left with no means of support. Eventually my father rebuilt and expanded the business. Although he was very successful, it was not without its ups and downs. I grew up with the name "Marlee Sales Corp." My father didn't change the name of his business to Arthur K. Marshall Associates until decades later. I still have a metal ruler with "MARLEE SALES CORP." written across it in large blue letters, with the name "Art Marshall" and the name of the salesman who worked for him underneath it.

19

———✧———

A Ghost and a Memory

My father saved the letters that his parents wrote to him during the three years that he served in the army. The letters are for the most part neatly typed (thanks to the skills they acquired taking business courses some twenty or thirty years earlier), and they are filled with good-natured reports of everyday life, local news, and gossip, as well as parental advice. My grandfather also displayed a strong paternal hand, providing instructions more than advice, and sometimes orders more than instructions, especially as he reported on his efforts to work through a business contact in Chicago to help my father get accepted to a special training program.

On December 23, 1945, my grandfather wrote a letter to my father, who was then stationed in the Philippines in the last months of his military service. My father was enrolled as a freshman at Brooklyn College when he was drafted, and in the army he was sent to the University of Oregon to be trained to be a meteorologist. He always told my sisters and me that if anyone asked what he did during the war, we should say that he sent up balloons. In the letter, my grandfather commented on some photographs that my father had sent, in particular a very small photograph of himself posing with a large weather balloon.

Arthur Marshall and his parents, World War II.

I have the photograph: my father stands confidently, holding an eight-foot-high balloon with a Mylar appendage folded into a triangle. He is wearing long pants and no shirt; a trailer bearing an army star, a ladder, and some sort of radar equipment are behind him, against a backdrop of palm trees. On the back, my father wrote in block letters: "HERE WE ARE FOLKS! MY JOB IN THE ARMY. I WANT THIS ENLARGED SO I CAN SHOW TO MY GRANDCHILDREN."

In his letter to my father, neatly typed, single-spaced, on three short pages, after discussing the end of the war and the pending induction of my father's younger brother, my grandfather responded: "You did not enclose a negative of yourself holding a balloon. When this comes, we will make an enlargement for you and not for the reason to show your

Arthur Marshall in the Philippines, November 1945.

grandchildren the part you played in the World War II. I remember the same old crap we tossed around when I was in service and what part we played in the World War I, when I was in the Army Transport Service division Finance and Accounts, that we would never live our home stay down when we got to talking about the war then . . . To me, this was very quickly forgotten and not a word was ever mentioned. So you see,

Sunday, 23,Dec.1945.

Dear Art:-

We received a surprise to-day by receiving
your letter dated the 11th,altho mailed the
14th of December. Note what you have to say
about Mel Zoler and his griping. He should
kick..Whatever happens, time will soon tell
what the score will be. Things are coming to
ahead real soon and when the Moscow conference
is over and an understanding is reached, I
feel that the need for the men in service
will be curtailed. The bottleneck at the
present moment is not releasing the men from
service but the bottoms and trains to bring
them home. Transportation facilities are in
a muddle and it is hard to say when this jam
will release. The housing shortage is presening
a serious problem plus employment is adding to
all the trials and tribulations of the veteran.
In my letter to you of the 22nd, sent to APO
351, I mentioned a few things of interest.
However, what matters is, the government does
not want to have you in the army any longer
than is necessary but someone must be kept.
As I mentioned in my letter that Stephen got
his induction notice and to report on Jan.15.
They are still taking the 18 and ups and
it is my opinion that the President wants to
put thru a training youth bill to keep the
armed forces to a certain par and train the
youngsters so as to make them prepared for
the future.

You did not inclose a negative of yourself
holding a balloon. When this comes, we will
make an enlargement for you and not for the
reason to show your grandchildren the part you

Page 2. Art Marshall.........

played in the World War 11. I remember the
same old crap we tossed around when I was in
service and what part we played in the World
War 1, when I was in the Army Trasport Service
division Finance and Accounts, that we would
never live our home stay down when we got to
talking about the war then...To me, this was
very quickly forgotten and not a word was ever
mentioned. So you see, what you are trying
to preserve is merely a ghost and a memory.
At least, you have something to remember and
that is the experience of going to College
at Oregon. your Canadian trip, your cross
country rides,then overseas Etc..... Yes
that is something to remember and if by
chance you have made some real friends in
the army, that is worthwhile.
According to your records, you have 40points.
The present number of points as announced
recently as at Jan.1, was 50. This means
that you will approach the mark when your
term will be near and the next thing to worry
about is that they do not freeze you or your
outfit. They may secure a number of re-enlist-
ments in Weather and if this is so, you will
have your chance to get out quickly. Your
branch of the service is much more sought
after because you have what we all call the
"snap." We have enjoyed seeing and receiving
the group of pictures you sent us recently
about your activities and some of the characters in your present quarters....
Mother and I visited with your Grandma at
the hospital. We met Uncle Irving, Jeanette
and genius Grace. She got to be a big girl.
Irving started to kid me that she was as tall
as I was..I retorted, that should be easy to
beat as I have lost my suit against the X CITY

what you are trying to preserve is merely a ghost and a memory."[1] The ellipsis marks are in the original typescript.

The paragraph stands out for its diction and its intensity. The letters that my grandfather sent to my father, including this one, are written in a light, often jocular tone. This letter includes news about "the Moscow conference" and "the trials and tribulations of the veteran," it comments on the pictures that my father had sent, it reports on my father's brother Stephen, what they had for dinner, and other family news, and it recounts comic stories, including one about losing a lawsuit against the city that concerned an encounter between the sidewalk and his "ass." It seems clear that in his inscription on the back of the photo my father was being flippant, ironic, when he imagined showing his grandchildren what he did during the war. He continued to make the exact same joke ten, fifteen, and twenty years later, and throughout our childhood. This is indeed exactly what my father told his grandchildren when he became a grandfather: "During the war I sent up balloons." Was my grandfather defensive about his "home stay" service during World War I? This Jewish cadet, this veteran of the prize-winning Hebrew Orphan Asylum cadet corps, was twenty-five when he registered for the draft in 1917. After his service as an accountant for the army, he was active in two American Legion posts in Brooklyn. In a brief account of his childhood, my father wrote: "I remember walking with my father—and the parades. Or maybe it's the wonderful picture we have of me in a white starched shorts pants linen suit waving an American flag while holding my father's hand. Was I 3 or older? I do remember the parades & the marching bands and the World War I veterans with the American Legion caps."[2] Holding his son's hand around 1927, he was a spectator to the parade. Writing to his son in 1945, did he still imagine the alternative future that might have followed his admission to West Point, or did that dream seem ridiculous in retrospect thirty-nine years later?

Somehow in those ellipsis marks there is some unexplained emotion: ". . . To me, this was very quickly forgotten and not a word was ever mentioned. So you see, what you are trying to preserve is merely a ghost and a memory." My grandfather goes on to suggest that my father's other experiences in the army (going to school in Oregon, traveling across country, to Canada, and overseas, his friends) would be "something to remember," but his admonition, if that is the right word, makes me wonder: What, in his mind, was something to remember? What was something to forget, without a word ever mentioned? What is the difference between a ghost and a memory, I wonder, as I think about the name that was forgotten, the word that was never mentioned, the unspoken word. What did my grandfather, David Warshafsky's grandson, remember as he cautioned his father's grandson against looking forward to a moment when, a grandfather, he would look back? If the silence of the ellipses indicates some omission (from the Greek *elleipein,* "to fall short, leave out") in the context of my grandfather's letter, it indicates anxiety about something that didn't happen—the part that he and his son did *not* play in the war. Yet the silence resonates further as my grandfather (who did not know his paternal grandfather, just as his son did not know *his* paternal grandfather, just as his grandson would not know *his* paternal grandfather) thinks about ghosts and memories, about words not spoken. There is also a story here "whose common theme," as Hamlet puts it, is the "death of fathers."

I have mentioned the reports and recollections that it was "utterly traumatic" for children to arrive at the Hebrew Orphan Asylum at the turn of the century, as well as the descriptions of its spartan regime, its often violent, English-boarding-school discipline, and its strict and anonymous institutional culture. I have recalled my father's and grandmother's recollections that my grandfather was bitter and resentful about his experience, that he wouldn't talk about his years there. David H. Marshall did not talk about his father, either; nor, according to his niece Adele, did his sister Millie, or his mother Lena. I thought about what must be forgotten, or left out, in recalling such memories, when I read an autobiographical account that Charles Dickens wrote for his biographer John Foster.

Dickens noted that until he wrote his autobiographical sketch, he had never before spoken about the period in his childhood when his parents, in and out of debtors' prison, sent him to work at the age of twelve in Warren's Blacking Warehouse for six shillings a week. After describing the experience, Dickens writes: "From that hour until this at which I write, no word of that part of my childhood which I have now gladly brought to a close, has passed my lips to any human being. I have no idea how long it lasted; whether for a year, or much more, or less. From that hour until this my father and my mother have been stricken dumb upon it. I have never heard the least allusion to it, however far off and remote, from either of them. I have never, until I now impart it to this paper, in any burst of confidence with anyone, my own wife not excepted, raised the curtain I then dropped, thank God." Dickens was bitter not only that he "could have been so easily cast away at such an age," but also that his mother had wanted him to continue working in the blacking factory even after the family's circumstances improved.[3]

I do not mean to compare the Hebrew Orphan Asylum, whatever its miseries, to the horrors of Victorian child labor in 1824—although one recent historian compares Hyman Bogen's account of the discipline imposed during the regime of Superintendent Herman Baar to Charlotte Brontë's descriptions of the boarding school in *Jane Eyre*.[4] As the twentieth century began, as I have said, the Hebrew Orphan Asylum was a national model and it prided itself on its benevolence, spirit of reform, and enlightened educational philosophy. Yet even in the best of circumstances, the experience of the orphanage left its wounds. In his memoir, Maurice Bernstein reprints excerpts from a debate that took place in the "Mail Bag" section of *The Rising Bell*, the newsletter of the HOA Alumni Association, about whether some alumni correspondents were recalling their experiences with too much nostalgia. In 1959—seven years after my grandfather died at the age of sixty-one—an authoritative summary was submitted by Hyman Bogen, who would become president of the alumni association as well as the author of *The Luckiest Orphans: A History of the Hebrew Orphan Asylum*. Bogen wrote:

> Although the H.O.A. rescued a great many of us from shattered homes, gave us each some wonderful moments, launched some on their present careers, and provided many with friendships that have endured—these things, heartening as they are, should not be permitted to obscure the basic

reality now being dimmed by time; that living there was a discouraging, even brutal and degrading experience. After having to violently re-arrange our lives upon admission, we were subjected to forces and pressures which often withered our feelings and destroyed our self-esteem and distorted our relationships. The effect of this damage is only now being felt by some alumni, but others are unwilling to recognize it because they cannot accept the memory of a terrible childhood.[5]

This surprisingly negative description by the author of *The Luckiest Orphans*, which is a candid but generally good-humored and admiring history, is no doubt informed by a survey that Bogen conducted of Hebrew Orphan Asylum alumni two years earlier. In 1957, Bogen sent seventeen questions to alumni and asked for their recollections, often following up with further questions and interviews. He asked seventeen questions about the experiences and recollections of the former inmates. Most of the typewritten answers held today in the archives of the American Jewish Historical Society are from alumni who were inmates in the period after my grandfather and his brothers were in residence (1903–06 for David and 1903–10 for Ruby and Isi), but there are some respondents who overlapped with them, or preceded or followed them by only two or three years.[6] According to one respondent labeled M-1, who left the asylum in 1901 at the age of fourteen, "The routine was military. We were organized into companies of about 20 with an older boy acting as captain, and he was usually a brute! We were actually banged with either the monitor's fists or a stick into discipline. We marched to meals, to classrooms, to the playground, and to bed. . . . We were identified by our numbers which were sewed in our garments like prisoners." In answer to Question 14, "Do you discuss your childhood freely with non-HOA persons?" he wrote: "Many oldtimers hesitate to discuss the H.O.A. because of the brutality they experienced[,] also the suppression of natural outlets of expression."

Respondent M-6, who entered the orphanage in 1897, wrote of the "discipline" and the monitor system: "I feel that this was one of the worst things that could ever happen anywhere. I don't think these customs were even practiced in prisons." Respondent M-3, who left in 1904, the year after David and his brothers arrived, wrote: "The conditions I was subjected to are today as archaic as gas-light." He offers a Dickensian image of the "awesome figure of Jacob Schiff"—the eminent Jewish millionaire, businessman, philanthropist, and HOA patron—with his "silk hat," "being conducted through the HOA" oblivious to the orphans. This alumnus said that his "unhappiest moments had to do with occasions when I was beaten by those in authority," adding: "My happiest moments were wan and pale compared to my unhappy moments." According to M-3, "The stress and accent were on uniformity, conformity, regimentation. The children were dealt with on a wholesale basis. There was no time nor means for individual treatment. All the boys wore the same ill-fitting uniforms, all had their hair clipped with barbers' clippers. They were as alike in appearance as peas in a pod. The kid who obtruded his personal problems was considered a nuisance."

Superintendent Coffee's brief tenure between 1903 and 1905 may have been a period of relative liberalization, a respite between the nineteenth-century institutional culture and the violence and brutality described by many alumni who were inmates in the two or three decades after my grandfather and his brothers left the orphanage. Yet Respondent M-17, who was an inmate between 1903 and 1912, and thus overlapped with the residence of my grandfather and his brothers, wrote: "I never accepted the discipline and conformity that was required of every inmate in the home." Although he described the "discipline" as "mainly in standing in a rigid position for an hour or two," he added: "As far as justification for discipline was concerned, I could never see it. I resented it all the nine years I spent at the institution." Respondent M-16, who was an inmate between the ages of five and twelve from 1904 to 1911, wrote: "I took many a beating from the monitors, Supt. and governors," although he suggests that "the discipline that I received at the HOA . . . helped me all through life, as honesty, and truthfull is always the best policy." All of the alumni who responded to Bogen's survey noted the terrible food (M-16, who overlapped with my grandfather, wrote: "Food worse than rotten"), and all spoke of the impersonality and emotional deprivation—what M-3 described as "the lack of any emotional relationships on my part. Nobody loved me or gave a damn about me in the HOA."

Bogen asked a specific question about homosexuality and lesbianism. According to M-3, describing an incident that would have occurred when my grandfather was an inmate: "Homosexuality was rife. I remember that Dr. Coffee once had each and every boy before him in a secret inquisition, in which each kid was asked if he had such relations. Such an official inquiry would only have been touched off by the widespread character of the situation." My grandfather would have been eleven or twelve at the time. He would have been sixty-six years old in 1957 if he were still alive. I can only imagine the answers that he would have given to Bogen's questions. We already know how he would have answered question 14: "Do you discuss your childhood freely with non-HOA persons?" Even if he were alive, however, I do not expect that he would have been part of the HOA Alumni Association. In the 1922 souvenir program commemorating the centennial anniversary of "the Organization of the Hebrew Orphan Asylum of the City of New York," there is a two-page "Honor Roll" of "Graduates of the Hebrew Orphan Asylum who Served their Country during the World War." I mentioned earlier that "Marshal, Isidore" and "Warshafsky, Reuben" appear on this list, but there is no mention of David Warshawsky, David Roshafsky, or David Marshall. Perhaps he didn't feel that his service in the war was something to remember. It seems most likely that he was not in touch with his fellow alumni.[7] Although active in clubs and veterans associations, he does not seem to have been proud to be a veteran of the Hebrew Orphan Asylum.

Bogen's survey and his surprisingly candid analysis of a "discouraging, even brutal and degrading experience," his acknowledgment of the emotional "damage" that resulted from "a terrible childhood," suggest that there were traumas apart from the actual living conditions in the orphanage. (Bogen also had a question in his survey about whether the alumni had sought any psychiatric help.) The trauma that Dickens evokes in his autobiographical account is not merely the experience of the blacking factory itself; just as painful are the shame and humiliation he felt in being sent there. He also evokes his unspeakable anger at his parents, especially his mother, for casting him away; and—remarkably—he pictures the entire family in a sort of unspoken conspiracy of silence on the subject. This is what resonates for me in the context of my grandfather's story. The sentiments that would strike him dumb, forbidding even an allusion, preventing him from entering into the confidence of anyone, even his own wife and his oldest son, likely would have encompassed his anger about the decision of his mother to send away her sons, no matter how reasonable or necessary that decision might have seemed to the adults in the family at the time.

Surely David Warshawsky's arrival at the Hebrew Orphan Asylum at the age of eleven was traumatic, as it would have been for most of the children sent there in early 1903, as it was for the children who later described their arrival in the 1957 survey and in the oral histories recorded in the 1980s, no matter how benevolent and nurturing the care was in the institution. What did Lena tell her sons? Ruby had just turned ten and Isi was seven. One of the women whose oral history is in the archives of the New York Public Library describes how her father told her to put on her best dress, brought her to the Hebrew Orphan Asylum, and left her there, without a word of explanation. Were the boys prepared for weeks, reassured that their stay would last only as long as it took for the family to get back on its feet, or were they told unexpectedly and suddenly that their lives were about to change? Only six days elapsed between Lena's application for admission and the entry of the boys into the orphanage. Was David, the oldest son, told to take care of Ruby and Isi? Did Daisy offer reassuring words to her younger brothers, or was she surprised when she came home from school that day that her brothers were gone?

I picture Lena and the three boys on the long trip from 132 Suffolk Street to 136th Street and Amsterdam Avenue on March 9, 1903. I don't know what combination of streetcar (some were still pulled by horses), electric car, and elevated train they would have taken. The Amsterdam Avenue electric car passed by the orphan asylum. The temperature that day was in the fifties; the *New York Times* forecast was: "Clear and colder; winds northeast to north." They would have brought nothing with them since the orphanage issued uniforms and their clothing would be taken from them as they were bathed and had their heads shaved upon entering the reception house for their two-week quarantine. One day David, Ruby, and Isi were children on the crowded streets of the Lower East Side; the next day they were numbered inmates along with a thousand other children wearing uniforms in an institution far from home, with two visiting hours four days a year.

Furthermore, Lena's difficult decision to send away her sons must have followed a precipitous and perhaps humiliating fall from prosperity to poverty, from the starched linen dresses in which David and Daisy posed in the Mandelkorn & Dombrow Photographic Art Studio on Essex Street to the "washing, etc." that Lena had to take in on Suffolk Street in order to feed her family. It also took place in the shadow of the death—and perhaps, even worse, in the shadow of the life—of Harris Warshawsky, whose ghost and memory became something to be forgotten, not a word ever mentioned. Did David, in the first dark nights in the dormitory, among a hundred boys in rows of beds, ever imagine his father's spirit admonishing him: "Remember me!" or (to again evoke Hamlet) was his father, dead two years ago, "not forgotten yet"? Such memories might strike a family dumb.

I have pictured David Warshawsky in 1906 as he prepared to leave the Hebrew Orphan Asylum, a month before his birthday, the world before him, the Bible that would name him David Marshall in hand. There is another moment I return to, a moment of return and retrospection. On April 10, 1910, David Warshawsky must have been among the five thousand spectators in the New York Hippodrome watching the remarkable spectacle of the fiftieth anniversary of the opening of the first building of the Hebrew Orphan Asylum. I imagine that the Warshawsky and Ruderman families came to see his brothers Ruby and Isi performing with the twelve hundred children on stage, just a few months before they would be discharged. Along with the other assembled alumni, he would have witnessed the exhibition drill of the "Special Company of the Cadet Corps," the march performed by the band, dances by the girls' gymnasium classes, and "exercises and games" by the boys' gymnasium classes. The children's exhibition culminated in "Rally Round the Flag" performed by the cadet corps and the singing of "The Star-Spangled Banner" by a chorus of boys and girls.

The audience was addressed by (among others) attorney and alumnus Meyer Cushner, "representing the former inmates" of the orphanage. He began by recalling his arrival at the orphanage as a young boy, "his heart heavy with an unspeakable grief," picturing himself "gazing longingly in the direction of the great 'East Side' from which he had just come." He then offered a stirring paean to "our Alma Mater" on behalf of the alumni. The audience also heard a speech by New York City Mayor William J. Gaynor. At the end of the program, following the performances and the speeches, there was a spectacular display of "Scenes of Institutional Life" projected in lantern slides on a large screen in what was billed as the largest theater in the world.

In his speech, Mayor Gaynor looked back to the early history of New York, telling the audience that his predecessor, Peter Stuyvesant, displayed bigotry and ignorance of "the history of your people" when he demanded that the first seven Jews wishing to land in Manhattan provide a bond promising that they would care for their own poor and orphans. He wryly noted that the city had never needed to search for this bond in its "archives," since "charity is the lineage of the Jewish race." He continued: "If we go back, I might almost say to the age of fable, or at any rate to that borderline where fable hardly ceases and history hardly begins, we find that even then among the Jewish people the weak and the orphan and the poor and the widow were not left unprotected or unprovided for." The mayor pictured the children, "some of them bereaved so early that they know not even the name of mother nor the name of father" and "carry that loss with them in their hearts as long as they live." Acknowledging the distinguished philanthropic supporters, the "great men," whose names were singled out in the introductory remarks of Hebrew Orphan Asylum President Louis Stern, the mayor paid tribute to the "many unnamed ones" and the "many widows and poor among you" who, although not "conspicuous," also contributed to the work of the orphanage.

Gesturing toward the twelve hundred Hebrew Orphan Asylum inmates present in the theater, as well as the alumni in the audience of five thousand, Gaynor offered an almost sublime image of the "thousands," "the tens of thousands" of orphans that had been cared for and had since "gone out into the world" over the preceding fifty years. "All that we do not see to-night," he said, "except in retrospect and imagination."[8] I doubt that my grandfather, having gone out into the world so recently, was nostalgic for his years in the Hebrew Orphan Asylum, even as the lantern slides with "scenes of institutional life" flashed before his eyes. Surrounded by those who had gone forth and those who had been left behind, the named and the unnamed, the shades of memory as well as the shadows on the screen, he would not look back, either in retrospect or imagination.

20

Searches and Signs

I have taken to reading the pages of the 1900 census for pleasure. It might be more accurate to locate my reading somewhere between idle and obsessive curiosity. I track down leads but also look for leads to follow. Amateur genealogical research is the new Internet addiction. *Ancestry.com*, one of the most popular genealogical websites, claims to provide over 13 billion records to over 2 million subscribers. *Familysearch. com*, the search engine of the Church of the Latter-Day Saints, has had billions of "hits" by amateur genealogists, as well as Mormons hoping to retroactively rescue other people's ancestors—by conversion rather than Kaddish. *Findagrave.com* claims to have 121 million burial records. There are Italian, Jewish, and other genealogical sites, often acting as portals for birth, death, marriage, naturalization, and other databases, while hosting online message boards and communities. Sometimes the *search engine*, that which drives the search, is more personal than technological. As I reached the end of this investigation, *Ancestry.com* ran television commercials that said: "You don't have to know what you're looking for. You just have to start looking." Do I know what I am looking for? The literary critic and memoirist Nancy K. Miller writes: "Memoirs about the loss of parents show how enmeshed in the family plot we have been and the price of our complicity in its stories. The death of parents forces us to rethink our lives, to reread ourselves. We read for what we need to find. Sometimes, we also find what we didn't know we needed."[1] If the story I am telling here is sometimes written in the ink of mourning, its story of a lost parent is about a father who was somehow misplaced. My father's father's father was lost in a family plot: a conspiracy of silence that we breathed like the invisible air around us. Do I know what I have found in these stories of lost parents?

As I return again and again to the search engines, the databases, the online newspaper archives, the websites filled with virtual warehouses of public documents, I wonder about the drive, the compulsion to search, to need to find one more piece of information. Besides the epistemological desire to know what can and can't be known, besides the forensic compulsion that drives the detective story forward in search of proof and evidence, there is also our contemporary compulsion (in our age of attention-deficit disorder) to check e-mail, Facebook, Twitter, blogs, text messages: the insatiable hunger for news feeds in an age that both denies and stimulates boredom.

In the case of Harris Warshawsky, where there are so many blanks and impasses, yet where I have discovered more traces of the story than I ever imagined possible, I keep hoping that another book scanned by Google, another government archive acquired by *Ancestry.com*, another family tree posted by an amateur genealogist, will suddenly speak his name; I search for new queries or combinations of search terms that will coax one more secret out of the literal-minded, Sphinxlike search engines. The case of Harris Warshawsky is not what the homicide detectives call a cold case, a cardboard box of leads, dead ends, and newspaper clippings—random pieces of evidence placed high on a basement shelf, waiting for a deathbed confession or the miraculous materialization of a clue. No one seemed to know that he was missing; no one wanted to view the scene of the crime. Yet like those cold cases that are solved by some previously unimagined forensic technology that can read DNA from an old hairbrush or diagnose a cause of death from the bones in a grave, it holds out the prospect of one more discovery. So I keep searching.

The origins of the word "search" are found in the early fourteenth century, in the Old French *cerchier*, which derives from the Latin *circare*, to go about, wander, or traverse, from the word *circus* or circle (from the Greek for "circle," which goes back to turn or bend). I keep returning to a line from a poem by Rainer Maria Rilke: "*Sehnsucht geht zu oft ins Ungenaue.*" An imprecise translation would be: "Longing leads so often into vagueness." *Sehnsucht* means longing, yearning, craving. *Sehnen* means to yearn, to long for, to desire. *Suchen* means to seek, to search for, to go in quest of, to look for, to try to find, to trace; to want, to desire. *Die sucht* means passion, mania, addiction. *Sehnsucht* lives somewhere in between longing, compulsion, mourning, and nostalgia. It names a vague yet insistent want, a lack, a desire that comes from missing what is not and perhaps was never there; a temptation to return; a need to look again, to circle back, to keep searching. All of these words name me. There is no end to looking back, to the search

Lower East Side, New York City.

for beginnings; the road has detours, dead ends, and wrong turns, and all offer signs of promise.

Reading through the census pages for New York City's Lower East Side, I feel like I am reading an author's outline for a novel. There are infinite plots implied in the large cast of characters and the details of families, marriages, children, neighbors, and boarders; details of race, religion, class, occupation, income, dwelling, education, literacy; stories of immigration and assimilation, of mother tongues, of parents and places left behind. I try to track down the secondary characters: the midwives who signed the birth certificates, the rabbis who signed the marriage certificates, the witnesses who signed the marriage certificates and the naturalization papers. I look up the neighbors; I try to find the entries for the census enumerators themselves. In 1894, Harris Warshawsky was a listed as a witness in the naturalization papers of Abraham Sametzsky, a tailor living at 17 Attorney Street. Was Harris Warshawsky a minor character in Abraham Sametzsky's story? He is a minor character in the story of the labor leader Meyer Schoenfeld and the tailors' strike of 1894—in cinematic terms, perhaps just an extra, a face in the crowd. He is a minor character in the story of Dr. W. A. McCorn, himself a minor character in the history of American psychiatry, and in 1899 briefly a major character in a flurry of newspaper articles after he shot and killed Clifton White, a boy who wandered into the wrong story to steal cherries on the grounds of the River Crest Sanitarium. He is, of course, a major character in the story of David H. Marshall, alias David Warshawky, alias David Roshofsky—although he is the face cut out of the family photograph.

Reading the census, it is difficult to know where to draw the line. Like the houses in Greek tragedy, these houses have too many stories, and each story opens onto a neighboring story. Through the census pages, I try to trace all of Harris and Lena's siblings. A family tree posted on *Ancestry.com* led me to a man who was a distant relative of Michael Ruderman, Lena's younger brother. He remembered his mother's "Auntie Ella and Uncle Mike." Through *Ancestry.com*, I made contact with a woman who might be my distant cousin—if I am right that Harris

Warshawsky's brother Jack is the same person as one Isaac Warshoff, who (according to the 1910 U.S. census) was a grocer from Russia living in Newark who married his wife Anna in 1893 and had children named David, Daisy, and Harry. She told me that her father changed names several times and that his family, which came from Minsk, was always "a mystery." She told me that as a child she heard that their original family name was Marshak or Marshall, and that Warshawsky was an Ellis Island name, later changed to Warshoff. Unless this is a coincidence, or a story from a parallel universe, it is a garbled version of my Warshawsky story. I accidentally uncovered a family secret about a relative of this family who long ago had been institutionalized in a home for the "feeble-minded." She said that there was "an undercurrent of shame" when they asked questions about her father's family. The census leads me to stories that might circle back to my story; or their uncanny phantasms might merely mirror my story. The census is a map of the underworld: a guide to the ghostly afterlife of untold stories.

The census looked both backward and forward. In 1890 and 1910, census enumerators asked about service in the Union or Confederate army or navy; in 1930, they asked if the family owned a radio set. (David Sarnoff of 275 East 69th Street, who, according to the 1930 census was the president of Radio Corp. and according to my father's cousin Millie almost was Daisy Warshawsky's husband, owned a radio.) The census is a collection of characters for a Borgesian anthology of histories and futures. One imagines what these people would become in the future that is now our past: the forking paths, the alternative futures at the crossroads or turning points of the past. Moving from page to page, from street to street, from language to language, inscribes one in the urban geographies of the novel. Walking down the street through the census pages, I am a sort of nineteenth-century *flaneur*; but unlike Baudelaire's observer of modern life, I am not aimless, and I am forced to follow the enumerator's prescribed path through the census district. The census enumerator is like Leopold Bloom in James Joyce's *Ulysses*, yet more systematic, wandering from street to street, in New York rather than Dublin, yet obsessive—as Joyce was—about facts. I, too, despite all my speculation, have become obsessive about facts. I am overinvested in the facts that stand for knowing. Yet each fact seems to launch a thousand stories, leaving me to read between the lines, to fill in the blanks.

Of course, Homer's Ulysses—Odysseus—was the original wanderer, but he was trying to get home, a victim of nostalgia (literally, homesickness). Most of the neighbors of the Warshawsky family found in the pages of the 1900 census had no desire to return home. They were cut off from their origins, never to return, even before the cataclysmic divide of the Holocaust. Their children were already orphaned, like the twelve hundred Hebrew Orphan Asylum inmates who paraded in uniform on the stage of the Hippodrome and sang "America." Even more than the parents who left worlds behind, they were like the orphans who populate so many eighteenth- and nineteenth-century novels: deprived of genealogies, fleeing fathers, in search of new social identities and classes, these characters changed their names and reinvented themselves in acts of conversion, metamorphosis, and autobiographical self-inscription. They were not nostalgic; they would have been baffled by *Ancestry.com*. My father's cousin Adele, Millie's daughter, was pleased to answer my questions, but after a while she told me that I should stop already. My mother found the story that I had to tell to be "sad." The Court of Justice of the European Union recently established what has been described as a legal "right to be forgotten." This right to privacy, founded in the French legal concept of *le droit à l'oubli* or "right of oblivion," would allow one under certain circumstances to expunge one's past from the Internet, or at least to erase online documents from the past, removing them from the reach of Google and other search engines.[2] Is there also a *droit d'oublier*, a right to forget? Would Harris Warshawsky have preferred to be forgotten?

Although I searched for public documents from Minsk and Gorodok in Russia, looking for Warshawskys, Rudermans, and Marshaks, I drew the line at visiting the old country in search of landsmen. This was a New York story. My father's cousin Adele, Millie's daughter, told me that she discovered that Warshawsky had been her mother's original name only because when her mother was hospitalized late in life, someone had assumed that she had been an immigrant. Millie demanded that Adele find a document proving that Millie had been born in New York City. Two generations later, I am invested in documents, proofs, and origins. When the census enumerator turns a corner, just a few buildings from the address of the building that I am hoping to explore, I am revealed to be someone trying to get somewhere after all, trying to get back to someone's home.

On a Sunday in August, I wandered up and down Norfolk, Suffolk, Essex, Rivington, and Broome streets, in search of the places where the

Rivington Street, New York City.

Rivington Street, New York City.

Warshawsky family lived, according to the pages of the census and New York City documents and city directories. The neighborhood today is again in transition: one finds gang graffiti, parking lots or overgrown, empty spaces where tenements and factories once stood, scaffolding that suggests gentrification. The young man with an accent who sold me a slice of pizza on Rivington Street is from Turkey; young couples line up on the street in front of fashionable bars that serve Sunday brunch. Thanks to the "street view" feature in Google Maps, I already had wandered down these streets in a virtual Internet dimension, navigating video images from a very recent past, now still and frozen in time, toggling facsimile photographs of census pages and seamless photographs of streets in search of addresses that may or may not still exist. Much of the old Lower East Side remains, but some buildings have been demolished, some replaced, some renumbered.

I search for addresses, for buildings that will speak to me. The old streets still resonate. Walking by the rows of buildings that form a backdrop in the old photographs of the streets that were crowded with pushcarts and wagons and hundreds of people, I am impressed by the dignified elegance of the architecture, the intricate, ornamental details now obscured by the zigzag lattices of fire escapes. I worry that if these buildings address me, if they speak of the past, they are only screen memories, facades that only stand in for images that can't be recalled.

Some New York City real estate records "estimate" that 151 Norfolk Street was built in 1912, the year that the *Forward* moved into its new ten-story building and the imposing Beaux-Arts Jarmulowsky Bank was built. Are the buildings in which the Warshawsky family lived in the last years of the nineteenth century ghosts, effaced behind facades that in the first years of the twentieth century marked a moment of class mobility for the neighborhood itself? Other records confirm that the six-story tenement building that was built in 1898 on a lot sold by the German Reformed Protestant Dutch Church (where John Jacob Astor worshiped) is the building that is there today. Regardless, the past hides behind the past. Building numbers on these streets may have changed over the years, like the names of the people who lived there. Some addresses direct one to an empty space, a vacant lot, where the numbers, like the names, have disappeared.[3]

On Rivington Street, at the corner of Clinton Street, I was struck by a strange two-story building painted with bright patterns and serpent-like shapes; across the awning of the shuttered storefront, stenciled in large block letters, I read: ALIAS. "Alias" is an old word, dating back to the fifteenth century, meaning "otherwise called," from the Latin word meaning "at another time, in another way." Cognates of "alias" meaning "other" and "different" echo through Greek, Sanskrit, Armenian, and Old English, among other languages. I, too, in my search for a name, am otherwise called. In my search for the familiar, I am named as an other. Dwelling on the resonant street names, as if they were the names of long-lost relatives, I look for the names hidden behind names, for another time and another place.

Rivington Street, New York City.

On that Sunday I walked down Rivington Street searching for No. 176, where the Warshawsky family lived between 1897 and 1900. At that address I found a six-story building joined to four parallel buildings in a seamless row. No. 176 is a bookend to the row, bordering a small park that interrupts the passage of Attorney Street—where my grandmother Jeanette was born in 1902. Plain yet elegant lintels and friezes frame the windows and a strange, gargoylelike face looks out from the center; the second story is covered with peeling paint, light blue, that stands out against the beige brick of the building and the rusting, red fire escape. As I approached the building from across the narrow street, camera in hand, I saw an awning over an empty storefront. Below the awning at

176 Rivington was a blank storefront, the window covered with faded newspapers; an open door revealed an empty store. On the awning I read the initials *DM* written in ornate cursive letters.

The sight of David Marshall's initials, the sight of my initials, appearing like a signature on the bottom right-hand side of the building, left me astonished. I could barely make sense of the letters, which were designed to look like they were written by hand. The abandoned sign seemed to name me, as if I were a character in a nineteenth-century novel with a plot punctuated by coincidences. How was I to read these letters? Beneath the letters *DM* appeared the words DANGEROUS MATHEMATICIANS. I later learned that this had been the site of a clothing design firm that had only recently relocated to Brooklyn. The garment industry still has a presence on the Lower East Side, in tailor shops, women's boutiques, and second-story windows stacked high with bolts of fabric. According to its website, this firm specialized in "revolutionary online design services" that allowed one to "enjoy the luxury of a New York City designer from anywhere." Some 150 years after the clothing industry was transformed by the Lower East Side tenements, shops, and factories in which garment workers produced ready-made clothes for the nation, this firm produced tailor-made clothing using mail, fax, and the Internet. One also can purchase online designer tee shirts with the letters *DM* emblazoned on the front. That Sunday, all that remained of the twenty-first-century designer's "signature clothing" at 176 Rivington Street were the initials on the abandoned sign. Life, like novels, like history, is filled with coincidences; only some of them speak to us. I cannot calculate the odds of finding such a sign in my search for my family name.

My search for a name led me to wander through records and archives. I savored the artifacts almost as much as the facts: the ink of signatures and handwritten names, the imprint of typewriters, the pages and photographs that threatened to crumble in my hands, the numbered boxes handed to me by librarians who spoke in hushed tones, as if they worked in a sanctuary. I skimmed thousands of names, some transcribed by Mormons, some catalogued by cemeteries and burial societies, some microfilmed or scanned. I clicked through thousands of document facsimiles found by

Rivington Street, New York City.

an Internet search engine swifter than thought. Each record, document, certificate, state report, newspaper article, and journal essay opens up onto more stories, more names, more histories, unfolding stories within stories. Some stories, like the documents I haven't found, like the document that Harris holds in the portrait with Lena, a text within a text, must be imagined. In looking back, even if we don't try to trace lineage to the end of the line, we see in retrospect and imagination. We walk the borderline where fable hardly ceases and history hardly begins.

Writing history, I have come to understand, can be an act of mourning. Freud understood mourning as a kind of hyper-remembering; he said that it had to come to an end. The name of the father has to be forgotten, after all. My search, started years ago, intensified after my father's death. If mourning is supposed to stop when the bereaved finds a substitute for the lost loved one, my mourning seemed to start when I found a lost father, a father who had been without a name: the lost father of the grandfather whose name I bore, who bore his grandfather's name. The Ashkenazi Jewish tradition, which is said to go back to the Egyptian Jews of the sixth century B.C.E., commands survivors to transfer the name of the deceased relative to the next child born. The child at once marks the absence of the lost relative and replaces the lost relative, completing the work of mourning by both remembering and forgetting.

If my search was meant to recover something that had been lost— the story of Harris Warshawsky—it also was meant to tell a story of loss; yet these efforts to recall to memory, to undo forgetting, were not meant to be elegiac. This was not a search for the ghost and memory of a lost father (or grandfather, or great-grandfather). It was a search for a story: a story about self-naming, a story that would make sense of the forgetting of a name. Despite my father's apparent lack of curiosity when his father was alive, and his fatalism about the limits of his knowledge, he would have been deeply interested in this story about David Warshawsky and his father. To tell this story thus inscribes me in loss, like those messengers in Shakespeare's tragedies who arrive with their letters too late. The story cannot reach its end any more than it can reach its beginning.

21

———✦———

Returning to Machpelah

Although my search for Harris Warshawsky's name in Machpelah Cemetery had reached a dead end, I began to get a better sense of the genealogy of the cemeteries themselves as I walked in the cities of the dead along Cypress Hills Street. Reading the names of the cemeteries and the residents, even without the pages of the census to guide me through names and neighbors, I began to understand the geography of their shifting borders and names. Back home in California, I continued to search the online databases that represent a sort of census of cemeteries. I returned to the *Find a Grave* website, which claimed to have 18,347,479 site visits "today" on the day of my last visit. The "mission" of *Find a Grave*, which sells baseball caps, tee shirts with pictures of half-buried gravestones, and tombstone-shaped lapel pins with question marks, is "to find, record and present final disposition information from around the world as a virtual cemetery experience." Harris Warshawsky does not appear in the 92 million grave records included on the website, but in searching the Machpelah Cemetery postings, I found a listing by a man in Alabama of a grave in Machpelah Cemetery for one Henry Rothchild, who died in 1902; it included a photograph posted by a *Find a Grave* volunteer of a stone sign above the main gate of the current Beth-El Cemetery that read, "New Union Fields Cemetery."

New Union Fields Cemetery.

The man in Alabama could give me no information, but I kept returning to this sign. At some point I suddenly realized that I had mis-read Dr. McCorn's handwriting on the death certificate. What I thought was "Machpelah—N.W. Fields," which I took to stand for the North West fields of Machpelah, was actually "Machpelah—N.U. Fields." This, I realized, meant "Machpelah—New Union Fields." New Union Fields today is adjacent to Machpelah Cemetery, part of what is now Beth-El Cemetery, and it contains a section called "Machpelah." In my walk around what is today called Machpelah Cemetery, I accidentally wan-dered into Beth-El Cemetery, not realizing that just behind the impos-ing mausoleums of the German-Jewish New York aristocracy was an old Machpelah, which at some point became the Machpelah section of New Union Fields. I found a telephone number for the office at Beth-El Cemetery, which, along with Salem Fields, is today the cemetery of the historic Congregation Emanu-El. The woman who answered the telephone did not seem surprised by my inquiry about a Harris or Aaron Warshawsky who died in February of 1901. Twice she came up blank, but I kept her on the line, and on the third try, she located a record for an Aaron Warschawski, buried in the old Machpelah section of New Union Fields. I was given an address: Grave No. 399 in the Order of B'rith Abraham section of the old Machpelah area. This is how I learned for the first time of Harris Warshawsky's association with the B'rith Abraham fraternal order. If he is named here as Aaron rather than Harris, this must be how he signed up for the lodge and its death benefits years earlier.

I pictured a book of the dead, a heavy, bound register, like the large register recording visits to inmates that I found in the archives of the Hebrew Orphan Asylum, with names inscribed in thick ink with neat handwriting. Later, when I asked for a copy of the page of the register, my correspondent replied: "Dear Mr. Marshall, I have enclosed a copy of the 'Dead Card' from the index. This unfortunately is the only information we have for Aaron Warschawski. If you have any information you would like to add to our records for Aaron I would be more than happy to put it on file." She sent a copy of what looked like a

WARSCHAWSKY, Aaron	
Died	Permit No.
Buried	
Plot No.	Section
Grave No. 399	Section O.B.A.
Remains removed to	Cemetery
Date:	

"Dead Card," New Union Fields Cemetery.

card from a library card catalogue. This "dead card," filled with blanks, turned out to be both testament and monument to what is missing.

Two months after my underground trip to Machpelah Cemetery, on a freezing Sunday toward the end of January, I returned to Cypress Hills Street, this time driving from New Jersey in the car that had been my father's. The Beth-El office is not on the cemetery premises and no one was in the gatehouse when I arrived. The grounds were covered with snow; unlike my first visit, this time I did not see a man carrying bundles of branches. I called the Beth-El cemetery office and someone was sent to help me. While I waited in the snow next to the tunnel-like arched entryway of the brick building, I tried to photograph the grand Rothschild mausoleum, but after taking only two photographs my camera flashed the message: MEMORY FULL. I had forgotten the memory card for the camera, the digital equivalent of forgetting to put film in the camera: another failure of memory and inscription. My inexpensive cell phone camera would have to document any discoveries. Eventually, a groundskeeper came and led me up a path through the snow, through a circle of crypts as elegant as a prestigious neighborhood in a European capital, to an old flat field filled with orderly rows of nondescript gravestones.

The Order of B'rith Abraham section today has a moderately ornate, stone, arched entryway (erected after 1901), but the gravestones are modest, small, mostly simple and thin. The groundskeeper brought me to the corner of the field, told me which section to look in, and left. I walked up and down the neatly ordered rows of gravestones, looking for Aaron Warschawski. In the late morning January light the graves cast no shadows, and the only footprints I saw in the snow were my own. I passed the graves of Rosie Fishel, Sarah Gass, Joseph Gluck, and Fannie Schnorman. The written tablets lined up in rows made me think of shelves in a library or bookstore: book covers facing out. I tried to decipher the worn letters through the erosion of writing that eventually returns the inscribed stone to a blank slate. So many gravestones are written in the first person rather than the third person: *Our Brother, Our Dear Father*; others seem to speak in the second person: *Dearest Papa,*

Beloved Mother. Familiar rather than proper names define the departed in relation to those left behind. It is the living who speak, who inscribe the texts that name the absent, that speak to the dead: those who cannot speak for themselves, who cannot say their names.

Aaron Warschawski was nowhere to be found. There are fewer blank or nearly blank stones than in the Machpelah Cemetery, but in the absence of a gravestone that speaks his name, I scrutinize every stone, imagining that the name I am looking for might be erased, worn away, just beneath the surface. Read from right to left, like Hebrew, the dates of death succeed in chronological order and form a sentence in which the date on the death certificate makes sense. Joseph Gluck died on January 30, 1901; Sarah Gass died on February 25, 1901; Aaron Warschawski, or Harris Warshawsky, who died on February 14, 1901, should be somewhere in between. In about the right place is a worn, almost blank stone. How ironic, I think, how appropriate, that at the end of my search I would come face to face with an illegible text, a memorial to effacement and erasure, the only gravestone in the row that withholds its name. There is no sign of Warschawski on the grave. As I kneel down in the brittle, white snow to try to read the letters at the bottom of the small, curved stone, below worn Hebrew letters I can almost decipher the name Rusman or Rudman.

The groundskeeper returns, and finds me at a loss. He leaves to again consult the map in the office, and then returns again. Like Virgil instructing Dante, my guide assures me that Grave No. 399 in the O.B.A. section must be the seventh grave from the right in the second row. This seems to correspond to the blank stone, but he insists that what I am looking for is not the grave with the blank stone but rather the blank space between the blank stone and the grave of Joseph Gluck. Wearing my father's gloves, I push away the snow with my hands; I claw the brown grass and the dirt beneath the snow, leaving rough fingerprints. Nothing meets the eye.

I later contacted my correspondent in the Beth-El office and asked for a list of the graves in the second row, number by number. Like the census enumerator, she reported:

New Union Fields Cemetery.

Rosie Fishel G# 402
Sarah Gass G# 401
Anna Rubman G# 400
AARON WARSCHAWSKI G#399
Joseph Gluck G#398
Fannie Schnorman G#397

The illegible stone belonged to Anna Rubman, who (I later ascertained) died on February 23, 1901, at the age of forty-three, nine days after the death of Harris Warshawsky and two days before the death of Sarah Gass.

Reading Harris Warshawsky's death certificate, I had found my way to Machpelah, New Union Fields. I had found Aaron Warschawski's grave. Yet there was nothing there, not even a blank slate on which to project fantasies, not even a blank page on which to write stories: just an interval, an invisible interval, a blank space in between. The name—the missing name—that was inscribed in the records of the cemetery office almost exactly 110 years earlier, was missing. Although I knew, after so many dead ends, that I might never find my grandfather's father's grave, I had imagined a culminating moment in my search in which I would come face to face with his name, written in stone, as if brought to the surface from the invisible ink that for so long had been his signature. I was prepared for a fading inscription, worn to effacement; for illegible Hebrew letters, for a blank page; but I found nothing.

It is not uncommon for old grave markers, often made of limestone, to fall over, to break, to disintegrate, to be buried themselves, like the settlements and tombs of the past buried by the layers of forgetting and rebuilding that mark civilization. Yet was there a meaning in this blank space, in the lack of even a blank page? Was Aaron Warschawski, alias Harris Warshawsky, fated to have his name erased, stricken from the book of life? It is possible that Harris Warshawsky's gravestone, perhaps an inexpensive limestone memorial, was the only marker in these rows of gravestones to fall over in a storm, to disintegrate, to become absorbed over the course of a century into the archeological strata of Machpelah. Or was there never a stone, never a speech act that said: *beloved husband, our father, our son?*

In Jewish practice, the unveiling, the dedication of the inscribed gravestone of the deceased, takes place long after the burial, up to a year later. The Order of B'rith Abraham section of the cemetery provided a modest burial. There are no family plots or monuments, only thin and narrow gravestones, closely spaced like tenement houses, erected one by one in order of death. An 1895 *New York Times* article reports that the death benefit provided by the Order of B'rith Abraham was $500, in addition to the expenses of the funeral.[1] Did Lena still have money for a gravestone in February of 1902? We know that by the time that Harry was born in August of 1901, six months after Harris's death, Lena lived next to the milk store that she operated with her brother, Abraham, at 130 Suffolk Street, and we know that by 1903 the milk store had become a grocery store. It is possible that when it came time to purchase the gravestone in February of 1902, a year after Harris's death, the money was already spent, invested in a store, needed by the living more than the dead. We know that a year later, in March of 1903, Lena was reduced to taking in washing, and Harris's three older sons were sent to the orphanage.

Or: Was Harris Warshawsky, after having burned his bridges on his way across the East River to Watkins Street, River Crest Sanitarium, and Machpelah, N.U. Fields, buried alone in an unmarked grave, without the presence of his family, with no gravestone to unveil? Are the names of the son and the grandchildren he never knew—Harry, Harold, Arnold, Adele, Arthur, or Aaron Kaddish—the only memorials to name the missing father? Does Aaron Warschawski's spirit haunt the graveyard, like the ghost questioned by Rabbi Akiva, unable to remember his name?

Perhaps, 110 years after his death, I am the first family member to visit the grave. Standing alone in the "Sons of Abraham" section of the cemetery named for "the tomb of the patriarchs," I cannot say Kaddish. Am I, David ben Aaron, called upon to redeem the soul of my great-grandfather? I find a few pebbles on the edge of the field and leave them on the frozen, vacant ground. The Jewish tradition of placing small stones on a grave is said to engage the visitors in the *mitzvah* of building the funeral monument, like the ancient tradition of building a cairn. In another interpretation of the tradition, the pebbles left by the visitors are said to hold the soul down; the small stones symbolize the boulder that, in prehistoric times, was supposed to keep the dead from escaping their graves: the rock that would stop up the mouth of the burial cave.[2] I wonder if I really want to recall Aaron Warschawski, or Harris Warshawsky, after all, to conjure him after so much forgetting. Placing a pebble on a grave is also an autobiographical mark; it says—to anyone who might follow and read the sign—*I was here*. In the place where his story ended, I have discovered another absence at the heart of the story: a lacuna that calls for a story that would tell why the name *Warshawsky* was buried, unwritten, unspoken. This is where I began; this is where my story begins.

Notes

In addition to providing references for citations, these notes offer additional historical background and bibliographical information for interested readers. However, the narrative is intended to stand on its own; the reader does not need to be distracted or interrupted by this scholarly apparatus.

Chapter 1. Presented to David Marshall

1. K. Kohler, *Guide for Instruction in Judaism, A Manual for Schools and Homes,* 4th ed. (New York: Philip Cowen, 1907), 117. According the 1903 *Jewish Ceremonial Institutions and Customs,* authored by William Rosenau, a leader in Reform Judaism, "The Bar Mitzvah ceremony, in the elaborateness of previous centuries, has fallen into disuse in many communities. With the ever-lessening attention paid by Jews to the study of Hebrew, a boy, who becomes a Bar Mitzvah, frequently does no more than recite the benedictions over a sub-section of the law read to him by the precentor of the synagogue. In those communities where the Bar Mitzvah ceremony has either disappeared altogether, or been modified as stated, an institution known as Confirmation, to which both boys and girls are admitted, has taken the place of the Bar Mitzvah. It may be celebrated at any time. In America, 'Shebuoth,' Feast of Weeks, is generally selected, because the existing tradition that on the sixth day of Sivan, the third month, the law was given to Israel at Mt. Sinai, and hence the time is best suited to impress on the Confirmants their religious responsibility. The

age of Confirmation is about the same age as that of the Bar Mitzvah. . . ." (William Rosenau, *Jewish Ceremonial Institutions and Customs* [Baltimore: The Friedenwald Company, 1903], 153–54).

2. Hyman Bogen, *The Luckiest Orphans: A History of the Hebrew Orphan Asylum of New York* (Urbana, Ill.: University of Illinois Press, 1992), 156. Rudolf I. Coffee's appointment as superintendent of the orphanage was announced in the April issue of *The Menorah*. It was reported that his predecessor, Mr. David Adler, would "sever his connection to the Asylum as soon as Mr. Coffee takes charge" (*The Menorah* 34:44 [1903], 255).

3. "Interview with Arthur Marshall," conducted by Cindy Marshall, April 6, 1991.

4. "Proceedings in Commemoration of the Fiftieth Anniversary of the Opening of the First Building of The Hebrew Orphan Asylum of the City of New York Held at the New York Hippodrome," April 10, 1910 in *Report of the Eighty-Seventh Annual Meeting of the Hebrew Orphan Asylum of the City of New York* (New York, 1910), 75. See Bogen, 169–70.

5. "Jesse Seligman Memorial," *New York Times*, April 24, 1896: 10.

6. Seymour Siegel and Laura Edwards, *An Orphan in New York City: Life with a Thousand Brothers and Sisters* (New York: Xlibris, 2000), 54.

7. *King's Views of New York* (New York: Sackett and Wilhelms Co., 1903), 80.

8. "Memorial Services for Titanic's Dead. Hebrew Orphan Asylum Trustees Pay Touching Tribute to Isador and Mrs. Straus," *New York Times*, April 29, 1912: 5. Bogen lists a number of "millionaires" who served as officers and trustees of the Hebrew Orphan Asylum, including Otto H. Kahn, Isador and Oscar Stauss, the Bloomingdales, the Sterns, the Lehmans, Henry Rice, Theodore Rosenwald, Marx Ottinger, Benjamin Russak, Jack A. Dreyfoos, Julius Ochs Adler, Jacob F. Bamberger, Julius Goldman, Jacob Goldsmith, Victor H. Rothchild, and Jonas Sonneborn. See Bogen, 139–40.

9. Bogen, 156–57.

10. *Report of the Eighty-Second Annual Meeting of the Hebrew Orphan Asylum of the City of New York* (New York, 1905), 62–63.

11. *Report of the Eighty-Third Annual Meeting of the Hebrew Orphan Asylum of the City of New York* (New York, 1906), 60. Bogen notes that with more than a thousand children—a ratio of about one adult to every hundred children—it was very difficult for Lowenstein to implement his agenda of "individualizing" the children. See Bogen, 162–63.

12. Maurice Bernstein, *All Still: Life Among a Thousand Siblings* (manuscript, 1991), 11, 60–61 (New York Public Library, Hebrew Orphan Asylum Oral Histories, Eldridge Street Collection: **P [Oral Histories, Box 147a]).

13. Bogen, 150.

14. Bernstein, 11, 17.

15. Bogen, 158.

16. Bernstein writes of his Bible: "Each Bar Mitzvah boy was given a Bible with his name engraved in golden letters. I had mine for more than fifty years and then it disappeared" (84).

17. "Interview with Arthur Marshall" (April 6, 1991). My father was very vague about the time frame here and knew none of the details of the boys' residence in the orphanage: "Let's say he was nine or ten. He was Bar Mitzvahed out of there, and when he came back to the family or when they came back, I don't know."

18. "Caring for Children After They Leave Institution for Orphans," *New York Times*, December 18, 1904: 2.

Chapter 2. Finding Names

1. *New York Times*, January 23, 1952: 27.

2. See *Guide to the Records of the Hebrew Orphan Asylum of the City of New York, undated, 1855–1985, 2004–*; I-42. Reprocessed by Dan Ma and Marvin Rusinek (February 2008). American Jewish Historical Society, Boston and New York. A portion of the original Hebrew Orphan Asylum records— almost entirely admissions records—are available in facsimile form on *Ancestry. com*. I have consulted both original and facsimile records.

3. "Applications for Admission, 1901–1903," Hebrew Orphan Asylum of the City of New York, records; I-42; Box 14; 1; American Jewish Historical Society, New York and Boston.

4. "Index of Children," n.d., Hebrew Orphan Asylum of the City of New York, records; I-42; Box 38; 1; American Jewish Historical Society, New York and Boston.

5. "Admissions and Discharges, 1884–1907," Hebrew Orphan Asylum of the City of New York, records; I-42; Box 19 (OS2); 1; American Jewish Historical Society, New York and Boston.

6. "Discharge Records, 1910–1911," Hebrew Orphan Asylum of the City of New York, records; I-42; Box 23; 4; American Jewish Historical Society, New York and Boston.

7. "Admission and Discharges, 1892–1901," Hebrew Orphan Asylum of the City of New York, records; I-42; Box 21 (OS1); 2; American Jewish Historical Society, New York and Boston.

8. *Annual Report*, 1906, n.p.

9. "Register of Visitors to Inmates, 1904–1905," Hebrew Orphan Asylum of the City of New York, records; I-42; 40 (OS1); 1; American Jewish Historical Society, New York and Boston. In his 1906 report, Superintendent Solomon Lowenstein described the policy of returning children to their mothers "as soon as possible" if they "no longer need the care of the Institution" (*Annual Report*, 1906, 54). He notes that during the preceding year, 353 children had been discharged.

10. "$1,000 in Cash Prizes for Hebrew Orphans," *New York Times*, June, 4, 1906: 18. The name "Kleinert" is misspelled as "Kleinent" in the article. Kate Kleinert was married to Isaac B. Kleinert, a patron and director of the Hebrew Orphan Asylum; he was a rubber manufacturer and inventor who held patents for earmuffs, the shower cap, the shower curtain, the dress shield, the garment shield, and other products.

Chapter 3. Inscribing Names

1. Perhaps David was born in the middle of the night, between the October 4 and 5. Rosh Hashanah in the Hebrew year 5652 began at sunset on October 2, 1891, so October 4 was the second day of the new year, but this doesn't really account for the confusion between 1891 and 1892. The birth certificates can be assumed to be the authoritative records of the Warshawsky children's birth dates. It is not clear why there are so many variations in subsequent documents for their birth dates. Variations could be due to translations from the Hebrew calendar, or minor mistakes by the midwives who filled out the birth certificate forms. Birthdays could be misremembered; the family would not have possessed documents or copies of documents to refer to. Orphan asylum registrars could have misheard or mixed up dates in conversations with a distressed mother, or with the children themselves. In later years, ages could be purposely misstated in order to make an oldest daughter more eligible for marriage or a son less eligible for draft registration. Daisy's marriage certificate shaves two years off of her age; some records indicate incorrectly that Daisy was born in 1891 or 1892 rather than 1890. The children may not have known their actual birth dates.

2. "Census Taking Begins," *New York Times,* June 2, 1900: 3; "Census Takers' Troubles," *New York Times*, June 3, 1900: 14; "Census Enumerators Making the Rounds," *Brooklyn Daily Eagle*, June 1, 1900: 1; "Census-Taking Begun. The Gigantic Task Which Must be Completed Within the Month of June," *Irish World*, June 9, 1900: 6.

3. Jacob A. Riis, *How the Other Half Lives: Studies Among the Tenements of New York* (New York: Charles Scribner's Sons, 1890), 125.

4. Strangely, the Ruderman family appears twice in the 1910 U.S. census. On April 18, two days after the census enumerator, Benjamin Kaplan, listed the Ruderman family as residing at 474 Saratoga Avenue, he appears to have found them all living together at 1357 East New York Avenue. Perhaps he got his notes mixed up. Today, a building that could coincide with 474 Saratoga Avenue one hundred years ago sits at the intersection of Saratoga and East New York avenues. If, like the building across the street, the Rudermans' building had two separate entrances, Kaplan could have become confused and visited their apartment twice, entering on Saratoga Avenue on April 16 and entering on East New York Avenue on April 18.

5. Meyer Ruderman, age seventy-three, is still identified a tailor. His son, Michael, age twenty-eight, is listed as "Mfg Cloaks." He will be married soon, on June 24, 1915, to Ella Spector. The Rudermans' son-in-law, Harry Novikoff, age thirty, married to Bessie, is also a tailor; by the 1920 census, he will be Harry Novick. The Rudermans' nieces, Rossie Ruderman, twenty-two, and Libby Ruderman, twenty, are both bookkeepers. There is a David Marshall recorded in the 1915 New York State census who is a twenty-two-year-old "actor" living in a "workhouse," but this document points to a novel that I do not intend to write.

6. *Brooklyn Daily Eagle*, April 20, 1913: 31. There is a University of Pennsylvania varsity football player named Dick Marshall who appears in the Brooklyn papers frequently in this decade, but there does not appear to be another local Dick Marshall.

7. See "Laws, Rules and Regulations Relating to Labor in Force January 1, 1915, Licensing of Trades, Chauffeurs," in *Journals of the Assembly of the State of New York, One Hundred and Thirty Eighth Session, 1915*, vol. 13, no. 49 (Albany. N.Y.: J. B. Lyon Co., printers, 1915), 271. There were earlier regulations in 1910 and 1911. See also: "A History of the Vehicle and Traffic Law in New York State," http://www.co.seneca.ny.us/history/A%20History%20of%20 the%20Vehicle%20and%20Traffic%20Law%20in%20New%20York%20State. pdf.

8. The *New York Times* published daily articles with detailed instructions under headlines such as "DRAFT QUESTIONS AND HOW TO ANSWER" (May 23, 1917), "FINAL INSTRUCTIONS FOR REGISTRATION" (June 2, 1917), "DRAFT REGISTRATION TUESDAY; ALL MEN 21 to 31 MUST ENROLL How to Register Without an Error" (June 3, 1917), and "QUESTIONS THAT MUST BE ANSWERED Instructions Prepared by the Government Should be Carefully Read Before Registering" (June 3, 1917).

9. There are many references in contemporary newspapers to "draft shirkers" who would lie about their age to avoid service.

10. The marriage license is announced in the *Brooklyn Daily Eagle* of November 7, 1922: 5.

11. "The Hebrew Orphan Asylum of the City of New York, 1822–1922: Souvenir in Commemoration of the Organization of the Hebrew Orphan Asylum of the City of New York," 1922, 76–77 (Hyman Bogen Collection; P-767; Box 1, American Jewish Historical Society, New York and Boston).

Chapter 4. A Posthumous Child

1. The Horatio Alger books are listed in the Hebrew Orphan Asylum library catalogues. See *Library Catalogue of the Hebrew Orphan Society* (New York, 1878) and *Supplement No. 1, Library Catalogue of the Hebrew Orphan Society* (New York, 1881). These catalogues are in the New York Public Library. In his memoir, Maurice Bernstein recalls reading the novels (57).

2. See, for example, www.jewishgen.org, which has a variety of census, tax, military, and other government documents with lists of local inhabitants.

3. Recalling that "Each Bar Mitzvah boy was given a Bible with his name engraved in golden letters. I had mine for more than fifty years and then it disappeared," Bernstein notes: "We were also given an Ingersoll watch" (84). In the 1905 annual report, Superintendent Coffee notes that twenty-four pupils will be confirmed "on Shebuoth," and then adds: "Nor must we forget the fifty-eight Bar Mitzvah boys who have been confirmed on Sabbath mornings during the past year, each receiving a present of a watch and a chain" (71–72). Bernstein may have conflated the gifts he received in these two ceremonies more than fifty years earlier. In any case, it makes sense that the Bible was presented at the time of the confirmation, which recognized Bible study.

Chapter 5. Traces of the Father

1. *The Newtown Register*, February 28, 1901: 4.

2. Aron and Wolf Warschawski are from "Wilkowisk, Russland." There is a Leib Aron Warschafsky, a "Tischler" from Kobrin, Russia, born about 1866, who departed Hamburg on June 3, 1888, on a ship called *Kaffraria*, bound for Montreal.

3. A tailor named Wolf Warshawsky was naturalized in New York in 1895, but although he states his date of birth as December 25, 1864, he claims to have arrived in New York on June 25, 1880.

4. I found an Isaac Warshoff, a grocer from Russia living in Newark in 1910, with a wife, Anna, whom he married in 1893, and children whose names include David, Daisy, and Harry. "Jack" might have been an Americanization of "Isaac." Is it a coincidence that Isaac Warshoff has a neighbor named Wolf Hecht, and that one of the witnesses at his wedding was one W. Hecht? I located the granddaughter of Isaac Warshoff, who recalls stories that the original family name was Warshawsky, but also remembers talk of the name Marshak. The 1900 census lists a Jake Warshafske in Manhattan, a married, thirty-year-old peddler from Russia, but he is living without his wife as a boarder with the family of Nathan Rosenblum, a tailor, at 142 Eldridge Street.

5. "Why Many People Change Their Names," *New York Herald*, June 6, 1890: 21.

6. Meyer, Anna, and Isaac Ruderman are all buried in Mt. Zion Cemetery, in the Chevra Gemeles Ches Anshe Haradok section, which is a burial society associated with the town of Garadok, near Minsk. Michael Ruderman lists Minsk as his birthplace on his World War II draft registration card.

7. As usual, the records, especially the census records, contradict each other. Lena's birth year ranges from 1870 to 1872, not counting the 1940 census, in which she appears to have given her age as sixty-five rather than seventy. I would privilege the marriage certificate and the Hebrew Orphan Asylum application for admission over the census records, since they presumably were based on a one-on-one interview. Her immigration year ranges from 1882 to 1887; again, based on the application for admission, which is consistent with the 1920 census and her father's 1930 census, I estimate her immigration year to be 1884, when she would have been fourteen. The 1910 census date for the immigration of the rest of the family, 1888, is consistent with both Isaac Ruderman's and Michael Ruderman's naturalization papers.

8. Annie Pollard and Daniel Soyer, *Emerging Metropolis: New York Jews in the Age of Immigration, 1840–1920* (New York: New York University Press, 2012), 113.

9. Riis, 105.

10. In the 1920 U.S. census, Lena reports that she was naturalized in 1891, which is within the normal margin of error for census records. "New laws of the mid-1800s opened an era when a woman's ability to naturalize became dependent upon her marital status. The act of February 10, 1855, was

designed to benefit immigrant women. Under that act, '[a]ny woman who is now or may hereafter be married to a citizen of the United States, and who might herself be lawfully naturalized, shall be deemed a citizen.' Thus alien women generally became U.S. citizens by marriage to a U.S. citizen or through an alien husband's naturalization. . . . In innumerable cases under the 1855 law, an immigrant woman instantly became a U.S. citizen at the moment a judge's order naturalized her immigrant husband. If her husband naturalized prior to September 27, 1906, the woman may or may not be mentioned on the record which actually granted her citizenship. Her only proof of U.S. citizenship would be a combination of the marriage certificate and her husband's naturalization record" (*Prologue Magazine* [Summer 1998] 30: 2). See http://www.archives.gov/publications/prologue/1998/summer/women-and-naturalization-1.html.

11. It appears that Hyman Lewis was born around 1868 or 1870, making him close in age to Harris Warshawsky. According to most of the records, he was born in England to Russian parents. He is referred to in some census records as a "private" teacher.

12. Riis, 124, 118.

13. "Relief for Poor Litigants is Now in Sight," *New York American*, November 26, 1898: 4.

14. Cited in *The Century: A Popular Quarterly* 43: 3 (January 1892): 327.

15. "The Lower East Side," *Library of Congress: Immigration . . . Polish/Russian:* http://www.loc.gov/teachers/classroommaterials/presentationsandactivities/presentations/immigration/polish6.html.

16. "Relief for Poor Litigants is Now in Sight," *New York American*, November 26, 1898: 4.

17. "Four New Schools Finished," *New York Times*, December 13, 1898: 14; "New East Side Grammar School," *New York Times*, April 8, 1897: 7.

18. *Fifty-Fifth Annual Report of the Board of Education of the City of New York for the Year Ending December 31, 1886* (New York: Hall of the Board of Education, 1897), 53.

19. "Some Schools Overcrowded," *New York Times*, September 12, 1900: 14; "Too Few Schools for New York's Children," *New York Times*, September 10, 1901: 3.

20. Abraham Cahan, "The Imported Bridegroom," in *Yekl and the Imported Bridegroom and Other Stories of Yiddish New York* (New York: Dover, 1970), 120. *The Imported Bridegroom and Other Stories of the New York Ghetto* was first published in 1898.

21. The photostat of Harris Warshawsky's naturalization papers on file with the District Court of the United States for the Southern District of New

York is long and rectangular, but perhaps new citizens would have been given some sort of certificate to take home with them.

22. An 1890s maternity dress with a tight-waisted bodice can be seen at: http://extantgowns.blogspot.com/search/label/1890s.

23. *Illustrated New York: The Metropolis of To-Day* (New York: International Publishing, 1888), 289. The studio is also listed in the 1890 New York City Directory.

24. The backs of the cards with the photographs of Harris and Lena give the address of the Newman Photographic Studio as No. 13 Avenue A. The photograph of Daisy and David was made by Mandelkorn & Dombrow "The Peoples" Photographic Art Studio, and it lists the address as 183 E. Essex Street, which had been the address of the Newman Photographic Art Studio. In 1894, Trow's Directory lists Sol. Dombrow, Photographs, and Israel Mandelkorn, Photographs, at 183 Essex Street. In 1897, Trow's lists Samuel Newman, Photographs, at 13 Avenue A. I have come across a wedding portrait from the turn of the century from the Wendel Photographic Art Studio at No. 13 Avenue A that notes that Wendel is "Successor to Newman." The advertisement also states: "Duplicates can be had at any time." Studios may have shared equipment and studios as well as sold their businesses (and their stock) to each other.

25. Hutchins Hapgood, *The Spirit of the Ghetto: Studies in the Jewish Quarter in New York* (New York: Funk & Wagnalls Co., 1902), 18, 24, 32–33, 37. Hapgood describes the old Jew who comes to America and "picks up only about a hundred English words and phrases, which he pronounces in his own way. Some of his most common acquisitions are 'vinda' (window), 'zieling' (ceiling), 'never mind,' 'alle right,' 'that'll do,' 'politzman' (policeman); 'ein schön kind, ein reg'lar pitze!' (a pretty child, a regular picture). Of this modest vocabulary he is very proud, for it takes him out of the category of the 'greenhorn,' a term of contempt to which the satirical Jew is very sensitive. The man who has been only three weeks in this country hates few things so much as to be called a 'greenhorn.' Under this fear he learns the small vocabulary to which in many years he adds very little" (10–11).

26. A registered Republican in 1919, when Republicans were "progressive," my grandfather was an adamant Republican in 1952, the year he died, according to my mother. See "List of Enrolled Voters, Twenty-Third Assembly District, Borough of Brooklyn," Board of Elections of the City of New York, December 31, 1919, 20. My mother recalls political discussions with her new father-in-law.

27. Arthur Marshall, "Growing Up in Bklyn," n.d.

28. Bogen, 157; "The Screen," *New York Times*, April 7, 1928: 22. There were long and positive reviews in the *New York Times* and the *Brooklyn Daily Eagle*. See also: "Harold Lloyd Unveils His New Comedy, 'Speedy,' at the Rivoli," *Brooklyn Daily Eagle*, April 9, 1928: 12A. Advertisements for Brooklyn screenings of the film appear in the *Eagle* from May 17 through August. See Bogen, 208. The scene with Babe Ruth can be seen online at: http://www.tcm.com/mediaroom/video/219160/Speedy-Movie-Clip-Babe-Ruth.html. In 1920, the New York Yankees almost bought the Hebrew Orphan Asylum so it could build a new stadium to compete with the Polo Grounds, but the deal fell through and the team ended up building Yankee Stadium in the Bronx. See "Terms Agreed Upon for Yankees; Park," *New York Times*, September 14, 1920: 21; and "Yankees Pick Site for New Ball Park," *New York Times*, January 30, 1921: 1.

Chapter 6. Traces of the Tailor: Becoming a Contractor

1. Abraham Cahan, *The Rise of David Levinsky* (New York: Harper & Brothers, 1917), 201. See Lawrence J. Epstein, *At the Edge of a Dream: The Story of Jewish Immigrants on New York's Lower East Side, 1880–1920* (New York: John Wiley & Sons, 2007), 65–68.

2. *The Men's Factory-Made Clothing Industry, Report on the Cost of Production of Men's Factory-Made Clothing in the United States*, Department of Commerce Bureau of Foreign and Domestic Commerce, Miscellaneous Series— No. 34 (Washington, D.C.: Government Printing Office, 1916), 12–13, 15.

3. *Seventh Annual Report of the Factory Inspector of the State of New York Transmitted to the Legislature January 1893* (Albany, N.Y.: James B. Lyon, State Printer, 1893), 205.

4. *Eighth Annual Report of the Factory Inspector of the State of New York Transmitted to the Legislature January 1894* (Albany, N.Y.: James B. Lyon, State Printer, 1894), 21.

5. New York Tenement Museum: http://www.tenement.org/encyclopedia/sweat.htm.

6. *The Men's Factory-Made Clothing Industry*, 18.

7. *Eighth Annual Report of the Factory Inspector of the State of New York, Transmitted to the Legislature January 1894* (Albany, N.Y.: James B. Lyon, State Printer, 1894), 275, 393; *Tenth Annual Report of the Factory Inspector of the State of New York, Transmitted to the Legislature January 1896* (Albany, N.Y.: Wynkoop Hallenbeck Crawford Co., State Printer, 1896), 463, 661; *Eleventh*

Annual Report of the Factory Inspector of the State of New York, Transmitted to the Legislature January 1897 (Albany, N.Y.: Wynkoop Hallenbeck Crawford Co., State Printer, 1897), 484–485; *Fifteenth Annual Report of the Factory Inspector of the State of New York, Transmitted to the Legislature January 1901* (Albany, N.Y.: James B. Lyon, State Printer, 1901), 151.

8. *Eighth Annual Report*, 12. However, according to Daniel Soyer, in many cases "contractors relocated their shops to tenements buildings converted entirely to manufacturing. Conditions in these places did not necessarily represent an improvement over those in the residential shops." ("Cockroach Capitalists: Jewish Contractors at the Turn of the Twentieth Century," in *A Coat of Many Colors: Immigration, Globalism, and Reform in the New York City Garment Industry*, ed. Daniel Soyer, [New York: Fordham University Press, 2005], 102). See Daniel E. Bender, *Sweated Work, Weak Bodies: Anti-Sweatshop Campaigns and Languages of Labor* (New Brunswick, N.J.: Rutgers University Press, 2004), 45.

9. *Eighth Annual Report*, 68. In 1903, four years after Harris Warshawsky is gone, we find a good deal of activity at 198 Broome Street. Manufacturing firms include: Simon Schlesinger (coats), Harris Brodsky (vests), Simon Kronenberg (underwear), Charles Weitzner (pants), and Louis Klenetzsky (tables). See *Eighteenth Annual Report of the Factory Inspection for Twelve Months Ending September 30, 1903* (Albany, N.Y.: Oliver A. Quayle, State Printer, 1904), 205, 295, 299, 376, 418.

10. Soyer, "Cockroach Capitalists," 94.

11. Henry White, "The Sweating System," *Bulletin of the Department of Labor*, 1: November 1895–November 1896 (Washington, D.C.: Government Printing Office, 1896), 369. According to White, "the new factory buildings were built expressly to accommodate the clothing trade under the new conditions. They contain 483 separate shops, and have legal space for 15,477 work people. Besides this, 371 tenements, formerly used for both working and living purposes, were cleared entirely of workers not members of the families living therein, and these tenements are now used for domestic purposes only. There were also 85 tenements buildings, which were cleared of residents and remodeled into shop buildings."

12. "Life in Sweating Shops," *New York Times*, April 28, 1895: 8.

13. "Over 50,000 Idle in Clothing Strike," *New York Times*, July 3, 1904: 16. The *Times* quotes "Secretary Chuck of the District Board, who has charge of the strikers," who explains that under "the task system which prevailed until three years ago," the "contractor would go down to the manufacturer and get a bundle of coats or pants" and then pay the tailors by the batch. The 1898

Annual Report of the Factory Inspector of the State of New York describes how the abolition of the task system was circumvented by methods that "relieve the boss or contractor of the odium of being called a 'task-master.' But, he reaps the full benefit of such a system just the same" (*Twelfth Annual Report of the Factory Inspector of the State of New York, Transmitted to the Legislature January 1898* [Albany, N.Y.: Wynkoop Hallenbeck Crawford Co., State Printer, 1898], 50). In an essay published in 1905, Isaac M. Rubinow wrote: "Because of the difficulties put in the way of sweatshops, the contract system is giving way in New York to small factories" ("Economic and Industrial Conditions, New York," in *The Russian Jew in the United States: Studies of Social Conditions in New York, Philadelphia, and Chicago, with a Description of Rural Settlements,* ed. Charles S. Bernheimer [Philadelphia: J. C. Winston Co., 1905], 117).

14. Riis, 121–22.

15. John M. Commons, "The 'Sweating System,'" in *Reports of the Industrial Commission on Immigration, Including Testimony, with Review and Digest, and Special Reports,* vol. XV (Washington, D.C.; Government Printing Office, 1901), 320. Soyer writes: "The contractor's main role in the industry was to take responsibility for recruiting the low-cost immigrant labor on which the industry thrived. His most important assets were, therefore, his social network and his knowledge of the language and conditions in the community. Contractors staffed their shops in a variety of ways. In the smallest shops, the boss and his family labored alongside the paid workers. He may also have employed other relatives. Perhaps most importantly, he hired his compatriots, people from his hometown in Europe" (103). See Irving Howe, *World of Our Fathers* (New York: Harcourt Brace Jovanovich, 1976), 81.

16. *The Men's Factory-Made Clothing Industry,* 14. "These Russian immigrants huddled together, the family keeping many boarders and lodgers, usually relatives or friends from their home towns or the unmarried sons and daughters of such friends and relatives. The lodgers usually entered the trade of the head of the house, and as the space afforded by the living rooms became too small for the work, the head of the house rented rooms elsewhere, thus creating the small shop apart from the home" (12).

17. The New York Tenement Museum: http://www.tenement.org/encyclopedia/sweat.htm.

18. Burton J. Henrick, "The Jewish Invasion of America," *McClure's Magazine* 40: 5 (March 1913), 130; Soyer, "Cockroach Capitalists," 94; Howe, 159. In *The Rise of David Levinsky,* the protagonist starts the cloak factory that will make him a millionaire with $400, which he has obtained from a combination of savings, loans, credit, and investments.

19. Commons, 322–23. In 1916, Meyer Schoenfeld, who was an organizer for the United Brotherhood of Tailors during the strikes of the 1890s, testified before the U.S. Congress: "The contracting system in the clothing trade is the stepping stone for the mechanic to become a manufacturer, and the contractor of to-day is apt to be a union man of yesterday; and you will find 25 per cent of the contractors of to-day, that they were strong union men a year or two or three or five or ten or fifteen years ago" (*Final Report and Testimony Submitted to Congress by the Commission on Industrial Relations*, II [Washington, D.C.: Government Printing Office, 1916], 2,026).

20. Jesse Eliphalet Pope, *The Clothing Industry in New York*, University of Missouri Studies, vol.1: Social Science Series (University of Missouri, 1905), 62, 114.

21. White, "The Sweating System," 363.

22. Cited by Pope, 113–14.

23. Soyer, "Cockroach Capitalists," 98; Commons, 321; Hendricks, 130.

24. Pope, 114, 283.

25. A September 15, 1895 *New York Times* article explains: "A little band of Russian refugees founded the Order B'rith Abraham in 1859 to bring together the Russian Israelites of New-York into one band of brotherhood, there to rejoice in the achievements of the successful brother and likewise to assist and cheer an unfortunate member of the clan." There was a schism between the Order of B'rith Abraham and the seceding Independent Order of B'rith Abraham in 1887, including a dispute in New York State courts over the right to use the name "B'rith Abraham." It would be very difficult to find the specific OBA lodge to which Harris Warshawsky belonged. Even if records survived, the *American Jewish Yearbook* for the year 5660 (covering September 5, 1899 to September 23, 1900) lists about sixty-five separate lodges in New York City and Brooklyn, mostly in the Lower East Side neighborhood where Harris Warshawsky lived and worked (*The American Jewish Yearbook* 5660 [Philadelphia: The Jewish Publication Society of America, 1899], 73–83). The *American Jewish Yearbook* for the year 5661 (covering September 24, 1900 to September 13, 1901), which lists 253 lodges nationally, lists eight lodges in Brooklyn and eighty lodges in New York City (of which twelve are women's lodges). Only nine lodges are said to "employ the English language." (*The American Jewish Yearbook* 5661 [Philadelphia: The Jewish Publication Society of America, 1900], 150–54). OBA lodges met twice a month on Broome, Suffolk, Norfolk, Rivington, and Essex streets, and on Watkins Street in Brooklyn. See Daniel Soyer, *Jewish Immigrant Associations and American Identity in New York,*

1880–1939 (Cambridge, Mass.: Harvard University Press, 1997), 62; and Anzia Yezierska, *The Bread Givers* (New York: Persea, 2003), 196.

26. Moses Rischin, *The Promised City: New York's Jews, 1870–1914* (Cambridge, Mass.: Harvard University Press, 1977), 176.

Chapter 7. Traces of the Tailor: On Strike

1. "Twelve Thousand Strike," *New York Herald*, September 4, 1894: 3; "Is a Giant Strike. Between 12,000 and 14,000 Coatmakers Now Arrayed Against the Sweating System," *New York Herald*, September 5, 1894: 3; "Ten Thousand Tailors Strike," *New York Times*, September 4, 1894: 5.

2. "Big Strike Begins To-Day," *New York Herald*, December 15, 1895: 5.

3. David O. Whitten, "The Depression of 1893," http://eh.net/encyclopedia/the-depression-of-1893/.

4. White, "The Sweating System," 371–72.

5. "Aimed at The Sweat System. Several Thousands Garment Workers On Strike," *New York Tribune*, September 4, 1894: 4.

6. "Is a Giant Strike. Between 12,000 and 14,000 Coatmakers Now Arrayed Against the Sweating System," New York Herald, September 5, 1894: 3.

7. "Big Strike Begins To-Day," *New York Herald*, December 15, 1895: 5.

8. "Is a Giant Strike. Between 12,000 and 14,000 Coatmakers Now Arrayed Against the Sweating System," *New York Herald*, September 5, 1894: 3. Years later, when Schoenfeld was employed by the American Clothing Manufacturers Association—an organization representing the contractors—he wryly admitted that in his union days "occasionally we did play up to the gallery a great deal" (*Final Report and Testimony Submitted to Congress by the Commission on Industrial Relations*, II [Washington, D.C.: Government Printing Office, 1916], 2031).

9. White, "The Sweating System," 371.

10. "Aimed At The Sweat System. Several Thousands Garment Workers On Strike," *New York Tribune*, September 4, 1894: 4.

11. "Strikers to Resume Work," *New York Tribune*, September 6, 1894: 9.

12. "Rioters in Brooklyn," *New York Tribune*, September 5, 1894: 1.

13. "Is a Giant Strike. Between 12,000 and 14,000 Coatmakers Now Arrayed Against the Sweating System," *New York Herald*, September 5, 1894: 3.

14. "Aimed At The Sweat System. Several Thousands Garment Workers On Strike," *New York Tribune*, September 4, 1894: 6.

15. "Confident Of Victory. The Garment-Workers Jubilant Over The Contractors Signing Bonds. Many Of The Employers," *New York Herald-Tribune*, September 11, 1894: 2; "Riot in Broome Street," *New York Herald*, September 16, 1894: 6.

16. "The Police Gone Mad," *New York Tribune*, October 12, 1894: 1.

17. "Aimed At The Sweat System. Several Thousands Garment Workers On Strike," *New York Tribune*, September 4, 1894: 4.

18. "Strikers to Resume Work," *New York Tribune*, September 6, 1894: 9.

19. "Strike Will Involve 15,000, *New York Times*, June 22, 1896: 8; "Contractors May Join Tailors," *New York Times*, July 18, 1896: 9; "Sympathy for the Tailors," *New York Tribune*, May 20, 1897: 12.

20. Mayer [sic] Schoenfeld, "TO ALL CLOTHING MANUFACTURERS OF NEW YORK," reprinted in Pope, 305–06.

21. "Strikers to Resume Work," *New York Tribune*, September 6, 1894: 9; "Strikers Victorious," *New York Herald*, September, 6, 1894: 3.

22. "The Employers Yield," *New York Tribune*, September 7, 1894: 2; "Confident of Victory," *New York Tribune*, September 11, 1894: 2.

23. "Riot in Broome Street," *New York Herald*, September 16, 1894: 6.

24. "The Ghetto of New York: The Daily Life of the Russian and Polish Inhabitants of the Jewish Quarter," *New York Herald*, August 18, 1895: 2.

25. According to the *New York Times*, "The principal cause of the strike was the refusal of the Contractors' Association to sign an agreement prepared by the Brotherhood of Tailors to date from Sept. 15" ("Many Tailors on Strike," *New York Times*, July 29, 1895: 1).

26. "Big Strike Begins To-Day," *New York Herald*, December 15, 1895: 5.

27. "The Ghetto of New York: The Daily Life of the Russian and Polish Inhabitants of the Jewish Quarter," *New York Herald*, August 18, 1895: 2; John M. Commons, "The 'Sweating System,'" in *Reports of the Industrial Commission on Immigration, Including Testimony, with Review and Digest, and Special Reports*, vol. XV (Washington, D.C.; Government Printing Office, 1901), 320.

28. "The Ghetto of New York: The Daily Life of the Russian and Polish Inhabitants of the Jewish Quarter," *New York Herald*, August 18, 1895: 2.

29. "Many Tailors Locked Out," *New York Times*, December 16, 1895: 2. According to the *New York Times*: "The lock-out of the tailors by the contractors who have repudiated the agreement they made last Summer with the Brotherhood of Tailors was begun yesterday." Bolaski continued: "Whenever [the contractor] refused to obey the shop delegate, the latter would get the men

to go out on strike, and then the union would declare a strike against him and refuse to supply him with other workers."

30. *The Men's Factory-Made Clothing Industry*, 18.

31. Abraham Cahan, "Summer Complaint: The Annual Strike," *Commercial Advertiser*, August 25, 1900, reprinted in *Grandma Never Lived in America: The New Journalism of Abraham Cahan*, ed. Moses Rischin (Bloomington, Ind.: Indiana University Press, 1985), 381–83.

32. *Fifteenth Annual Report of the Factory Inspector of the State of New York Transmitted to the Legislature January 1901* (Albany. N.Y.: James B. Lyon, State Printer, 1901), 150–51.

Chapter 8. Special Circumstances of the Case

1. Application No. 3180, April 22, 1903; Application No. 3030, October 6, 1902.

2. "Interview with Arthur Marshall" (April 6, 1991).

3. Cahan, *Yekl: A Tale of the New York Ghetto*, 13–14. The novella originally was published in 1896.

4. Yezierska, *The Bread Givers*, 92, 97.

5. "Sold Impure Milk," *Daily People*, September 19, 1901: 1; "Thirty Milk Dealers Fined," *Daily People*, September 23, 1902: 3.

6. Rose Cohen, *Out of the Shadow: A Russian Jewish Girlhood on the Lower East Side* (New York: George H. Doran Company, 1918), 212.

7. "Personal Reminiscence." My father misspoke or miswrote or momentarily misremembered the number of children in his father's family; he elsewhere correctly referred to six children and often named his father's siblings: Daisy, Ruby, Millie, Irving, and Harry. The admission records, as well as birth certificates and other documents, confirm the number of children in the family.

8. Brooklyn Hebrew Orphan Asylum, Volume 19, 319. As usual, there are some inconsistencies in ages, but it appears that Nathan and Rueben Ruderman, half-orphans, were admitted to the Brooklyn Hebrew Orphan Asylum on September 25, 1896, and then on July 1, 1897 "discharged to their father who remarried and lives at 556 Vanderbilt Avenue." A Fannie Ruderman died on May 4, 1896 of "Septicaemia following birth of full term child" (Coroner's Certificate of Death, #8013). The boys are sent to the orphanage for the first time on May 26. Isaac Ruderman married Ida Scholtsky on February 21, 1897. On September 13, 1898, Nathan and Ruben Ruderman are again admitted. Under "mother" is listed "Fannie (dead)," and under "father" is

listed "Isaac unknown." There is a slight discrepancy in the ages recorded for these brothers between these two records of admission, but the latter entry is clearly linked to Lena's family. Ruben Ruderman is "taken off roll 16 yrs old" on September 14, 1908, but Nathan appears to remain until he is eighteen, when he is discharged "to Uncle 474 Saratoga" on February 18, 1911. This is the address of the Ruderman family in the 1910 census. Isaac is reported to be living there at the time, as well as two Ruderman granddaughters, Rossie and Liebie (Rosie and Lilie), who are also living with the family in 1905. Rosie seems to have been born in 1895 and Lilie in 1897, but ascertaining accurate birth dates from census data is difficult. When Nathan Ruderman registers for the draft in 1917, he gives his address as 494 Saratoga Ave Brooklyn," down the block from 408 Saratoga Avenue, where Lena's family lives at about this time. The birth date, September 15, 1892, matches the 1898 Brooklyn Hebrew Orphan Asylum record. He lists "two Sisters & Brother" and notes that he supports "Grand Parents." He is living with the Rudermans on Saratoga Avenue at the time of the 1920 census. On his World War II draft registration form, Nathan Ruderman lists next to "Name and Address of Person Who Will Always Know Your Address, "MARSHALL –SAME," indicating that he is still living with a branch of the family at the age of forty-nine. In 1920, the two younger Ruderman sisters are living with Lena's sister Fannie—they are listed as "roomers" in the census—who is married to Max Gottlieb. I surmise that Lena's brother Isaac's two sons were sent to the orphanage after his wife died, while his two daughters remained with the Ruderman family. He withdrew his sons after he remarried, but then abruptly sent the boys back. Did his second wife die? Did the marriage not last? Did the stepmother resent the children from the first marriage? What happened to Isaac? Isaac does not appear to be living with the Rudermans during these years, at least until the end of the decade. He died on February 28, 1912, and he is the only child of Meyer and Anna Ruderman to be buried with his or her parents, in the Haradok Society section of Mt. Zion Cemetery.

9. *Annual Report of the Committee on Fire Patrol to the New York Board of Fire Underwriters* (New York: Lauter Press, 1903), 154. See "Yesterday's Fires," *New York Times*, May 17, 1902: 20. According to the U.S. census, by 1910, Solomon Hartman had become a rabbi. He lived at 290 Stanton Street. Perhaps, in the old-world tradition, he read the Torah in the back room of the grocery store while his wife and children tended to the customers.

10. According to the *Daily People*, "Meat that formerly cost eight cents a pound now sells at 18 and 20 cents, and even at those prices the butchers refuse to 'trim' the meat. Fat, bones and all goes in at the same price" ("Disorder in

the Ghetto. Women Continue Fight Against Kosher Butchers," *Daily People,* May 17, 1902: 3).

11. "East Side Riot," *Daily People,* May 16, 1902: 3.

12. "Fierce Meat Riot On Lower East Side," *New York Times,* May 17, 1902: 3.

13. "Protest Against Sale of Meat," *Daily Tribune,* May 16, 1902: 1.

14. "Fierce Meat Riot On Lower East Side," *New York Times,* May 17, 1902: 1, 3.

15. "Trouble Renewed on Lower East Side. Butchers' Shops and Customers Again Attacked," *New York Times,* May 17, 1902: 2.

16. "A Real Police Problem," *New York Times,* May 24, 1902: 8. Paula E. Hyman describes the editorial comments in the *New York Times* as "fierce and vitriolic." The first editorial on May 17, criticizes the monopolies and suggests that the violence has been caused by a "densely-crowded mass of ignorant men and women, especially women" (Editorial, *New York Times,* May 17, 1902). By May 24, after the rioting has spread to Brownsville in Brooklyn, the *Times* opines: "The class of people, especially the women, who are engaged in this matter have many elements of a dangerous class. They are very ignorant. They mostly speak a foreign language. They do not understand the duties or the rights of Americans." See Paula E. Hyman, "Immigrant Women and Consumer Protest: The New York City Kosher Meat Boycott of 1902," *American Jewish History* 70.1 (1980), 96 and *passim.*

17. "Mob Tries to Storm Jail for Women," *New York World,* May 17, 1902: 1. The *Times* also reported: "The Hebrew newspapers in their evening editions charged the police with brutality, describing their treatment of the women demonstrators as 'murderous,' and as worse than would have been meted out to them by the gendarmes of Russia" ("Trouble Renewed on Lower East Side," *New York Times,* May 17, 1902: 2).

18. "Trouble Renewed on Lower East Side," *New York Times,* May 17, 1902: 2.

19. Hyman writes: "The wholesale price of kosher meat was rolled back to nine cents a pound so that the retail price would be pegged at fourteen cents a pound. Kosher meat cooperatives . . . continued in existence. While meat prices began to rise inexorably again in the period following the conclusion of the boycott, the movement can still be considered a qualified success" ("Immigrant Women and Consumer Protest," 96).

20. "Protest Against Sale of Meat," *Evening Tribune,* May 16, 1902: 1.

21. "Women Resume Riots Against Meat Shops," *New York Times,* May 18, 1902: 3.

22. Hyman, "Immigrant Women and Consumer Protest," 96–101, and *passim*. Although the articles in the newspapers sometimes seem sympathetic to the cause of the women, from the outset they describe them as angry, hysterical, violent, and out of control. One exception is an admiring profile of one of the organizers of the boycott, Mrs. Esther (or Sarah) Edelson, in the *World* that credits her with starting the strike: "She wears her hair cut short and covered with a wig, in the Russian fashion, yet even this disfigurement does not rob her of attractiveness. She is forty-eight years old. She has large hazel eyes that light up when she speaks and her complexion is pink and white. Her smile is especially winning." Although she is described as a "leader" and quoted at length, the article seeks to reassure by feminizing her. See "One Woman's Protest Started Big Meat Strike," *The World*, May 17, 1902: 2.

23. See "East Side Milk Famine," *Daily People*, May 19, 1902: 3. According to the *Daily People*, "As a result of the shops being closed, a much larger number of push-cart pedlers than usual were selling greens, vegetables, and fish on the streets" ("Disorder in the Ghetto," *Daily People*, May 17, 1902: 3).

24. "Panic in Tenement," *Daily People*, May 20, 1902: 3.

25. "Trouble Renewed on Lower East Side," *New York Times*, May 17, 1902: 2; "A Real Police Problem," *New York Times*, May 24, 1902: 8.

26. Trow's *Business Directory of Greater New York* (New York: Trow's Directory, Printing and Bookbinding Co., 1902), 594, 232.

Chapter 9. Reading the Death Certificate

1. "Brooklyn's Ghetto," *Brooklyn Daily Eagle*, December 4, 1899: 9.

2. http://www.firecompanies.com/MFC/public/userfiles/image/watkinsst/ladder-120-history-complete.pdf.

3. "Letter to the Sheriff," *Brooklyn Daily Eagle*, May 21, 1900: 5.

4. Cahan, *The Rise of David Levinsky*, 464.

5. Wendell E. Prichett, *Brownsville, Brooklyn: Blacks, Jews, and the Changing Face of the Ghetto* (Chicago: University of Chicago Press, 2002), 13–14. In contemporary directories, most of the addresses associated with Watkins Street are unnumbered. For example, in the 1897 Lain's Directory for Brooklyn, the address for Aaron Teplitzkey, a tailor, is "Watkins n[ear] Livonia av." The same is true in the 1899 *Trow's Business Directory of Brooklyn, City of New York*. The atlas pages of this directory show Watkins Street intersecting with Belmont, Liberty, Livonia, and Lott avenues, among others. Today, Watkins Street is interrupted several times and exists in small sections between Linden

Boulevard and Pitkin Avenue. Watkins Street appears to have run continuously as late as 1926, according to the aerial-view map provided at http://gis.nyc.gov/doitt/nycitymap/. See Ellen Levitt, *The Lost Synagogues of Brooklyn: The Stories Behind How and Why Many Brooklyn Synagogues, Now Old "Ex-shuls," Were Converted to Other Uses, Primarily As Christian Churches* (Avotaynu, 2009).

6. *Thirteenth Annual Report.*

7. "Preparing to Cleanse Brownsville Ghetto. Health Officer Black and a Sanitary Committee Make a Tour of Inspection. Improvement in Sweat Shops," *Brooklyn Daily Eagle*, December 15, 1899: 18; "Finkelstein Rearrested," *Brooklyn Daily Eagle*, April 18, 1901: 2.

8. Upington's 1901 *Elite Directory of Brooklyn*, which promises "27,000 Names of First-Class Families" listed by street address, along with "Envelopes Addressed" and "Circulars Folded" for use by businesses, does not include Watkins Street.

9. Four and a half years after Harris Warshawsky's death, nine of the eleven families at 88 Watkins Street are Italian immigrants, most of whom have been in the U.S. for less than ten years. Only two Russian Jewish heads of households live in the building: Morris Stark, a glazier, whose twenty-three-year-old son, Isador, is a lawyer and twenty-year-old daughter, Bertha, is a seamstress; and Isidor Madoff, a barber, who has a boarder, Samuel Rossky, a real estate agent.

10. Cahan, 464. David Levinksy writes: "Deals were being closed, and poor men were making thousands of dollars in less time than it took them to drink the glass of tea or the plate of sorrel soup over which the transaction took place."

11. Epstein, 95.

12. The possibility of Harris's desertion also raises the question of Harry's paternity. Lena had five children between November 5, 1890 (ten months after she was married) and December 21, 1895, and then none until Harry was born on August 17, 1901, when she was thirty years old. Assuming that she became pregnant sometime in November of 1900, she would have been less than three months pregnant when Harris died. Might she have become pregnant while he was absent? It is possible that there were miscarriages. I have found no evidence of any infants who died. I searched for children named Warshawsky who died during this period and found a child named Max Warshawsky who was born on July 28, 1897, and whose death was recorded on August 14, 1897 (listed as "Max Warsehawsky, 4 days old"). However, this was the child of a "Sam. Warshawsky" who was a sugar maker born in Germany. My father's cousin Adele told me that Lena resented her husband because she was pregnant so often.

13. Alter F. Landesman, *Brownsville: The Birth, Development and Passing of a Jewish Community in New York* (New York: Bloch, 1969), 271. The house was razed in 1909 and a dedication ceremony for a new building took place on May 10, 1910. See: "Hebrew Educational Society's New Building in Brownsville," *Brooklyn Daily Eagle*, November 29, 1899: 13; "The Hebrew Educational Society in the Field," *Brooklyn Daily Eagle*, December 28, 1899: 9; "Hebrew Educational Society," *Brooklyn Daily Eagle*, October 21, 1900: 42; "Hebrew Educational Society," *Brooklyn Daily Eagle*, November 30, 1900, 17.

14. According to the list of hospitals and dispensaries contained in the *Annual Report of the State Board of Charities for the Year 1900*, its "objects" were to "provide free medical assistance for the sick poor." The dispensary treated 4,116 people in 1900: 6,522 treatments, with 5,329 prescriptions dispensed. Medical treatment, including medicine, cost twenty cents (*Annual Report of the State Board of Charities for the Year 1900*, 3 vols. [Albany, 1901], 337).

15. According to Soyer, the contract doctors hired by societies "preserved the immigrants' sense of dignity" since they "did not have to resort to public dispensaries or hospital clinics, or other major health-care providers for the poor, which carried the stigma of charity" (*Jewish Immigrant Associations*, 94).

16. "Shiva—Mourning in the Jewish Tradition." *Lower East Side Tenement Museum Encyclopedia*, http://tenement.org/encyclopedia/jews_shiva.htm. Louis Meyers, who founded the Riverside Memorial Chapel in New York, which grew into a funeral home empire, began as Meyers Livery Stable on Norfolk Street in 1897. See James Trager, *The New York Chronology* (New York: HarperCollins, 2003), 254.

Chapter 10. Reading the Death Certificate: The Place of Death

1. *River Crest, Astoria, Long Island, New York City; a private sanitarium for the care and treatment of mental and nervous diseases and selected cases of alcoholic and drug habituation* (New York, 189–?), 21 pp. illus., map. Research Call Number *C p.v. 189–, no. 3.

2. *Medical Record: A Weekly Journal of Medicine and Surgery* 52 (July–December 1897); 22 (May 28, 1928): 34.

3. *Medical News: A Weekly Medical Journal* 77 (July–December 1900): 14; *The Alienist and the Neurologist* 22.1 (1901): 212; *Twelfth Annual Report of the State of New York Commission in Lunacy, October 1, 1899 to September 30, 1900, Transmitted to the Legislature, February 7, 1901* (Albany, N.Y.: James B. Lyon, State Printer, 1901), 212. By 1917, the sanitarium had grown; it

had country club–like amenities, including "a park of about 30 acres" with a herd of twenty-four cows and a golf course, tennis courts, and a bowling alley. According to *The Institutional Care of the Insane in the United States and Canada*, published in 1916, "River Crest is situated on a plateau on Lawrence Point, Long Island. It is about 50 feet above sea level and commands an attractive view of Long Island Sound, the East River and the City of New York" (Henry H. Hurd, et al, *The Institutional Care of the Insane in the United States and Canada* [Baltimore: Johns Hopkins University Press, 1916], 276–77). See *Medical Review of Reviews* 20 (January–December 1914), xxvii.

4. "Della Fox Recovers," *New York Times*, June 28, 1900: 8; "Della Fox Leaves Sanitarium," *New York Times*, June 29, 1900; "The Barrymores in Peril," *New York Times*, April 2, 1901: 6; "Steinitz in Bellevue," *New York Times*, April 27, 1900: 16; "Mrs. Richman's Insanity," *New York Times*, October 18, 1902: 2; "Say S.T. White is Sane," *New York Times*, September 23, 1900: 7; "Woman's Will Contested," April 10, 1910: 6; "Dr. Wilde in Workhouse: Escaped Sanitarium Patient Found and Returned to Asylum," *New York Times*, February 13, 1900: 7; "Became Demented in China," *New York Times*, November 4, 1900: 14.

5. *State of New York State Commission in Lunacy Twelfth Annual Report* (Albany, N.Y.: James B. Lyon, State Printer, 1901), 98.

6. "Steinitz Soon To Be Free," *Brooklyn Daily Eagle*, April 5, 1900: 16; "Noted Chess Player Free," *Oswego Daily Times*, April 11, 1900: 8; *The Steinitz Papers; Letters and Documents of the First World Chess Champion*, ed. Kurt Landsberger (North Carolina: McFarland and Co., 2002), 262.

7. The article in the *New York Times* announcing Steinitz's death at the Manhattan State Hospital on Ward's Island details his "tragic" final years, noting that "he became so violently insane that he was sent to Bellevue Hospital. From there he went to Ward's Island and later he was sent to the Rivercrest Sanitarium in Astoria. He was discharged from there in March last, and returned to his home, where he remained two weeks. Again he had to be sent back to the Manhattan State Hospital, where he remained until his death on Sunday" ("William Steinitz Dead," *New York Times*, August 14, 1900: 5).

Chapter 11. Reading the Death Certificate: The Name of the Physician

1. *The Alienist and Neurologist* 25: 2 (May 1904): 238. See *The Ten-Year Book of Cornell University*, IV, 1868–1908 (Ithaca, N.Y. 1908), 335. See also

the notice in the *Journal of the American Medical Association* 42:10 (1904), 664. Someone has posted on a family genealogy website the transcription of a wedding announcement found in the scrapbook of a Mrs. John L. Puff of Newfield, New York: "Wedding bells have been ringing again in Newfield (NY). The house of Mr. and Mrs. Wm H. Weatherell was the scene of joyous festivity yesterday afternoon at the marriage of their daughter Maggie to Wm. A. McCorn. The bride was elegantly attired in wine-colored silk, *en train*. The floral decorations were very beautiful, and were artistically arranged by Mrs. David Keppel and excited considerable comment. Among the guests present were Mrs. Geo. Cox, Miss Rose Broadhurst and Mr. Thomas Bradley, all of Elmira; Mrs. O. D. Smith of Syracuse, Rev. Noble Palmer of Buffalo performed the ceremony according to the Episcopal rite. Mr. and Mrs. McCorn left on the 6:25 p.m. train for Buffalo where Mr. McCorn is to pursue his medical studies at the Buffalo Medical College. May joy and prosperity go with them is the wish of their many friends." Presumably the wedding took place in or around 1879, since this is when McCorn completed his studies at Cornell and began his medical studies at Buffalo. I cite this not because it is important to my story but because it illustrates the strange crossing of stories, both in life and on the Internet, and it illustrates the different worlds in which Harris Warshawsky and Dr. McCorn lived. Neither Harris nor Lena had left Russia at the time that McCorn was married in upstate New York. (http://growingupinwillowcreek. blogspot.com/search/label/McCorn).

2. *Medical Record* 65:14 (April, 1904): 544.

3. "A Doctor Shoots a Young Man," *Daily Star*, June 24, 1899: 1. This article reports that McCorn himself returned to the scene of the shooting with a blanket for the boy, and notes that when searched at the police station, he had a "little metal case containing the necessary instruments for administering a hypodermic injection and several small bottles containing tablets. . . . When asked about having the hypodermic arrangement with him he replied laughingly that he took it along in case the boy needed it."

4. "Clifton White Dead," *New York Times*, June 25, 1899: 13; "Young Clifton White Died This Forenoon," *Brooklyn Daily Eagle*, June 24, 1899: 16; "Dr. McCorn Arraigned," *Brooklyn Daily Eagle*, July 3, 1899: 2; "Dr. McCorn Exonerated," *Brooklyn Daily Eagle*, July 7, 1899: 7; "In Dr. McCorn's Behalf," *Brooklyn Daily Eagle*, July 9, 1899: 12; "Dr. McCorn Released," *Brooklyn Daily Eagle*, July 18, 1899: 16; "Dr. McCorn Acquitted," *Brooklyn Daily Eagle*, September 15, 1899: 14. Some early accounts claimed that the bullets had not hit anything before hitting the boy. The boy's mother, Mrs. Susannah White of Astoria, later sued McCorn for $15,000. See: *Brooklyn Daily Eagle*, December

5, 1901. For other accounts, see *New York Herald-Tribune*, June 6, 1899; and *New York Herald-Tribune*, July 11, 1899.

5. *The Institutional Care of the Insane in the United States and Canada*, 211, 273, 278, 858. See "Hyoscyamine in the Treatment of the Insane," *The Medical Record: A Weekly Journal of Medicine and Surgery* 33 (June 2, 1888): 608. Articles were reprinted in the *Milwaukee Daily Journal*, July 27, 1888 and the *Atchison Daily Globe*, August 6, 1888. See also: *The Blue Book for the State of Wisconsin*, 1893; and *Biennial Report of the Board of Trustees of the Milwaukee Asylum for the Insane for the Two Years Ending September 30, 1888* (Madison, Wis.: Democrat Printing Company, State Printers, 1889), 47. McCorn would publish on topics related to criminal insanity in the following years. He was a member of a committee that submitted a lengthy report entitled, "Report on Reformatories and Penitentiaries," to the Wisconsin State Conference of Charities and Corrections in 1893. See *Annual State Conference of Charities and Corrections* (Madison, Wis.: Democrat Printing Company, State Printers, 1894), 152–63. *The Institutional Care of the Insane* also identifies McCorn as having been an assistant physician at the Long Island Home.

6. McCorn was listed on the payroll for the hospital in 1895 and 1896. See *Tenth Biennial Report of the Illinois Eastern Hospital for the Insane, September 1, 1896* (Springfield, Ill.: Phillips Bros., State Printers, 1897), 114. See *Medico-Legal Journal* 15:4 (1904): 453. McCorn corresponded with the journal to express opinions in a debate about cigarettes and insanity, or "cigarette fiends" (454, 469–70).

7. See Lawrence Davidson, "The Strange Disappearance of Adolph Meyer," *Orthomolecular Psychiatry* 9.2 (1908), 137.

8. McCorn's letter to Meyer, dated July 22, 1900, refers to "charges" being "preferred against Dr. Van Gersow" and states that "his removal will of course follow and the next matter is who will be his successor." He refers to a friend who is advocating Meyer for the position and offers to "assist to do what little I can for this purpose." The John Hopkins archives contain two drafts from Meyer to McCorn dated July 24, 1900, insisting that he does not want to get involved and that the question is "one which I should not care to precipitate either myself or through well-meaning friends" (Adolf Meyer Collection, the Alan Mason Chesney Medical Archives, Johns Hopkins Medical Institutions, unit I: 2487, folders 1 and 2).

9. McCorn's resignation is announced in the January 1887 issue of the *American Journal of Insanity* (482), but he announces his acceptance of the McLean position in a March 6, 1898, letter to Meyer. His appointment to a temporary position is announced in the *Eighty-Fourth Annual Report of the*

Trustees of the Massachusetts General Hospital (Boston: The Barta Press, 1897), 136.

10. "Lawyer Spann's Suit," *New York Times*, December 30, 1900: 3; "Suing for $15,000," *Brooklyn Daily Eagle*, December 5, 1901: 8.

11. McCorn writes that the Grand View owner "and his wife are constantly quarrelling, cursing and blackguarding each other about the house frequently, using language that would make a sailor blush and finally worst of all he, Donohue, the owner, goes on frequent sprees, when he tries to wreck the house in every way by breaking furniture, assaulting the help and making himself a spectacle generally before the patients." After describing this slapstick scene, McCorn asks Meyer: "how is Dr. Crothers and his work regarded by the profession at large, as well as by those who have devoted themselves to the study of allied conditions, nervous and mental troubles particularly?" (June 14, 1901) (Adolf Meyer Collection, the Alan Mason Chesney Medical Archives, Johns Hopkins Medical Institutions, unit I: 2487, folders 1 and 2).

12. The 1904 issue of the *Alienist and Neurologist* identifies him in different articles as both "Supt. Elizabeth General Hospital, Elizabeth, N.J." and "late Supt. Elizabeth General Hospital, Elizabeth, N.J" (26, 199, 292, 437), suggesting that he held this appointment at the time of his death. See also *Journal of American Medical Association* 42.10 (1904), 664.

13. W. A. McCorn, "Degeneration in Criminals as Shown by the Bertillon System of Measurement and Photographs," *American Journal of Insanity* 53.1 (1896): 46–56. The article was based on a paper that he delivered at the Association of Assistant Physicians of Hospitals for the Insane on May 8, 1896. McCorn was elected to the association at this meeting; the following year, his resignation from the Eastern Illinois State Hospital was announced.

14. W. A. McCorn, "Hallucinations: Their Origin, Varieties, Occurrence and Differentiation," *American Journal of Insanity* 57.3 (January, 1901), 417–28. McCorn gave a paper called "Genesis of Hallucination" at the Association of Assistant Physicians of Insane Hospitals on September 26, 1900 (*Indiana Medical Journal* 1900 [19.1], 155).

15. "Medical Society to Meet," *Brooklyn Daily Eagle*, November 19, 1899: 35.

16. *Medico-Legal Journal* 18.4 (1901): 639.

17. Arthur MacDonald, *A Plan for the Study of Man With Reference to Bills to Establish a Laboratory for the Study of the Criminal, Pauper, and Defective Classes with a Bibliography of Child Study* (Washington, D.C.: Government Printing Office, 1902), 161–62. McCorn is identified as "resident physician River Crest (nervous diseases), New York City."

Chapter 12. Reading the Death Certificate: The Name of the Disease

1. Frank G. Hyde, "Notes on the Hebrew Insane," *Proceedings of the American Medico-Psychological Association* (American Medico-Psychological Association, 1901), 133–34. The article was subsequently published in the *American Journal of Insanity* 58 (January 1902): 469–71.

2. M. Beadles, "The Insane Jew," *Journal of Mental Science* 46.195 (1900): 731–37; Harvey Baird, "Some Observations on Insanity in Jews," *Journal of Mental Science* 54 (1908): 528–32. Researchers generally agreed that despite the increase in numbers caused by unprecedented immigration and squalid working and living conditions, the rates of insanity among Jews were actually relatively low.

3. He writes: "On the first show of returning reason the relatives or those dependent on Hebrew patients make continued importunities for their release and in cases where these requests are complied with the patients are at once permitted to resume their struggle for riches, with the result, in a great many cases, of prompt return to the hospital" (134).

4. Applications 3131, 3143, 3171, and 3030.

5. For a general history of the diagnosis, see Juliet D. Hurn, "The History of General Paralysis of the Insane in Britain, 1830–1950," Dissertation, University of London, March 1998.

6. "Sample Your Symptoms: Perhaps You are Eligible to Membership in the Paresis Club," *Daily Inter Ocean*, May 11, 1890.

7. "The Relentless Paresis," *New York Sun*, November 10, 1895: 7.

8. *State of New York State Commission in Lunacy Twelfth Annual Report* (Albany, N.Y.: James B. Lyon, State Printer, 1901), 410.

9. "Medical Men Meet," *Brooklyn Daily Eagle*, March 29, 1901: 5.

10. Th. Tiling, "Alcoholic Paresis and Infectious Multiple Neuritis," *American Journal of Insanity* 55.2 (1888): 301–12.

11. "The Clinical Differation of Brain Syphilis and General Paresis," *Brooklyn Medical Journal* 16.2 (February 1902), 80–107. Subsequent citations from this article refer to this publication. The lecture before the Brooklyn Society for Neurology is mentioned in the *Brooklyn Daily Eagle* of March 29, 1901. In the *Annual Reports of the Board of Charities to the Governor for the Years Ending September 30, 1901 and 1902* (New Haven, Conn.: The Tuttle, Morehouse and Taylor Press, 1903), Grand View Sanitarium is listed under "Private Sanitaria for Mental and Nervous Diseases." Located in South Windham and at Stamford Hall, with "accommodations for more than two hundred inmates," it is described as "one of the latest of its class established in

the State, and at present is devoting especially attention to the care of nervous and mental diseases, at the same time providing a separate department for the treatment of alcoholism and drug habits." (52, 133). In the discussion of McCorn's paper transcribed in the proceedings of the Brooklyn Medical Society, McCorn is remarkably prescient about the future directions of psychiatry: "the future of mental medicine, as well as of many, if not all, physical diseases lies within the domain of physiological chemistry, and when we have mastered the problems of altered metabolism we will find a ready explanation and likewise the proper therapy for most diseases. Why research in this direction has not accomplished more I do not understand, but in this great age of advancement I believe we may look for wonders to be accomplished in this direction, and at no distant future" (107).

12. *The Alienist and Neurologist* 22.3 (July, 1901): 453. In the proceedings of a "Symposium on General Paralysis or Paresis" in 1902, Dr. Edward Cowles writes of the effect of the disease on the family: "The patient needs immediate protection when the outset of the disease is an acute attack of melancholia or mania; when the dementia comes on insidiously, protection is equally important of the personal and business interests both of the patient and the family" ("Treatment of Paresis: Its Limitations and Expectations," *Transactions of the Medical Society of the State of New York* [New York, 1902], 176). In the same symposium proceedings, Dr. Charles G. Wagner offers a demographic analysis of thousands of patients diagnosed with paresis, concluding that "while no particular profession, trade, business or occupation predisposes the individual to an attack of general paresis, every walk is of life is represented." He notes that "Dr. Asher found a definite hereditary predisposition in thirty-three per cent., and syphilitic infection in thirty-five per cent." He concludes: "Overwork, sexual excesses, alcoholism, irregular habits of sleeping and eating and such accidents as sunstroke and cerebral traumatism appear to be great factors in the production of this disease" ("The Comparative Frequency of General Paresis," 173, 175). For a comprehensive overview published in the following decade, see Emil Kraepelin, *General Paresis*, trans. J. W. Moore, *Nervous and Mental Disease Monograph Series*, no. 14 (New York: The Journal of Nervous and Mental Disease Publishing Company, 1913). McCorn translated some of Kraeplin's work.

Chapter 13: The Case of H. W.

1. Here, and elsewhere in this section, I am borrowing citations from McCorn's composite pictures of symptoms to reconstruct and imagine Harris Warshawsky's story.

2. "The Relentless Paresis," *New York Sun*, November 10, 1895: 7.

3. "Insane at 'L' Station," *New York American*, December 31, 1898: 2.

4. *Thirtieth Annual Report of the New York Visiting Committee of the State Charities Aid Association for Bellevue Hospital and Other Public Charitable Institutions* (New York: October 1, 1902), 58–59. It was in the 1890s, following the New York State Care Act of 1890 and other legislation, that state "lunatic asylums" began to be called "state hospitals."

5. "The Barrymores in Peril," *New York Times*, April 2, 1901: 6.

Chapter 14. The Pavilion for the Insane

1. *Twenty-Ninth Annual Report of the New York Visiting Committee of the State Charities Aid Association for Bellevue Hospital and Other Public Charitable Institutions* (New York: October 1, 1901), 15–16.

2. He notes that "the great bulk of our admissions have come through the department of charities of the city of New York, after examination at the pavilion at Bellevue Hospital" (*State of New York State Commission in Lunacy Twelfth Annual Report* [Albany, N.Y.: James B. Lyon, State Printer, 1901], 814). According to a note in the report, "there is no place in New York City (Manhattan), since the removal of the Bloomingdale Asylum to White Plains, to which a person seized with sudden and violent mania in a hotel or private house can be taken except to the wards for the insane at Bellevue" (1056).

3. Cohen, *Out of the Shadow*, 233.

4. *Twenty-Eighth Annual Report of the New York Visiting Committee of the State Charities Aid Association for Bellevue Hospital and Other Public Charitable Institutions* (New York: October 1, 1900), 27; *Twenty-Ninth Annual Report*, 11.

5. "Inquiry Into Death of Insane Patient," *New York Times*, December 16, 1900: 14; "Hilliard Inquest Begins," *New York Times*, December 28, 1900: 3; "Grand Jury Denounces Bellevue Management," *New York Times*, February 1, 1901: 3. See the *Twenty-Ninth Annual Report*, "Hilliard Case," 24–27.

6. *The Medico-Legal Journal* 18.4 (1901): 642.

7. *Thirtieth Annual Report of the New York Visiting Committee of the State Charities Aid Association for Bellevue Hospital and Other Public Charitable Institutions* (New York: October 1, 1902), 71.

8. *State Commission in Lunacy Twelfth Annual Report*, 817.

9. *Twenty-Ninth Annual Report*, 61.

10. *State Commission in Lunacy Twelfth Annual Report*, 185.

11. *State Commission in Lunacy Twelfth Annual Report*, 814.

12. The recommendations of the grand jury that was convened after the Hilliard case included: "That the fee system in connection with transfers of patients to private hospitals be not resumed, but that all formalities in connection with these transfers shall be made a part of the duty of the examining physicians" (*Twenty-Ninth Annual Report*, 26).

13. "Further Revelations of the Workings of the Bellevue Insanity Trust," *Daily People*, December 28, 1900: 3. The article also accused Bellevue of incompetence and errors, and reports the "astounding revelation" that "a perfectly sane woman taken to Bellevue Hospital for medical treatment had been sent in mistake for another and really crazy woman to the insane pavilion, that she had been beaten and ill-treated there." Dr. Fitch is accused of having "made many errors in his examinations," and the plight of the victim of the error, who was beaten by an insane patient, is recounted in detail.

Chapter 15. The Place of Burial: Machpelah

1. Genesis 49: 30–31 and 50: 24; Exodus 13: 19; Joshua 24: 32.

2. "Our Hebrew Cemeteries," *Brooklyn Eagle*, June 20, 1886: 11. A total of 1,491 people were buried in Mt. Zion, where Lena's parents, Meyer and Anna Ruderman, would later be buried. See Joseph Jacobs, "Notes on the Jewish Population of New York," *Jewish Charity* 3.8 (1904): 193.

3. "Our Hebrew Cemeteries," *Brooklyn Daily Eagle*, June 20, 1886: 11. The anonymous author writes: "The Jews were the first pilgrim fathers, and in their anxiety to be buried in the grave of their kindred there was a consciousness of this pilgrimage, a sense of national unity, a natural piety, and, as the writer of the letter to the Hebrews in the New Testament scriptures argues, an evidence of faith in a Promised Land, a declaration that they sought a country and 'looked for a city that hath foundations.'"

4. Soyer notes that "the acquisition of a cemetery was often among a society's first acts" (*Jewish Immigrant Association*, 88). See "Death Benefits," 87–93.

5. *New York Times*, February 18, 1901: 3.

6. Henry Roth, *Call It Sleep* (New York: Picador, 1991), 60–61.

7. Soyer, *Jewish Immigrant Association*, 90. See also "The Death of Abraham Rogarshevsky," Lower East Side Tenement Museum, http://www.tenement.org/encyclopedia/97_rogarshevsky.htm#death.

8. William Wordsworth, *The Prelude* (1805–06), VII, 599–623, in *The Thirteen-Book Prelude*, ed. Mark L. Reed (2 vols., Ithaca & London, 1991), 1: 208.

9. "Houdini's Final Trick, a Tidy Grave," *New York Times*, October 31, 2008, http://cityroom.blogs.nytimes.com/2008/10/31/houdinis-final-trick-a-tidy-grave/?module=Search&mabReward=relbias%3As%2C{%221%22%3A%22RI%3A11%22}.

Chapter 16. Saying Kaddish for a Ghost

1. *The Jewish Encyclopedia*, 12 vols., ed. Isidore Singer, et al. (New York: Funk and Wagnalls, 1906), 401–02.

2. Lewis Naphtali Dembitz, *Jewish Services in Synagogue and Home* (Philadelphia: The Jewish Publication Society of America, 1898), 110–11.

3. *The Jewish Encyclopedia*, 401–02.

4. Leon Wieseltier, *Kaddish* (New York: Vintage, 1998), 170.

5. This version from the *Zohar Hadash* is cited and discussed by Wieseltier in *Kaddish*, 132. See also 40–43.

6. *Jewish Services in Synagogue and Home*, 121–22.

Chapter 17. Picturing a Future

1. "Applications for Admission, 1901–1903," Hebrew Orphan Asylum of the City of New York, records; I-42; Box 14; 1; American Jewish Historical Society, New York and Boston.

2. Pollard and Soyer, *Emerging Metropolis*, 122.

3. "Interview with Arthur Marshall" (April 6, 1991).

4. See *Annual Report*, 1903; *83rd Annual Report of the Hebrew Orphan Asylum of New York*, 1906.

5. *Annual Report*, 1905, 63. See Library Catalogue of the Hebrew Orphan Society (New York, 1878) and *Supplement #1, Library Catalogue of the Hebrew Orphan Society* (New York, 1881). These catalogues are in the New York Public Library. See *Report of General Inspection of the Hebrew Orphan Asylum of the City of New York, May 19th 1916, Department of Public Charities*, reprinted in Bernstein, 265. See also *The Chronicle of the Hebrew Orphan Asylum, Published by the Literary Society of the Institution*, September, 1904, vol. 1, no. 2, 2. Bogen writes: "Three editions of the Chronicle were published but no copies exist today" (157). I located two issues in the Hebrew Orphan Asylum archives in the Center for Jewish History. These issues give a sense of the educational culture of the asylum. In this issue, a short essay entitled "Character

and Reputation" discusses the "famous negro of Haiti—Toussaint L'Overture." The author writes: "He was one of the greatest statesmen and fighters the world has ever produced. He was as bold as Napoleon, and as straightforward as our own model, President George Washington, but why did people hate him? Simply because he was a negro. He was the highest of his fellowmen in regard to character, but the lowest in the line of reputation" (6).

6. *The Chronicle of the Hebrew Orphan Asylum, Published by the Literary Society of the Institution*, 1904, vol. 1, no. 3, 4.

7. *The Menorah: A Monthly Magazine for the Jewish Home* 36 (January to June 1904): 260.

8. "$1,000 in Cash Prizes for Hebrew Orphans," *New York Times*, June 4, 1906: 18.

9. Ladies Sewing Society of the Hebrew Orphan Asylum (New York, October 1903). The list of items given to the thirty-nine graduates includes: "20 bosom shirts, 108 plain shirts, 62 negligé shirts, 47 canton flannel drawers, 202 pairs stockings, 90 pairs shoes, 107 suits, 178 night shirts, 62 singlets, 62 drawers, 128 handkerchiefs, 77 hats and caps."

10. *The Mad Heiress* is a mechanical imitation of a late eighteenth-century novel in which an orphaned young woman is imprisoned in an insane asylum by her unscrupulous guardian to prevent her from marrying Henry Marshall.

11. Bogen, 121, 115–22.

12. "Jewish Cadets," *The American Hebrew*, New York Sivan 24, 5656; (June 5, 1896), 135–36. Levy was New York City coroner and president of the Jewish Immigrant Protective Society.

13. *Annual Report*, 1903; *Annual Report*, 1906, 20, 56. Special praise is given to the bandleader, Mr. Phillip Egner. In other sections in the report we can read: "The Cadet Corp of the Institution has maintained its usual high state of efficiency, as has been abundantly shown by its record in two competitive drills, and by the unusually fine exhibition furnished on the evening of April 21, 1906" ("Report of President and Board of Trustees," 45–46); and "Our Cadet Corps participated in the competitive drill at the Twelfth Regiment Armory, and succeeded in winning the banner. The Corps and Band also paraded on Decoration Day with the Grand Army of the Republic" (40). See 45–46.

14. "Hughes Reviews Cadets; Both are Delighted," *New York Times*, November 30, 1906: 4.

15. *Annual Report*, 1907, 28.

16. The article notes that "a drill by a special company . . . won a flag at the Twelfth Regiment Armory last year" and continues: "These boys, doffing their khaki jackets, went through a series of movements which brought forth

round after round of applause. They wound up by a skirmish and a volley of shooting which entirely disposed of an imaginary enemy" ("400 Boys Drill Like Veterans," *New York Times,* April 26, 1908: 57).

17. *Proceedings in Commemoration of the Fiftieth Anniversary of the Opening of the First Building of The Hebrew Orphan Asylum of the City of New York Held at the New York Hippodrome, April 10, 1910* in *Report of the Eighty-Seventh Annual Meeting of the Hebrew Orphan Asylum of the City of New York* (New York, 1910), 75. See Bogen, 169–70.

18. Edward Chauncey Marshall, *The History of the United States Naval Academy* (New York: D. Van Nostrand, 1862), 68–82, 133.

19. See "Stuyvesant Wins Shoot: High School Boys Make Good Marks in Tripartite Match with Rifle," *New York Times,* December 21, 1907: 7; and "Eighteen Schools in Championship Shoot—Boy Runners in Stuyvesant Games," *New York Times,* December 22, 1907: 32. Stuyvesant High School no longer has student records from this period. A yearbook publication called *The Indicator* has a two-page profile of the rifle club, which includes a student named Warshawsky, along with a photograph. Unfortunately, none of these publications includes first names for the students. I am guessing that this was Ruby, who became an automobile mechanic after he left the orphanage. One of the boys in the photograph of the rifle club resembles photographs of my father at that age. I am grateful to Mr. Henry Grossberg, executive director of the Stuyvesant High School Alumni Association, for sending me copies of these pages.

20. *Annual Report,* 1906, 21.

21. *Annual Report,* 1910, 24.

22. Bob Moon, USMA Band History, chapter 12, TEACHERS OF MUSIC WITH THE U.S.M.A. BAND 1817–1974," 173–74; http://usma-bandalumni.org/hist_main.htm.

23. According to the *New York Times*: "Considerable testimony came out relating to the matter of religious tolerance." Cadet Leo Israel Samuelson of Texas denied that he had ever been "interfered with on account of your religion." One cadet, who denied ever calling another cadet "a --- Jew," insisted that he considered a Jewish cadet to be "a Jew" rather than "an American." See "Congressmen Score West Point Hazers," *New York Times,* January 19, 1901: 5.

24. "Says West Point is Not Anti-Semitic," *New York Times,* December 7, 1915: 3. According to the *Times,* this correspondence, which was to be entered into the congressional record, was "due to the fact that there are few applicants of the Jewish faith in Mr. Chandler's district for appointments to the Military Academy, and the New York member investigated the cause of the lack of

Jewish interest in a military career." Chandler states: "During my term of office as Congressman I have held several preliminary competitive examinations after due notice to all the people of my district to fill vacancies at West Point and Annapolis." Chandler, a progressive and then Republican representative of the 19th District, was an advocate of religious freedom. According to a *New York Times* article on April 28, 1921, "CHANDLER PLANS BILL TO LET JEWS ENTER," "An amendment to the immigration bill before the Senate providing that an exception shall be made in the case of Jews who apply for admission to this country, and can show that they fit all the present requirements will be offered to the House of Representatives by Representative Walter M. Chandler of this city he said last night at a meeting in the Lexington Avenue Opera House. Henry Ford was vigorously attacked by Mr. Chandler. He said that it was Mr. Ford's contention that the Jews were trying to get control not only of the United States, but of the whole world. 'If 10 per cent. can get control of the other 90 per cent. in this country,' said Mr. Chandler, 'then let them do it. Henry Ford is influencing Congress today with the assertion that the Jews are trying to get control of the earth.'"

25. *Official Register of the Officers and Cadets of the United States Military Academy* (West Point, New York: U.S.M.A. Press and Bindery), June 1906, 47.

26. "Failed to Enter West Point," *New York Times*, February 3, 1909: 8; "West Point's Candidates," *New York Times*, October 15, 1911: 14.

27. "The Political Campaign of 1898. New York State. Platforms, Letters of Acceptance, Portraits and Sketches of Candidates of Both Parties," *Brooklyn Eagle Library*, no. 30, vol. XIII no. 9, October 1898, 18. See *Brooklyn Daily Eagle Almanac* 1909, 112.

28. "O'Brien's Defiant Hosts: Smith and Goetz Renominated in the Eighth. Jacob Hess Lends a Hand at John J. O'Brien's 'Citizens' Meeting Last Night," *New York Times*, October 26, 1899: 1; "Indictments Trifles in O'Brien's Eight. 'Silver Dollar' Smith and Alderman Goetz Renominated for the Offices They Hold . . . Distinguished Citizens of the East Side Insist that Indicted Officials Are Worthy of their Suffrage," *New York Herald*, October 26, 1899: 3. See: "Now She is Mrs. Dreyfus. 'Silver Dollar' Smith's Oldest Daughter Takes a Husband," *New York Times*, December 22, 1892: 2; and Albert Fried, *The Rise and Fall of the Jewish Gangster*, revised edition (New York: Columbia University Press, 1993), 28. Abraham Cahan describes Silver Dollar Smith's Essex Street saloon in *The Education of Abraham Cahan*, trans. Leon Stein, Abraham P. Conan, and Lynn Davison (Philadelphia: The Jewish Publication Society of America, 1969), 290–91.

29. *City Record*, vol. XXXIII, New York, November 6, 1905, 9292–93.

30. *Official Register of the Officers and Cadets*, 48. My grandfather's 1942 registration card lists his height (at the age of forty-nine) as five foot four, but my father described him as "5 foot 3, a short portly man" in recalling a moment from 1947 ("Personal Reminiscence").

Chapter 18. Picturing a Past

1. "Interview with Arthur Marshall" (April 6, 1991).

2. The register includes in its list of students: "Ruderman, Michael, 82 Essex street" (*Fiftieth Annual Register, 1898–1899, College of the City of New York* [New York: John Polhemus, 1899] 85). According to Irving Howe, City College was at this time attracting more and more Eastern European immigrants. He writes: "City College was actually a combination of high school and college. Upon graduating from grammar school, boys could take an entrance examination and those scoring at least seventy would be admitted to the 'sub-freshman class' in which they were expected to cram somewhat less than an equivalent of high school into one's year's work. High-school students who had done well in their first year were allowed to transfer to the 'sub-freshman' or freshman classes. This meant a fairly liberal policy of admissions and a high rate of casualties. . . ." I have not been able to ascertain whether Michael Ruderman was registered after 1899. Howe reports that in 1903, "more than 75 percent of the students were Jewish" (281).

3. Cahan, *The Rise of David Levinsky*, 156.

4. "250 Youngsters Start at Office Boy Trade," *New York Times*, October 9, 1906: 4; "Opportunities for Education," *American Educational Review: A Monthly Review of the Progress of Higher Education* 30.2 (1908): 81.

5. "Interview with Arthur Marshall" (April 6, 1991); "Personal Reminiscence."

6. "Told Round the Ticker," *New York Times*, October 22, 1906: 9. The article continues: "The messengers in the Stock Exchange houses are accustomed to association on the waiting bench with the sons, relatives, and protégés of their employers, but it isn't often that a star football man and a United States Army officer to boot finds himself at the call of the office force of a brokerage house. Mr. Daly served this painful period of apprenticeship with Post & Flag."

7. "Topics in Wall Street," *New York Times*, June 21, 1908: 23. A 1913 article has this story: "An employer who has a large number of boys as runners interrupted an animated conference around a typewriter a few afternoons ago and discovered the following notice at the head of a number of subscription

blanks: 'Xmas comes but once a year,/When it does it brings good cheer;/ If you would feel the Xmas joy,/Remember the faithful office boy.' 'When you have made your rounds with that,' he said to the ringleader, 'I shall expect you to come back and divide with me.' Conditions, however, are not as bad as that. The broker, a little blue just now, knows that 1914 is going to bring him prosperity again" ("Dullness in Stocks May Chill Santa," *New York Times*, December 8, 1913: 6).

8. "Personal Reminiscence;" "Interview with Arthur Marshall" (April 6, 1991).

9. Franklin P. Adams, "This Little World," *Post-Standard* (Syracuse, N.Y.), February 19, 1946: 1. Adams also recalled this story in his column in the *New York Tribune* in 1917: "It is seven or eight years since this department has had an office-boy contrib[ute] with more than mediocre poetical ability. Incorrigible and aged readers will recall David Warshawsky's famous epithet: If Donlin only joins the Giants,/ The fans would drink his health in pints" ("The Conning Tower," *New York Tribune*, August 19, 1917: 3). See Bruce Nash and Allan Zullo, *The Baseball Hall of Shame 4* (New York: Pocket Books, 1990), 172. "That Double Play Again" appeared in the July 12, 1910 *New York Evening Mail* (not on July 10, as numerous sources state). The *Chicago Daily Tribune* reprinted it as "Gotham's Woe" on July 15, 1910. Three days later, on July 18, it appeared in the *New York Evening Mail*.

10. "Work Wanted," *New-York Daily Tribune*, October 6, 1909: 11; *Report of the Eighty-Fifth Annual Meeting of the Hebrew Orphan Asylum of the City of New York* (New York, 1908), 42.

11. "Advertisements," *Daily People*, February 6, 1906: 4.

12. There is an unusual 1909 New York City directory listing for "Meyer Ruderman, tailor" with an address of 21 East 136th Street. I haven't found any other Meyer Rudermans in the city directories of the period. Might the Warshawsky and Ruderman families have tried moving back to Manhattan from Brooklyn for a few years? They are in Brooklyn in 1906 and in 1910, but at different addresses: 474 Saratoga and 441 Hopkinson. From what I can tell from birth certificates and directory listings, there was one other David Warshawsky in New York City who was about the same age as my grandfather.

13. *Brooklyn Daily Eagle*, September 15, 1922: 15.

14. Michael Ruderman is an accountant with H. Herman Sternback and Co., a cotton importer at 23 East 23rd Street; David H. Marshall is an accountant with William E. Wiener, Inc. at 5 West 37th Street, which is associated with a woman's clothing manufacturer.

15. The 1916 *Yearbook of the American Institute of Accountants* describes

the rigorous process through which New York State licensed CPAs, following Section 80 of the legislature's 1896 Act, amended in February of 1909 and May of 1913 (*1916 Year-Book of the Institute of Accountants in the United States of America* [New York: The Institute of Accountants, 1916], 196–98).

16. "Ordered to Camp By Draft Boards," *Brooklyn Daily Eagle*, August 1, 1918: 17; "Men for Camp Upton and Other Stations," *Brooklyn Daily Standard*, August 1, 1918. 5. An 802-page *Manual for the Quartermaster Corps United States Army* published by the War Department describes in great detail the duties that an accountant would perform in the "Finance and accounting division" of the "Army Transport Service." See *Manual for the Quartermaster Corps United States Army 1916* (Washington, D.C.: Government Printing Office, 1917), 55, and *passim*.

17. "Men Picked from Draft to Go First to Yaphank," *Brooklyn Daily Eagle*, September 7, 1917: 9. The *Eagle* includes Isadore Marshall on a list of "Brooklyn-Long Island Soldiers Home from War" on July 20, 1919.

18. See "Rapaport-Gans Post Plans Affair," *Brooklyn Daily Eagle*, November 16, 1919: 68; "Brownsville Post Favors Bonus," *Brooklyn Daily Eagle*, March 14, 1920: 71. The first article refers to the Rapaport-Gans Post, which is planning a fundraising dinner to erect a monument in Brooklyn, to which General Pershing is invited. The second refers to the election of officers at the Brownsville Post. These organizations would have been composed of World War I veterans. The *Brooklyn Standard Union* also reported these events. See *Brooklyn Standard Union*, November 14, 1919 and March 8, 1920. See "American Legion Post $25,000 Drive a Success," *Brooklyn Standard Union*, April 11, 1920: 7.

19. "Huron Club Elects Officers," *Brooklyn Standard Union*, n.d. 1918: n.p.; "Buys $500 in Thrift Stamps," *Brooklyn Daily Eagle*, April 10, 1918: 19. The Huron Club in Manhattan was a notorious political and social club associated with Tammany Hall and the Democratic Party. It does not appear to have been connected to the Brooklyn Huron Club.

20. "Will Entertain Candidates," *Brooklyn Standard Union*, October 28, 1919: 5.

21. "Huron Club Dance A Success," *Brooklyn Standard Union*, October 27, 1919: 6.

22. "Heard Where Pitkin Ave. Meets Eastern Parkway," *Brooklyn Standard Union*, 1920, n.d.; n.p. These were the years before my grandfather married. A November 16, 1933, article lists "Mrs. Dick Marshall" among "committee women" involved in a "Community Milk Fund" (*Brooklyn Daily Eagle*, November 16, 1933: 6). I have a small leather-bound booklet that is a 1947–1948 publication of New York University called "The Waverly: A Guide to Washington

Square College." The staff, listed and photographed in the front matter, includes my father, who is identified as the advertising manager.

23. I am grateful to Mr. Thomas M. Savini, Director of the Chancellor Robert R Livingston Masonic Library of Grand Lodge in New York City, for his assistance.

24. There is another Bible in my possession besides the one inscribed to David Marshall in 1906; on its blue cover, embossed in gold, is the familiar Masonic symbol of a "compass and square" framing a *G*, along with "Gothic" and "NO. 934, F. & A.M." in gold letters. Inside, the "Presented by . . . to Brother . . ." pages used for Apprentice initiations and promotions to Fellowcraft and Master Mason are blank, uninscribed. I assume that this Bible was given to my father, along with the folded and apparently unused Mason's apron that I found in a drawer after his death. It is strange that he never discarded it; perhaps he associated it with his father.

25. "Marriage Announcements," *New York Times,* March 12, 1922: 27. According to the 1930 U.S. census, Louis Levitt manufactured "merchandise" and had an income of $20,000. His son-in-law, David, who lived with his family at the same address, is listed as a "manager" for "machines" and has an income of $7,500. The 1925 New York State census indicates that Louis Levitt was retired. The 1910 and 1915 censuses list him as a manufacturer of shoes. The 1900 census, which lists him as living at 59 Attorney Street, shortly before my grandmother was born, reports him working as a shoemaker.

26. *Brooklyn Blue Book and Long Island Society Register* (Brooklyn: Rugby Press, 1922), xii. According to the advertisement, "The Chateau Rembrandt is the Brooklyn ideal social center for receptions, banquets, bazaars, concerts, recitals, dances and bridge parties."

27. "Chateau Rembrandt Opens in Splendor," *Brooklyn Daily Eagle,* February 23, 1922: 7. The manager was said to be "formerly of the Ritz, London, Paris, and Switzerland, whose services at the Peace Conference in France won him the personal friendship of Woodrow Wilson."

28. Rabbi Levinthal, who was especially concerned with the Americanization and assimilation of the children of Jewish immigrants, as well as American materialism, wryly noted that second-generation Jews were more likely to attend a "center" than a synagogue or a temple. I do not know if either the Levitt or the Marshall families had any connection with the Brooklyn Jewish Center, or if they had been members of Temple Petach Tikvah or Levinthal's first congregation, Temple Beth-El in Greenpoint, Brooklyn. Levinthal, who had a J.D. as well as a doctorate, was known as a charismatic speaker as well as an influential author. See Kimmy Caplan, "The Life and Sermons of Rabbi

Israel Herbert Levinthal," *American Jewish History* (March 1999); and Samuel P. Abelow, *History of Brooklyn Jewry* (Brooklyn: Scheba Publishing Company, 1937), 73–90.

29. *The New York Red Book* (Albany, N.Y.: J. B. Lyon Company, 1916), 726. Dresher's political career appears to have begun in 1899, when according to the *Brooklyn Daily Eagle*, he was appointed an "assistant dump inspector" in the Brooklyn Street Cleaning Department ("New City Appointees," *Brooklyn Daily Eagle*, July 25, 1899: 6).

30. Born in 1891, he married in 1917 at the age of twenty-six, after what one biographer called a "lengthy courtship," some five years after Daisy married. See Daniel Stashover, *The Boy Genius and the Mogul* (New York: Broadway Books, 2002), 39.

31. Cahan, *Yekl: A Tale of the New York Ghetto*, 13–14.

32. "Interview with Arthur Marshall" (April 6, 1991).

33. Peter P. Wahlstad and Walter Seely Johnson, *Credit and the Credit Man* in *Modern Business*, vol. 8 (New York: Alexander Hamilton Institute, 1917). See chapter XI, "The Credit Man," 175–91.

34. Elias St. Elmo Lewis, *The Credit Man and His Work* (Detroit: The Book-Keeper Publishing Co, 1904), 293–94.

35. "Interview with Arthur Marshall" (April 6, 1991).

36. *Brooklyn Daily Eagle*, September 7, 1926: 26; *Brooklyn Daily Eagle*, May 5, 1929: 53.

37. "Growing Up in Bklyn," n.d.

38. "Interview with Arthur Marshall" (April 6, 1991); "Personal Reminiscence."

39. "Interview with Arthur Marshall" (April 6, 1991).

40. No. 437,841, Serial No. 524,338, published December 28, 1947, Class 20, *Official Gazette of the United States Patent Office*, vol. 608, 1948, ix; 896.

41. "Interview with Helene Marshall," conducted by Cindy Marshall, April 6, 1991.

Chapter 19. A Ghost and a Memory

1. Personal letter, December 23, 1945; ellipsis in original. I have corrected some obvious typographical errors.

2. "Growing Up in Bklyn," n.d. According to the June 1, 1926 *Brooklyn Daily Eagle*, twelve Civil War veterans, as well as some Spanish War veterans,

marched in the 1926 Memorial Day parade ("Twelve Civil War Veterans Lead East New York Parade," *Brooklyn Daily Eagle*, June 1, 1926: 15).

3. Dickens continues: "Until old Hungerford Market was pulled down, until old Hungerford Stairs were destroyed, and the very nature of the ground changed, I never had the courage to go back to the place where my servitude began. I never saw it. I could not endure to go near it. For many years, when I came near to Robert Warrens' in the Strand, I crossed over to the opposite side of the way, to avoid a certain smell of the cement they put upon the blacking-corks, which reminded me of what I was once. It was a very long time before I liked to go up Chandos Street. My old way home by the Borough made me cry, after my eldest child could speak" (John Forster, *The Life of Charles Dickens*, [1927; rev. ed., New York: Dutton, 1966, 1: 32–33]).

4. Naomi Wiener Cohen, *What the Rabbis Said: The Public Discourse of Nineteenth-Century American Rabbis* (New York: New York University Press, 2008), 91.

5. Bernstein, 339. The letter is dated March 14, 1959. In his book, Bogen describes the mission of Superintendent Lionel J Simmons, a former inmate who took over in 1920, in these terms: "An institutional man all his life, he apparently wanted only to change [HOA's] image—to convert it from a military school to a private boarding school, or, in short, an orphanage purged of its nineteenth-century practices" (197). In *An Orphan in New York City: Life with a Thousand Brothers and Sisters*, Seymour Siegel, who entered the orphanage in 1929, describes reminiscing with other alumni who had many positive memories: "it was all true. But, unlike the other men around the table, I also remembered much that was dehumanizing, mean, cruel, unfeeling, and unjust. . . . I remembered nights when a nine-year-old cringed in his bed, praying that he wouldn't be hurt again; I remembered indignities to my person, episodes of stark hopelessness, years of futility, and periods of depressing isolation. My fears and injuries, my pain, had not come because of separation from my parents but because of direct maltreatment by some of the orphanage staff, and the institution's lack of professionally trained counselors. My friends seemed to be denying a significant part of our common experience, the painful part" (12).

6. Bogen notes in the preface to *The Luckiest Orphans* that he received one hundred replies (including four from "alumni who had grown up in the 1890s") but adds that "the questionnaire apparently released" five alumni "to write about their lives in the HOA for the first time, and they seemed eager and relieved to do so" (vii).

7. "Answers to Questionnaire, Male, 1957–58, Answers to Questionnaire, Female, 1957–58," Hyman Bogen Collection; P-767; Box 6; American Jewish

Historical Society, New York and Boston. Bogen drew upon and quoted from these answers in his book. Box 1 contains the "Souvenir in Commemoration of the Organization of the Hebrew Orphan Asylum of the City of New York," as well as other Seligman Solomon Association dinner programs.

8. *Proceedings in Commemoration of the Fiftieth Anniversary of the Opening of the First Building of The Hebrew Orphan Asylum of the City of New York*, 75, 79–81, 91; see also Bogen, 169–70.

Chapter 20. Searches and Signs

1. Nancy K. Miller, *Bequest and Betrayal: Memoirs of a Parent's Death* (Bloomington, Ind.: Indiana University Press, 2000), xiii.

2. Court of Justice of the European Union, Judgment in Case C-131/12, Google Spain SL, Google Inc. v Agencia Española de Protección de Datos, Mario Costeja Gonzále, http://curia.europa.eu/jcms/upload/docs/application/pdf/2014-05/cp140070en.pdf. See Jeffrey Rosen, "The Right to Be Forgotten," 64 *Stanford Law Review*. Online 88, February 13, 2012.

3. The German Reformed Protestant Dutch Church sold the lots to Isidore Jackson for $60,000 in 1897, who also acquired the building that was at 155 Norfolk. (See "In the Real Estate Field, *New York Times*, May 25, 1897: 10.) According to the *New York World* of April 23, 1897, "This is one of the oldest churches in the city, having been established in 1758 in Nassau st. It has been for thirty-six years in Norfolk st., near Rivington, but recently sold its property there for $60,000 cash. The original John Jacob Astor was an officer of the church for many years, and some of the old minutes are in his handwriting" ("Monmouth Park Unsold," *New York World*, April 23, 1897: 8). Newspaper accounts of real estate transactions, maps, and atlases showing building lots, conveyance records, and city register tax assessment records suggest that the building was built before 1900 and not in 1912.

Chapter 21. Returning to Machpelah

1. "Order B'rith Abraham," *New York Times*, September 15, 1895: 17. According to the *Seventh Annual Report of the Bureau of Labor Statistics of the State of Connecticut for the Year Ending November 30, 1891*: "The benefit is $500 on death of a member and $500 on the death of the member's wife" (444).

Irving Howe cites an 1897 *Evening World* article that estimates that a funeral would cost over $140, "a staggering sum for most immigrant workers," 221. See Soyer, *Jewish Immigrant Associations*, 81–93.

2. See Theodor *Reik, Pagan Rites in Judaism (New York:* Farrar, Straus, 1964), 44, 48.